Tourism Development, Go and Sustainability in The]

This book focuses on the complex issues of tourism development, governance and sustainability in the long-standing popular island destination, The Bahamas, where tourism remains one of the primary fiscal industries.

The book achieves this by looking at the impacts of mass tourism development from social, economic and environmental perspectives; panarchy and resilience; assessing sustainability; moving towards a blue economy; impacts of climate change and innovative alternative tourism offerings to ensure sustainable tourism – a welcomed but challenging essential contemporary focus of the tourism industry. It further looks at how development, governance and sustainability come together in the aftermath of a recent natural disaster, Hurricane Dorian, which proved to be a strong catalyst for action, innovation and change in The Bahamas.

Given the complexity of these key concepts and The Bahamas as an established popular tourism destination archipelago which relies so heavily on the industry, this book offers significant insight for other tourism regions and will therefore be essential reading for upper-level students and academics in the field of Tourism research.

Sophia Rolle is Graduate Programmes Coordinator and Senior Lecturer of Tourism Management in the Centre for Hotel and Tourism Management, Faculty of Social Sciences at the University of the West Indies.

Jessica Minnis is a Professor of Sociology in the School of Social Sciences at the University of The Bahamas.

Ian Bethell-Bennett is an Associate Professor and former Dean of Liberal and Fine Arts at the University of The Bahamas.

Contemporary Geographies of Leisure, Tourism and Mobility

Series Editor: **C. Michael Hall**, *Professor at the Department of Management, College of Business and Economics, University of Canterbury, Christchurch, New Zealand*

The aim of this series is to explore and communicate the intersections and relationships between leisure, tourism and human mobility within the social sciences.

It will incorporate both traditional and new perspectives on leisure and tourism from contemporary geography, e.g. notions of identity, representation and culture, while also providing for perspectives from cognate areas such as anthropology, cultural studies, gastronomy and food studies, marketing, policy studies and political economy, regional and urban planning, and sociology, within the development of an integrated field of leisure and tourism studies.

Also, increasingly, tourism and leisure are regarded as steps in a continuum of human mobility. Inclusion of mobility in the series offers the prospect to examine the relationship between tourism and migration, the sojourner, educational travel, and second home and retirement travel phenomena.

The series comprises two strands:

Contemporary Geographies of Leisure, Tourism and Mobility aims to address the needs of students and academics, and the titles will be published in hardback and paperback.

Titles include:

Tourism in China
Policy and Development Since 1949
David Airey and King Chong

Tourism and Innovation 2nd Edition
C. Michael Hall and Allan M. Williams

Routledge Studies in Contemporary Geographies of Leisure, Tourism and Mobility is a forum for innovative new research intended for research students and academics, and the titles will be available in hardback only.

Titles include:

Authenticity in North America
Place, Tourism, Heritage, Culture and the Popular Imagination
Edited by Jane Lovell and Sam Hitchmough

Tourism Development, Governance and Sustainability in The Bahamas
Edited by Sophia Rolle, Jessica Minnis and Ian Bethell-Bennett

For more information about this series, please visit: www.routledge.com/ Contemporary-Geographies-of-Leisure-Tourism-and-Mobility/book-series/SE0522

Tourism Development, Governance and Sustainability in The Bahamas

Edited by
Sophia Rolle, Jessica Minnis
and Ian Bethell-Bennett

LONDON AND NEW YORK

First published 2020
by Routledge
2 Park Square, Milton Park, Abingdon, Oxon OX14 4RN

and by Routledge
52 Vanderbilt Avenue, New York, NY 10017

Routledge is an imprint of the Taylor & Francis Group, an informa business

British Library Cataloguing-in-Publication Data
A catalogue record for this book is available from the British Library

Library of Congress Cataloging-in-Publication Data
Names: Rolle, Sophia, editor. | Minnis, Jessica, editor. |
Bethell-Bennett, Ian, editor.
Title: Tourism development, governance and sustainability in the Bahamas /
Edited by Sophia Rolle, Jessica Minnis and Ian Bethell-Bennett.
Description: Abingdon, Oxon; New York, NY: Routledge, 2020. |
Series: Contemporary geographies of leisure, tourism and mobility |
Includes bibliographical references and index.
Identifiers: LCCN 2020007155 (print) | LCCN 2020007156 (ebook)
Subjects: LCSH: Tourism—Bahamas. | Tourism—Government
policy—Bahamas. | Sustainable tourism—Bahamas.
Classification: LCC G155.B25 T67 2020 (print) | LCC G155.B25
(ebook) | DDC 338.4/7917296—dc23
LC record available at https://lccn.loc.gov/2020007155
LC ebook record available at https://lccn.loc.gov/2020007156

ISBN: 978-0-367-46967-2 (hbk)
ISBN: 978-0-367-51228-6 (pbk)
ISBN: 978-1-003-03231-1 (ebk)

Typeset in Times New Roman
by codeMantra

My contributions to this book are dedicated to my daughter
Eboni Deanne Adderley who is the sum of my being. She
listened and offered advice on many occasions during the
writing and editing process. She became my calming force.
Thank you, "pumpkin", I love you. I also wish to thank
members of my immediate family and special friends for their
contributions with initial editing. A heartfelt thanks to both
Jessica and Ian for whom this book would not be a reality.
They are the epitome of class and professionalism.

Sophia Rolle

By His Grace, I give tribute to my family and friends for their
encouragement, and a listening ear during the production of this
publication. I extend thanks to my colleague William Fielding
for his assistance with data creation, to the University of The
Bahamas, as well as the participants in the study in two chapters
to which I am associated. To Sophia and Ian, thanks for sharing.

Jessica Minnis

I give thanks and honour to my family, especially my late
father who introduced me to so many islands of The Bahamas,
and passed on to me a love of the sea, to my wife and children,
to The University of The Bahamas, formerly the College of
The Bahamas, for a research grant that facilitated some of the
early research for this project, and to The Bahamas National
Development Plan and its team on which and with whom the
three of us worked to create data for this, as well as to William
Fielding. I thank Sophia and Jessica, with whom I worked
closely. I also thank the others who worked on Family Island
Development.

Ian Bethell-Bennett

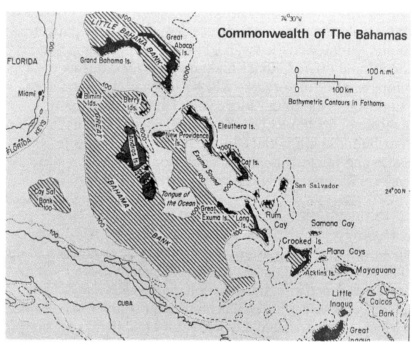

Image courtesy of Media Enterprises and Neil Sealey
Copyright © 1999

Contents

Figures

Tables

About the editors

Sophia Rolle is Bahamian-born, and driven by her passion for, and development of, the peoples of The Bahamas. Dr. Rolle is an "Educator Extraordinaire", who is a well-respected and highly sought-after resource in the areas of sustainable tourism development, education and research, both locally and internationally. She holds four earned degrees in the areas of Hotel Management; Business Management; Hotel, Restaurant, and Institutional Management; and Family and Consumer Sciences Education with emphasis in Tourism Management.

Professionally, Dr. Rolle has kept busy in the world of academia and industry – researching, teaching, and consulting over various pedagogical areas of tourism development and its impact on small island developing states (SIDS), such as The Bahamas. She is also the proud recipient of a plethora of distinguished scholarly certifications, awards, and accolades including the prestigious Cacique Award for Human Resources Development presented to her in 2005 by The Bahamas Ministry of Tourism. Besides teaching and research, Dr. Rolle was recommended by the Governor General for the Commonwealth of The Bahamas to serve in the capacity as Justice of the Peace for the entire Bahamas. She maintains active affiliations with many local and international organizations and is a board member for the Governor General Youth Awards; a member of the Board of Directors for the Bahamas Civil Aviation Authority, a founding director of Friends of The Arts, a member of the Rotary Club of Nassau Sunrise, and a lifetime member of Delta Sigma Theta Sorority Inc. The remainder of her time is spent mentoring her daughter, Eboni Deanne, and engaging in her new-found passion – fine arts painting.

Contact Information: Dr. Sophia Rolle; Graduate Programmes Coordinator and Senior Lecturer of Tourism Management in the Centre for Hotel and Tourism Management, Faculty of Social Sciences at the University of the West Indies.; P.O. Box N-4863, Nassau, The Bahamas. Email address: sophia.rolle@uwimona.edu.jm

Jessica Minnis is a Professor of Sociology in the School of Social Sciences at the University of The Bahamas. She has collaborated with a number of faculty members at the University of The Bahamas and Dr. Richard Stoffle, University of Arizona on several projects and papers related to marine protected areas, male under achievement, school-based sexual behaviour studies, community service, family, civil society, the profile of sentenced inmates, and currently tourism and tourism development on small island states. She is also a co-editor of the book *Junkanoo and Religion*.

She was also a member of the National Crime Commission and Steering Committee-Strategic manpower review of the Police Force.

Contact information: Jessica Minnis; Faculty of Social and Educational Studies; University of The Bahamas, P.O. Box N-4912, Nassau, The Bahamas. Email address: jessica.minnis@ub.edu.bs

Ian Bethell-Bennett is an Associate Professor and former Dean of Liberal and Fine Arts at the University of the Bahamas. He holds degrees in Trade Policy, Cultural Studies, English, and Spanish. Dr. Bethell-Bennett's research interests include gender in development and migration. His recent publications focus on unequal development in the Caribbean, particularly in The Bahamas and Puerto Rico where resorts take over land and disenfranchise locals. Dr. Bethell-Bennett writes on art and culture, and has participated in NE7 and NE8 as well as in 2018 Double Dutch Hot Water with Plastico Fantastico as a part of the Expo 2020 collective. Dr. Bethell-Bennett works around Haitian and Cuban migration to and through The Bahamas, and is currently working on a project on Statelessness in The Bahamas. He writes in the daily newspapers on gender and development.

Contact Information: Dr. Ian Bethell-Bennett; Faculty of Liberal and Fine Arts; University of The Bahamas; P.O. Box N-4912; Nassau, The Bahamas. Email address: ian.bennett@ub.edu.bs

Contributors

Lisa Benjamin, B.A., LL.B., LL.M., PhD Killam Postdoctoral Fellow at Dalhousie University, Halifax, Nova Scotia at Schulich School of Law. She is a former Assistant Professor of Law at the University of The Bahamas. Dr. Benjamin is a lawyer by training and a member of the Compliance Committee (Facilitative Branch) of the United Nations Framework Convention on Climate Change, The Bahamas National Climate Change Committee, and the Public Education and Outreach Subcommittee of the National Climate Change Committee. Dr. Benjamin is also a co-founder of the Climate Change Initiative at the University of The Bahamas and founder of the Environmental Law Clinic, a collaboration between the University of The Bahamas LL.B. programme and the Eugene Dupuch Law School. She is a Director of The Bahamas Protected Areas Fund and has been an advisor to the Bahamian national delegation to the United Nations Framework Convention on Climate Change process. Dr. Benjamin's current research looks at climate change in small island developing states, trade and environmental law, and access and benefit sharing. She received her PhD from the University of Leicester, and her dissertation investigated legal and non-legal mechanisms which mediate corporate greenhouse gas emissions.

Margo Blackwell is an Associate Professor of Literacy in the Faculty of Social and Educational Studies at the University of The Bahamas. She has collaborated with faculty on numerous research projects relating to education, gender, and sustainable development. She is a member of the University's Board of Trustees.

Joshua Carroll is an Associate Professor of Recreation, Parks and Tourism at Radford University. Dr. Carroll's teaching and research focus on sustainable, nature-based tourism and how this can be used as a pathway toward positive community and economic development as well as ecological integrity. He has worked on many projects with agencies and organizations such as the US National Park Service, US Forest Service, State Parks, various beach communities, and river systems. His work has made valuable contributions in several locations such as New England, California, Colorado, The Bahamas, Virginia, and Alaska.

Teo Cooper is an Assistant Professor of Science Education and Dean of Students at the University of The Bahamas (UB) North Campus in Freeport, Grand Bahama. Dr. Cooper holds a Bachelor of Education degree in Biology with Combined Science from the former College of The Bahamas (now UB). Dr. Cooper's graduate education includes a master's degree in Higher Education Administration, an Educational Specialist degree in Science Education, and a Doctor of Education degree in Curriculum and Instruction specializing in Science Education and Environmental Science, each from Florida International University (FIU). He has led and consulted on several initiatives towards developing environmental education policy and programmes in The Bahamas.

Mayuri Deka is an Assistant Professor at the School of English Studies in the University of The Bahamas. Dr. Deka has published and presented numerous papers on the areas of American literature with a focus on multi-ethnic identities, Transnational and Postcolonial literatures, cognitive psychology, and pedagogy. She is in the process of writing her book on pro-social pedagogy and social justice. Dr. Deka has taught a wide range of American and World literature and theory, including Caribbean narratives and its interactions with other cultures and races.

Jay Jones-Mills is Bahamian, a widow with one adult son. She is a registered nurse by profession and practised nursing in England before returning to The Bahamas. In addition, she holds a certificate in Secretarial Science and also had a short foray in Catering. More recently, she worked in the Administration area at a foreign language school. Currently, she is a Sales Manager with Heritage International (Bahamas) Limited and the local distributor of a Canadian-based tertiary education savings plan. Jay Jones-Mills enjoys a good thriller, novel, or movie; solving crossword puzzles; theatrical productions; and fitness walking. She is active in her church particularly in the Children's and Small Group Ministries.

Zhivargo Laing is a Bahamian business consultant. He is a former Minister of Economic Development and Minister of Finance in The Bahamas who lead the government's policy efforts in the areas of financial services, international trade, foreign investment, and e-government development for some ten years. He is a graduate of the University of Western Ontario, with graduate studies at The George Washington University, the Robert Kennedy College/University of Cumbria School of Business, and Bangor University in Wales, England UK. Mr. Laing's training is in economics, finance, business, and leadership. Mr. Laing was a key government leader during the Great Recession of 2007/2008. He was responsible for leading the country's fiscal stimulus programme, developing the country's 24/7 E-government platform, laying the foundation for the country's small- and medium-size business development legislation, and re-engineering the country's business license and fiscal reform regime. Mr. Laing's work with the Bahamas Financial Services Board helps to craft the country's strategic direction for the industry. He was also the lead policy negotiator on the country's response to a number of international regulatory developments impacting the financial services sector. Mr. Laing is now the Executive Director and Senior Policy Fellow at the University of The Bahamas. He is also an author, radio talk show host, and columnist. He is married and has four children.

Michelle McLeod is an Acting Programme Director at the Centre for Hotel and Tourism Management at the University of the West Indies (UWI), Nassau, The Bahamas. Dr. McLeod's tourism industry experience spans over 25 years, and she is a graduate of UWI, University of Surrey, and Bournemouth University where she obtained a doctorate with no corrections after her viva. Dr. McLeod received the Principal's Award for the Research Project with Greatest Economic Impact for the Faculty of Social Sciences for the project entitled "Open Data and Interactive Community Mapping: Empowering Local Community Tourism" in 2018; the Principal's Award for Research Project Attracting the Most Research Funds in the Faculty of Social Sciences for the project entitled "Harnessing Open Data to Achieve Development Results in Latin America and the Caribbean" in 2016; Best Researcher in the Mona School of Business and Management in 2016; the Institute of Travel and Tourism, PhD Research Student of the Year in 2010; and the UKAIS (United Kingdom Academy of Information Systems) PhD Consortium, Winner of PhD Consortium Best Presentation Prize in April 2008. Dr. McLeod's two co-edited books are entitled *Knowledge Networks and Tourism* and *Tourism Management in Warm-Water Island Destinations.* Her present research interests are in the subject areas of tourism, knowledge networks, open data ecosystems, policy networks, destination networks, and service productivity.

Edward Minnis holds a Master of Art in History from Carlton University, Canada. He is an accomplished artist and a playwright. He is a junior Full-Stack Web Developer and Software Supply Analyst.

Bridgette Rolle is a highly specialized and experienced professional in education and training who has contributed to the development of education policies, administration, and programmes in the Commonwealth of The Bahamas. Dr. Bridgette Rolle's career started as the principal Adviser to the Minister of Education and Training through executive management activities that included the assessment and restructuring of the Ministry's portfolio which included analysis and evaluation of special educational projects. As Administrator for the University of the West Indies Medical School, Dr. Rolle's role and responsibilities expanded and to become less about restructuring, analysing, and assessing, to one of decision-base management. Her current role as Deputy Permanent Secretary in the Ministry of Health finds her again assisting with policy, planning, and development but with direct oversight for the management of the Bahamas National Drug Council. Some of her previous works include but was not limited to developing a mechanism for delivering The Bahamas' first Bachelor of Pharmacy Degree, currently offered at the University of The Bahamas, and developing a comprehensive Customer Service Manual for The Bahamas Ministry of Tourism. Over the years, Dr. Rolle became certified as a Drug Prevention Specialist, obtained CARIAD Certificates in Addiction Studies and Motivational Interviewing. She is also an Adjunct Lecturer for the University of the West Indies and has training in Grant Writing. Dr. Rolle has written five children's books pending publication. She has one son, Sy Bradford LaRoda.

Neil Sealey was educated in the West Indies and England, completing his graduate and postgraduate studies at Oxford and London Universities. He was a Senior Lecturer in Geography at the College of The Bahamas now University of The Bahamas for many years. He now manages the book publication and distribution arm of Media Enterprises Ltd. in Nassau. Mr. Sealey has authored several books on the geography of The Bahamas.

Adelle Thomas is Senior Caribbean Research Associate for the IMPACT project and part of the Science team. Dr. Thomas's foci are on aspects of social vulnerability, adaptation strategies, and loss and damage. Prior to joining Climate Analytics, Adelle was an Assistant Professor and Director of the Climate Change Initiative at the University of The Bahamas. Dr. Thomas maintains an affiliation with the University of The Bahamas as a Visiting Researcher where she is involved with small island sustainability initiatives. As a human-environment geographer, she is interested in the particular vulnerabilities and adaptation potentials for small island developing states. Dr. Thomas is a contributing author to the "Intergovernmental Panel on Climate Change's Fifth Assessment Report", and her publications also appear in academic journals such as *Geography Compass* and *International Journal of Climate Change Strategies and Management*. She is the Chairperson of the Public Education and Outreach Subcommittee of the National Climate Change Committee, the co-founder of the Climate Change Initiative at the University of The Bahamas, and a member of the UNFCCC Technology Executive Committee.

Stacey Wells-Moultrie was born and raised in New Providence in The Bahamas but spent many summers with her grandmother in Savannah Sound, Eleuthera, where she learned to appreciate the beauty of the Bahamian natural environment. Her interest in science was fostered by her father who would watch National Geographic episodes on television with her.

He passed his love of the sea to her, and she decided to study marine sciences. After receiving a Bachelor of Science degree in Zoology (specializing in Marine Sciences and Fisheries) from the University of the West Indies, Moultrie-Wells completed further studies at Dalhousie University, where she obtained a master's in Marine Management. She returned to The Bahamas and worked for several years as an environmental officer in the public service and a senior policy advisor for a non-governmental organization. She is now employed as an environmental consultant, specializing in environmental policy and planning. In 2016, Moultrie-Wells was awarded a master's in Urban Planning at the University of Florida with a sustainability specialization. She plans to continue her research on indicators and development of an assessment tool specific to Small Island Developing States to aid in their achievement of sustainability.

Foreword

There are few economic sectors, if any, as complex as tourism. That complexity is perhaps best reflected in the powerful but little used tourism satellite accounting system introduced by the United Nations World Tourism Organization (UNWTO) to measure the effects and flows of tourism expenditure throughout an economy. That complexity is further reflected by the resignation of many countries to measuring tourism simply by a headcount of visitor arrivals, a measure that is akin to banks using turnstile counts to measure the profitability of their operations.

But economies such as that of The Bahamas that are highly reliant on tourism have no choice but to venture far beyond simple headcount in determining strategies; policies; and the economic, environmental, and social effects of tourism. And the complexities are compounded by the now mandatory and welcomed focus on "sustainable development", a phrase that may have as many meanings depending on the authors. The definitions of "sustainable development" considered and selected in these chapters have the wonderful combination of a solid core and enough flexibility to recognize that one size never fits all.

Then there are the conversations about culture. Not the narrower view of the artistic aspects of culture only but the generic aspects that take into consideration the desires and wishes of the people who often eagerly embrace that which brings higher incomes and higher standards of living as often measured against those of visitors.

One suspects that much of the acculturation that is often attributed to the influences of visitors on local culture could just as easily be attributed to the pervasive access to and impact of cultural expressions delivered via the ubiquitous electronic media. But it is precisely those kinds of differing effects that the authors of this volume attempt to identify from the voluminous data found in the rich references and from their own seminal and original studies.

The slow-motion crisis of climate change is deserving of much greater discussion. While all of the issues addressed in this compilation on tourism would be of high interest in Small Island Developing States (SIDS) it will be our collective inertia in the face of climate change (and possibly brain drain) for which our grandchildren will give us eternal hell if we maintain our current posture. And it is the subject of climate change that places all SIDS of our region and beyond clearly in the same boat that transports us all.

The chapter "Vacation Rental Market in The Bahamas" is easy reading and should be required reading across The Bahamas and our region. The evolution described is likely to be found throughout the Caribbean that is arcing to the benefit of a broader involvement of local providers, a universal objective of nearly all communities. "Room rates" have always been a misnomer as very few travellers select a destination for the room. The evolution of accommodations highlights the desire of many travellers to engage safely with local people and live actually and vicariously, for a short period of time, as a member of the local community.

This book would have been incomplete without the marketing people weighing in. They have always known that the many attempts at the commoditization of tourism are impossible because of the many variables involved, the very reason for its complexity. Travel and tourism have always been about experiences, and there has never been any such thing as a unit of experience. Even the recent introduction of such terms as "the Blue Economy" which is covered herein is marketing and promoting an always-present opportunity that is made so much more attractive by this new moniker.

Then, there is the gorilla in the room: hurricanes that appear to be increasing in intensity if not frequency. The crisis of Hurricane Dorian has become a catalyst for action, innovation, and change in The Bahamas. It has already engendered the implementation of policies and practices in air and sea transportation, more resilient construction, and sustainable practices that have long been only discussion points in academic debates. So, the timing of this volume from academia just might be perfect in the current atmosphere that is more welcoming of thoughtful change than any other in recent memory.

No one should mistake this book as it is about The Bahamas despite its title. The Bahamas is merely the locus of many of the citations. It is really a book about tourism in SIDS, and anyone interested in that subject would profit from reading it thoroughly.

The Bahamas and the Caribbean together comprise the world's most tourism-dependent region, and there has long been a cry suggesting that The Bahamas and the Caribbean should therefore be the world's most tourism conversant and tourism competent regions.

This small volume is not intended to be anything close to an exhaustive treatment of tourism. But it is a serious attempt to address the complexities of tourism and tease out some of the more important factors that affect this most vital economic sector.

As much as anything else, it begins to fill a void by delivering a *highly readable* display of tourism knowledge that is easily accessible to many of our citizens across The Bahamas and the Caribbean and which should thereby redound to their and our collective benefit.

Vincent Vanderpool-Wallace

Acknowledgements

This text would not have been possible had it not been for the hard work, dedication, and professionalism of each contributing author. We are deeply indebted to all 13 authors. We are especially thankful to the former Director General of Tourism, Mr. Vincent Vanderpool-Wallace for his contributions to the Foreword and Dr. Joshua Carroll for the concluding chapter in the text. We give a special thanks to Emma Travis, Nazrine Azeez and their teams for their acceptance, advice, and support for and throughout this publication. Finally, we are grateful for having such a fertile landscape in which to write such a text. The Bahamas consisting of its many Islands and Cays provided a wonderful opportunity to the researchers to delve into areas of tourism development, governance, and sustainability. This is the first of many books in this area and we are very happy to have written it for the people of The Bahamas, the Caribbean Diaspora and scholars, enthusiasts, and others wanting to study tourism.

Abbreviations

5M	Measuring, Monitoring, Mapping, Modelling and Managing
AMOEBA	A Multidirectional Optimum Ecotope-Based Algorithm
AOSIS	Alliance of Small Island States
ANT	Actor Network Theory
BACUS	Bahamas Association for Cultural Studies
BEST	Bahamas Environment, Science and Technology Commission
BHA	Bahamas Hotel Association
BNFC	Bahamas National Festival Commission
BPoA	Barbados Programme of Action
BSD	Bahamian Dollar
CARICOM	Caribbean Community
CAS	Creativity, Activity, Service
CBD	Convention on Biological Diversity
CEDAW	Convention on the Elimination of Discrimination Against Women
CO_2	Carbon Dioxide
CCCCC	Caribbean Community Climate Change Centre
COFCOR	Council of Foreign and Community Relations
CLDCSID	Countries, Landlocked Developing Countries and Small Island Developing States
CTO	Caribbean Tourism Organization
DMO	Destination Management Organizations
DSF	Destination Sustainability Framework
ECLAC	Economic Commission for Latin America and the Caribbean
EF	Ecological Footprint
EIA	Environmental Impact Assessment
EVI	Environmental Vulnerability Index
FAO	Food and Agriculture Organization
FOC	United Nations Statistical Commission Friends of the Chair
GCF	Green Climate Fund

GHG	Greenhouse Gases
FDI	Foreign Direct Investment
FNM	Free National Movement
FTU	Friendliness Through Understanding
GDP	Gross Domestic Product
GIS	Geographic Information System
IAEG-SDG	Inter-Agency and Expert Group on Sustainable Development Goal Indicators
IAS	Invasive Alien Species
ILAC	Spanish acronym for Latin American and Caribbean Imitative for Sustainable Development
InVEST	Integrated Valuation of Ecosystem Services and Trade-offs
IPCC	Intergovernmental Panel on Climate Change
IUCN	International Union for Conservation of Nature
LDC	Less Developed Country
LTO	Local Tourism Organisation
NEMA	National Emergency Management Agency
MATH	Marijuana Agro-Tourism Habitat
MHA	Member of the House of Assembly
MOU	Memorandum of Understanding
MPA	Marine Protected Area
NDP	National Development Plan
NEMA	National Emergency Management Agency
NPACC	National Policy for the Adaptation to Climate Change
PGCE	Postgraduate Certificate in Education
PLP	Progressive Liberal Party
ODA	Official Development Assistance
PM	Particulate Matter
PoU	Prevalence of Undernourishment
PPP	Public, Private Partners
R&B	Rhythm and Blues
SD	Sustainable Development
SDG	Sustainable Development Goals
SFO	Satellite Fisheries Outpost
SDSN	Sustainable Development Solutions Network
SEEA-EEA	System of Environmental-Economic Accounting and Experimental Ecosystem Accounting
SIDS	Small Island Developing States
SIDSNET	Small Island Developing States Network
SIS	Small Island States
SIE	Small Island Economies
SNA	Social Network Analysis
SME	Single Market Economy
SOPAC	South Pacific Applied Geoscience Commission
SPC	Secretariat of the Pacific Community

TFC	Total Final Consumption
TSA	Transport Security Agency
UBP	United Bahamian Party
UK	United Kingdom
UN	United Nations
UN DESA	United Nations Department of Economic and Social Affairs
U.S.	United States
UNCTAD	UN Conference on Trade and Development
UNEP	United Nations Environmental Programme
UNEP ROLAC	United Nations Environment Programme Regional Office of Latin America and the Caribbean
UNICEF	United Nations International Children's Fund
UN-OHRLLS	The United Nations Office of the High Representative for the Least Developed Countries
UNSD	United Nations Statistics Division
UNSC	United Nations Statistical Commission
UNWTO	United Nations World Tourism Organization
USD	United States Dollars
VAT	Value Added Tax
VR	Vacation Rentals
VRBO	Vacation Rentals by Owner
WCED	World Commission on Environment and Development
WGEI	Working Group on Audit of Extractive Industries
WHO	World Health Organisation
WTTC	World Travel and Tourism Council
WWFN	World-Wide Fund for Nature

Introduction

This book addresses issues regarding tourism and tourism development, governance and sustainability in The Bahamas. These areas have a special relationship between visitors, the industry, the environment and local communities. Tourism and tourism development are important impelling causes that move the Bahamian economy and society. This book is specifically focused on The Bahamas as not enough information is written on these areas and not compiled into a book such as this. The chapters are written by several authors with differing expertise and differing views. They all however provide some new perspectives into the workings of the country's most important industry, tourism, and additionally, provide insight into different strategies this small island nation used to remain relevant as a tourist destination.

This book further draws together diverse concepts and understandings that really speak to a changing geography of tourism and development as well as the need for a better understanding of how to build smarter for a stronger tourism product that includes local community welfare and wealth.

Finally, this book will provide university students especially those in tourism, business and the social sciences disciplines with a robust and intellectual discussion on matters of sustainability, governance and development from the perspective of small and resilient multi-island destination.

The Bahamas are an archipelago of approximately 700 islands and 2,400 uninhabited islets and cays laying 50 miles off the east coast of Florida to the north and east coast of Cuba. Only 30 islands are inhabited. Some of the islands are New Providence on which the capital Nassau is found, Grand Bahama – Freeport, Abaco, Bimini, Eleuthera, Cat Island, Mayaguana, Exuma, Ragged Island and Inagua (www.bahamas.com).

Tourism in The Bahamas grew from a very small industry in the 19th century to a multi-million-dollar industry in the 21st century and is one of the main generators of employment in the country (Cleare, 2007). Approximately 65% of the Bahamian workforce is directly employed with in tourism (www.bhahotels.com), and tourism accounts for approximately 50–70% of the country's GDP (www.cia.gov).

Across the 1920s through the 2010s, tourism has made an impact on the natural and built environments, in addition to the well-being and culture of host and visitor populations. For instance, some of the Bahamian islands have experienced loss of mangroves due to dredging to accommodate marinas and mega hotel resorts, soil erosion, loss of natural habitat and increased pollution (Rolle et al., 2015). At the same time, residents and visitors participated in local festivals such as Junkanoo, regattas and Goombay summer. The interaction between visitor and resident often provides a learning opportunity and cultural exchange among them. Additionally, tourism has played a role in insuring the sustainability of the overall tourism sector because the 1 million plus tourists who visit The Bahamas annually help to maintain the livelihood of stakeholders such as hotel operators, restaurants, tour guides, water sports and dive companies (Bahamas Investment Authority (ND); Ministry of Tourism, 2019a). Potential negative impacts are income inequalities, commoditization of cultural heritage, increased socio-economic disparity, sense of disenfranchisement and loss of cultural identity (Rolle et al., 2015; Vison 2040 (2016) UNEP&WTO, 2005). These challenges are exacerbated by natural disasters worsened by sea level rise and global warming.

Climate change must also be added to the mix when addressing tourism governance, development and sustainability because climate change affects the environment, social well-being and economies. Tourism and its related sectors are highly vulnerable to a wide range of crises such as terrorism, climate change, pandemics, natural disasters (hurricanes) and economic disruptions (COMCEC, August 2017). As pointed out in a report by UN World Tourism Organization (UNWTO) and partner organizations (2008), the tourism industry and governments have the responsibility of developing mitigation and adaptation strategies to respond to the challenges that global climate change will have on tourist destinations and allied industries. Moreover, the tourism sector and governments should capitalize upon new opportunities that may emerge from climate change economically, environmentally and socially.

Climate change, recognized as a major global issue (UNWTO, 2008; IPCC Report, 2018), has significant implications for tourism in The Bahamas, particularly as The Bahamas is one of the SIDS to be greatly impacted by climate change and sea level rise (Hartnell, 2016; Rolle, 2019). In terms of sea level rise, studies have indicated that "if projected sea level rise is reached by 2050, between 10–12% of the Islands of The Bahamas – Abaco, Grand Bahama, New Providence etc. – will be lost, particularly in coastal zones where the main tourism products are located" (ECLAC, 2011; Mycoo & Donovan, 2017; Rolle, 2019). Additionally, the impact of climate change-sea level rise on the Bahamian tourism market will affect the country's income and government revenues because tourism contributes to around 50–70% of the country's GDP.

Natural disasters such as category 5 hurricanes, which may be tied to climate change (ECLAC, 2011), also impact Bahamian tourism and economy

(Nair, 2019). The Bahamas sits in the hurricane zone of the Atlantic Ocean, so is vulnerable to hurricanes (Granvorka & Strobl 2013). The hurricane season is typically from June to the end of November, and over the years, The Bahamas has experienced mild to severe hurricanes that have affected either all The Bahamas or various islands in the archipelago – Ragged Island, Long Island, Eleuthera (ECLAC, 2011) – with slow moving Hurricane Dorian in 2019 being the most destructive and economically challenging for The Bahamas. It decimated two important economic and tourist-centre islands in the Country – Abaco and Grand Bahama – with damages appraised between $3 and $5 billion and hundreds dead or missing (IADB, 2019; The Bahamas Investor, 2019). The government estimated that it will also take billions of dollars and several years to rebuild Abaco and Grand Bahama (Hartnell, 2016).

Prior to Hurricane Dorian two intense and slow-moving Hurricanes – Joaquin (2015) and Irma (2017) – hit the southern Bahamas. Both caused considerable damage to infrastructure and homes; for example, Hurricane Joaquin's damage was $104.8 million (Hartnell, 2016; Neely, 2019). Both impacted tourism, the economy and environment in that, there was a drop in visitor arrivals for a while, plus the recovery process has been slow. The positive side of this is that many of the affected islands were minimally populated, and so the loss of life and property was not as calamitous as Dorian. However, these hurricanes combined showed weaknesses in the preparation, recovery process, the vulnerability of the economy so reliant on tourism and the need for government and private sector to upgrade their preparedness to tackle hurricanes predicted to be stronger in the future. According to UNWTO et al. (2008), future tropical cyclones (typhoons and hurricanes) will become more intense, with higher wind speeds and more heavy precipitation associated with ongoing increases of tropical sea surface temperatures. This prediction for the future has implications for the Bahamian tourism industry, economy and livelihood (UNWTO et al., 2008; Bahamian Investor, 2019). The environment is the greatest asset of the Bahamian tourism industry; hence, its preservation is paramount to sustainability.

Governments also have an important role to play in creating the context and stimulating actions to ensure that tourism is supported and is more sustainable in the future (United Nations Environment Programme and World Tourism Organization Report, 2005). In The Bahamas, the Government is obliged to provide infrastructural developments such as roads and electricity production and piped-water facilities, schools and hospitals/clinics. While residents have benefited from increased jobs and increased income, they have been plagued with infrastructural challenges like the sustained provision of electricity, access to medical clinics, increased illegal immigration and adequate school facilities particularly in the family islands (Bethell-Bennett, Rolle, & Minnis, 2016).

Governance is also a focal point as local communities' inclusion or exclusion from the decision-making process around how development will look on their island determines how they feel and act. These decisions also impact their quality of life as overcrowding leads to other environmental problems and social ills.

As stated above, tourism in The Bahamas initially began in the 1800s when the Americans came to improve their health in the warmer climates and the British would take extended leaves from the cold and damp of the UK or for medical reasons, and tourism in the islands began to grow (Craton & Saunders, 2000; Cleare, 2007). The 1898 Hotel and Steamship Service Act established Nassau as a winter tourist destination (Cleare, 2007; Ministry of Tourism, 2019). Several other events also contributed to the rise and importance of tourism in the country. Tourism grew due to other sources of income in the islands such as plantations, sponging and fishing, that mainly failed due to bad soil and disease, followed by rum running and wrecking (Craton & Saunders, 2000).

The Bahamas' tourism industry further developed along with a vast number of tourists into South Florida, due to Henry Flagler, founding father of Miami and his railway and cruise line, plus his push into Cuba. These two markets, along with a sea and air, link directly with New York and Florida allowed the free flow of wealthy eastern seaboard residents into the region inclusive of The Bahamas (Cleare, 2007).

Additionally, tourism development occurred, as noted in Gail Saunders' and Angela Cleare's 2007 work on tourism in The Bahamas, with the 1959 Castro Revolution in Cuba that saw that country closed itself off from North American tourists because of the US embargo based on Castro's declaration of his socialist position. When Cuba closed itself off to the US in the 1960s, The Bahamas benefited tremendously. Many of the hotels and businesses left Cuba and moved to other areas and casinos moved to New Providence as Castro nationalized many of American assets in Cuba (Craton & Saunders, 2000).

It must be noted that the Bahamian tourism industry exists as an inside-outside industry as it always developed reliant and in response to external events and conditions such as the 1992 Gulf War crisis. Then in 2001 when the US closed its border as a result of the attacks on September 11, a decreased air travel to The Bahamas resulted in low hotel occupancy. The Bahamas was directly affected as tourism employees were put on day's work or sent home while the downswing continued (www.tourismtoday.com). Then, as mentioned previously, the annual hurricanes, over the years, damaged the islands, especially the devastating Dorian in September 2019. In different ways hurricanes have shaped the tourism sector, employment, development and overall economy of The Bahamas. Despite the setbacks, The Bahamas has been able to rebound, market and rebrand in promoting itself and tourism. For example, over the years, rebrands are as follows: "It's Better in The Bahamas", "Just Off the Coast-Familiar", "Hip to Hop Through the Islands", "Islands of The Bahamas... Fly Away" and, post-Dorian, "14 Islands, Welcome You With Open Arms." Ultimately then, it is essential when examining tourism in The Bahamas to read it not as if it were an exogenous industry and not at all endogenous. This is an important consideration for any valuable study of tourism and development in The Bahamas.

Built on the design implemented by the Minister of Tourism at that time, Sir Stafford Sands, in the 1950s, tourism has remained a Foreign Direct Investment (FDI)-focused industry. Sands encouraged large hotel, steamer and tourism companies to come to The Bahamas through legislation such as the Hotels Encouragement Act of 1954 of which in part was responsible for the development of three of the early major hotels: the British Colonial, the Royal Victoria and the Montague Beach, the latter two have since been demolished (Cleare, 2007). Today, the Sands model of FDI has not been altered; in fact, it has been expanded by successive governments, where major foreign hotel chains own the development and provide Bahamians with jobs (Bethell-Bennett, 2017).

As the tourism product evolved over the years, there have been differing policies by successive governments regarding the size and types of developments, development incentives and commitment to sustainability of tourism resorts and commitment to sustainability of the lifestyles and culture of the local communities in which these resorts are located (Smith. L, 2012; Rolle et al., 2015; Bethell-Bennett, 2017). For example, this was seen in the Resorts World project in Bimini, where residents questioned the wide scope of the development on their small island and how many of the 300 jobs will materialize for them (Alexander, 2014).

Little of that money filters into the local communities aside from through minimum-wage jobs, tours, foods and souvenirs. Resorts and investors offer dreams of wealth and large-scale community success, yet many of them fall flat, as many of the properties in the nation's second city, Freeport in Grand Bahama, can attest, for example, with the closure of the Jack Tar resort and the Four Seasons resort in Exuma (Smith, 2007a, tourismtoday.com).

The focus of tourism shifted in the 1980s and early 1990s to a more mass-marketed approach. This included cruise ships, large-scale resorts with all-inclusive offerings and gated residential communities where gambling and casino life were a draw (www.tourismtoday.com). The mass approach to tourism has meant that tourists usually spend money for travel arrangements in the home market. As Pattullo (1996) indicates, travel packages are purchased and paid for in advance of arrival in the destination, i.e. The Bahamas. Also noted by the Minister of Tourism that on average, cruise ship passengers spend $69.00 and stopover visitors spend approximately $1,500 (Mckenzie, 2017). So, this means that there must be a consideration of the balance between local empowerment, sustainability and tourism development.

Little critical work has been done on the tourism industries in The Bahamas and their impact on the environment apart from Sullivan-Sealy et al.'s (2007) study on the environmental impact of Baker's Bay development on Guana Cay in the Abaco's that can bear this out. The resort promised sustainable models of development and to incorporate environmental impact assessment and ongoing evaluation, as well as efforts to protect the local ecosystem along with other partners; these promises became more pipedreams, and the façade quickly fell. According to their study, a number of environmental issues arose, for example, there was

> unknown material dumped in two landfills; invasive alien plants displacing native vegetation; invasive alien insects (Lobate Lac Scale Insect) impacting the health of native trees, especially after hurricane disturbances; erosion of beaches from the removal of dunes and natural vegetation along Baker's Bay; erosion of beaches from Australian pine (invasive alien plants) and an accumulation of trashes and unregulated dumping to name a few.

The interstitial space between tourism and sustainability has been little explored and even less implemented in The Bahamas because the Government seems to be of the opinion that regulations and controls are unwarranted as they continue to open doors to rather uncontrolled and unpublished Heads of Agreements that give away developments and land to foreign companies in the name of development (Anchor Projects) for the country and economy (Gibson, 2019). An example of this was a joint venture with the Government and the I-Group of investors involving 10, 000 acres of land in the sparsely populated island of Mayaguana. According to Smith (2007b), the project promised $1.8 billion of investments over 15 years and has yet to materialize and to date, still has not. As opined by Fred Smith QC (The Nassau Guardian, 2015), the stated Heads of Agreement is to cut through red tape so a development can proceed as swiftly as possible which leads to the subversion of numerous laws put in place to protect The Bahamas and its environment such as Local Government Act, The planning and Subdivision Act and the Customs Management Act.

It is against this backdrop that this book explores the effects of tourism and tourism development in The Bahamas both positive and negative. The book is divided into three major parts: development, governance and sustainability.

Part I: Development

The chapters brought together here explore different aspects of tourism and development in The Bahamas that have been little explored. The Bahamas is one of the more famous tourism destinations; it seems that little critical apparatus has been employed to examine tourism and to see how tourism can be used to drive more equitable development to keep the natural beauty of the islands, preserved culture and a balance struck between economic development and environmental preservation.

Tourism has become the bedrock of many island economies because of their idyllic lifestyle and picturesque beauty. Tourists desire the experience of being on an island far away from all their worries, but this desire changes lives for locals as land is consumed by development, prices rise and daily essentials such as potable water or electricity become hard to access due to the strain placed on these by an increasing tourist population.

Small island communities like Ragged Island, The Bahamas, offer alternatives to mass-tourism development that are sought after but not at the same levels or by the same people who are interested in the Nassau-based resorts of Atlantis or Baha Mar, and these are as valuable to a diversity of tourism offering as are the former.

Also the chapters in this part addressed tourism and tourism development response to climate change and natural disasters (hurricanes) given that The Bahamas is vulnerable to such climate crises.

Chapter 1 – *Identities in flux: psychological acculturation and developing tourism in The Bahamas* by Mayuri Deka – explores the historical and transnational impacts on nationalism and identification tourism has when it pulls up the ancestral roots of communities and replaces them with gated communities and resorts that remove local access to coastal areas as experienced in Abaco, New Providence and Bimini, for example. The entire community revolves around tourism service, so people are unwilling to challenge their erasure through unbridled development as noted in Chapter 2.

Chapter 2 – *The impact of tourism development on small island communities in The Bahamas: the case of Abaco, Bimini and Exuma* by Jessica Minnis, Sophia Rolle and Ian Bethell-Bennett – also demonstrates that as tourism development in a community gets older, the results or positive correlations with quality of life, improved access to infrastructure and so forth tend to become tempered so that persons in the communities see the resort as more disconnected from them than being there to improve their lives.

Chapter 3 – *Living on islands: tourism and quality of life on the islands of Abaco, Bimini and Exuma The Bahamas a case study* by Jessica Minnis and Margo Blackwell – examines the impact of tourism development-anchor projects on the quality of life of residents on three islands in the archipelago; quality of life as it relates to quality of life indicators such as human, social and built capital. Have these anchor projects really improved the residents' quality of life although they benefitted from increased employment and income? The authors show the respondents belief that tourism and tourism development improved their quality of life even though they recognized the environmental costs of the developments in their islands.

Chapter 4 – *Vacation rental market in The Bahamas* by Jay Jones-Mills – examines the extent to which hotels in the islands are becoming a relic of the past while vacation rentals and Airbnbs are the wave of the future because they have become popular among tourists.

Chapter 5 – *Case study on Bahamian Carnival* by Ian Bethell-Bennett – examines how carnival a festival that has no socio-cultural connection to a traditional Bahamian masquerade, Junkanoo, is justified and incorporated into the established Bahamian Junkanoo and Bahamian culture.

Chapter 6 – *Junkanoo Carnival, Bahamas as a strategy for tourism development* by Ian Bethell-Bennett – shows that moving away from indigenous cultural practices in favour of tourism engineered attractions need to be more closely thought-through. Tourists are not offered access to Junkanoo and would like to experience it. They would also like a cultural product, where guest is immersed in the urban cultural settings of a destination.

Part II: Governance

The focus of this part is the role of governance in tourism and its role in achieving and maintaining a sustainable tourism destination. De Bruyn and Alonso (2012) conceptualized governance as a system to define and implement strategies in which decisions are the result of interaction between public and private institutions (international and local) and society. Further, these sectors need to work together with set values and principles, dialogue, innovation, strong leadership effectiveness and more to achieve a viable tourist destination.

Tourism governance is important in creating and implementing inclusive management process. It is a means by which tourist destinations achieve sustainable development. The chapters in this part examine tourism governance from an economic standpoint but from three different angles, the Panarchy and Actor Network Theory (ANT), the Experienced Economy and a smile and courtesy campaign. It must be noted that Chapter 7 examines tourism governance, panarchy and resilience in The Bahamas, and also addresses the country's response to and mitigation against natural disasters.

Chapter 7 – *Tourism governance, panarchy and resilience in The Bahamas* written by Michelle McLeod – examines the nature of tourism and the role of governance in supporting the economic viability and sustainability of tourism in The Bahamas using the theoretical framework of Panarchy and ANT and the physical and non-physical characteristics of the Bahamian society as a case study. This chapter explains how governance through the cooperation between relevant government and private agencies can build a resilient and sustainable tourist destination.

Chapter 8 – *Atlantis: a case study in the experience economy* written by Zhivargo Laing – uses the Atlantis Resort, Paradise Island, as a case study for the application of the "Experienced Economy" (EE) by Pine and Gilmore (1999) to show a company in this case a tourist service, and intentionally use their product and goods as props to create a memorable event and experience for their customer (tourist). In other words, the EE becomes the experience. A "co-creation" where the buyer (tourist) and the seller (tourist destination), together create a unique tourist experience. It further suggests that the experienced economy can be a mechanism for promoting economic prosperity in the development of the tourism product as well as sustaining its development.

Chapter 9 – *The economics of smiling: a history of the Bahamian courtesy campaign 1955–1970* written by Edward Minnis – analyses how a smile and a courtesy campaign is utilized as a strategy by relevant government sector agencies to emphasize to employees in the tourism industry, and how important these campaigns are in improving the economic well-being of Bahamians and maintaining tourism as the number one industry of the country is discussed.

Part III: Sustainable development

As noted by United Nations Environmental Programme (UNEP), sustainability is based on principles of sound husbandry of the economical and sensible management of resources and on equity in the way that these resources are used and in the way in which the benefits obtained from them are distributed (UNEP, 2005, p. 8).

According to the World Tourism Organization (WTO), sustainable tourism is "tourism that takes full account of its current and future economic, social and environmental impacts, addressing the needs of visitors, the industry, the environment and host communities" (UNEP, 2005, p. 12).

Developed without concern for sustainability and climate change, tourism can not only damage societies and the environment, it can also contain the seed of its own destruction (UNEP, 2005, p. 10). In this regard, the chapters in this part address various aspects of tourism, climate change, tropical cyclones/hurricanes and sustainability.

Chapter 10 – *Assessing sustainability in small island developing states: a comparative analysis of sustainability assessment tools and their applicability to small island developing states* by Stacey Wells-Moultrie – sought to examine existing sustainability assessment tools and how they may or may not be applicable to small island development states (SIDS). Assessment tools were selected based on their uniqueness and features. A secondary look at development of assessment tools, should none already exist, was also examined. Some 304 indicators were initially examined for relevance and based on a series of questions such as SIDS with vulnerability to sea level rise issues, individual and community well-being, external dependence and SIDS with low human capital and weak institutional structures.

This part also brings attention to the blue and green economies that need to be considered.

Chapter 11 – *Toward a blue economy: **Ragged Island:** a case for sustainable development for the islands of The Bahamas* by Bridgette Rolle – initiates a discussion on the sustainable development on Ragged Island, The Bahamas, using the concepts of a "Blue Economy" defined loosely as a long-term strategic plan for development of small island states using ocean-related activities. In fact, it was at the United Nations' General Assembly in 2015 where a resolution to the Sustainable Development Goals (SDGs) was adopted that embraced the notion of small island developing states making more use of the oceans, seas and marine resources for sustainable development of their islands.

Chapter 12 – *Climate change, tourism and sustainable development in The Bahamas* written by Adelle Thomas and Lisa Benjamin – take us through a series of impact scenarios on climate change and their overall impact for the Islands of The Bahamas. It's because of the very nature of the country – being small and archipelagic in nature makes it highly susceptible to climate change and its residual effects. This vulnerability becomes even more pronounced because the country is heavily dependent on tourism as its major driver of the economy. Governments grapple with the decision to spend money on impact mitigation or tourism development. This chapter proffers several policy interventions that, if implemented, will provide excellent strategies for the way forward for small island development states (SIDS) like The Bahamas regarding climate change adaptation.

Chapter 13 – *Marijuana Agro-Tourism Habitat* by Sophia Rolle – proffers the question through a survey of millennials on whether the Government of The Bahamas ought to develop a sustainable Marijuana Agro-Tourism Habitat (MATH) on one of the Out Islands in The Bahamas as a means of diversifying the tourism economy. Millennials saw this as an opportunity for The Bahamas to diversify the tourism industry and introduce an experience that is not found anywhere else in the Caribbean. The chapter further suggests the development of the MATH that will not only bring a "new tourist" to The Bahamas, but it also has the potential of contributing significantly to the overall GDP as well as creating a number of new Bahamian entrepreneurs in the country separate and apart from the traditional tourism products.

Part IV: Development, governance, sustainability. A look at hurricanes

Chapter 14 – *Sustaining tourism after a hurricane* by Neil Sealey – draws on the experiences of Abaco and Grand Bahama, The Bahamas, after they were destroyed by Hurricane Dorian in 2019. Sealey discusses actions that must be addressed and taken by tourist destinations to protect tourists in the eventuality of a hurricane if they are to remain lucrative and sustainable. He makes recommendations that tourist destinations can take to mitigate adverse publicity from tourists and media in order to remain sustainable.

Chapter 15 – *Hurricane Dorian: a case for building comprehensive climate change resilience frameworks for small island developing states in the Caribbean* by Teo Cooper – discusses events of Hurricane Dorian that severely impacted The Bahama islands of Abaco and Grand Bahama in September 2019. Cooper discusses a number of factors such as sea level rise, flooding, state of infrastructure in the islands, level of disaster preparedness, climate change legislation, food and water supplies, climate migration and the need for community building and capacity building, in regard to how small island states (SIDS) respond to climate change and natural disasters. He builds a case for comprehensive climate change resilience frameworks that SIDS can utilize to build climate change resilience, even if financial capacity was limited.

Part V: Conclusion

Chapter 16 – *Toward an understanding of the tourism experience* by Joshua Carroll, weaves together the differing perspectives on tourism development, governance and sustainability in the previous chapters noting there are many differing perspectives regarding both tourism and the most appropriate courses of action to handle tourism. He discusses how these differing views can sometimes be challenges to tourism development on the islands. Alternatively, these views become unique opportunities for tourism and tourism development, particularly with regards to sustainability, growth, and how subtle changes in political atmosphere can have lasting impacts on visitors and the communities that host them. These elements work to shape the views that visitors have of a destination, and to an extent the views that the communities within these visited sites hold of themselves.

References

Alexander, H. (2014). Islands in the stream: The battle for the soul of Bimini. 06 July 2014, www.telegraph.co.uk. Retrieved 1 February 2019.

Bahamas (2015) "Strewn with rotting remains of failed resort projects". 14 August 2015, www.tribune242.com. Retrieved 1 February 2019.

Bahamas Investment Authority (ND). Bahamas Investment authority. Hotel and Resorts https://www.bahamas.gov.bs/wps/portal/public/Guide%20for%20Investors/For%20Hotels%20and%20Resorts/

Blanchet, P. (15 November, 2019). Damages and other impacts on Bahamas by hurricane Dorian estimated at $3.4 billion: Report. News Release. https://www.iadb.org/en/damages-and-other-impacts-bahamas-hurricane-dorian-estimated-34-billion-report. Retrieved 5 November, 2019.

Bethell-Bennett, I. (2017). Tourism and anchor projects: The Bahamian panacea. *The Nassau Guardian*, www.thenassauguardian.com. Retrieved 1 February 2019.

Cleare, A. (2007). *History of tourism in The Bahamas: A global perspective*. Philadelphia, PA: Xlibris.

COMCEC (August 2017). Risk & crisis management in tourism sector: Recovery from crisis in the OIC member countries. https://www.sbb.gov.tr/wp-content/uploads/2018/11/Ris_and_Crisis_Management_in_Tourism_Sector-.pdf. Retrieved 14 April 2020.

Craton, M., & Saunders, G. (2000). *Islands in the stream* (Book 2). Athens: University of Georgia Press.

de Bruyn, C., & Alonso, A. F. (2012). Tourism destination governance, in Eduardo Fayos-solà (ed.), *Knowledge management in tourism: Policy and governance applications* (Bridging tourism theory and practice, Volume 4). Bingley: Emerald Group Publishing Limited, pp. 221–242.

ECLAC (22 October 2011).An assessment of the economic impact of climate change on the tourism sector in the Bahamas. https://www.caribbeanclimate.bz/2010-2011-review-of-the-economics-of-climate-change-recceclacc/. Retrieved 15 December 2019.

Gibson, A. (2019). A young man's view: Signing away The Bahamas. 4 February 2016, www.tribune242.com. Retrieved 1 February 2019.

Granvorka, C., & Strobl, E. (2013). The impact of hurricane strikes on the tourism in the Caribbean. Retrieved, 8 December, 2019. https://pdfs.semanticscholar.org/adcf/d044dfc9d6172b34661f691c75a4038f3693.pd

Hartnell, N. (2016). Bahamas facing $500m climate impact by 2025. Wednesday, December 2016, www.tribune242.com. Retrieved 1 February 2019.

IADB (15 November 2019). Damages and other impacts on Bahamas by hurricane Dorian estimated at $3.4 billion: report. Retrieved 8 December, 2019. https://www.iadb.org/en/damages-and-other-impacts-bahamas-hurricane-dorian-estimated-34-billion-report

IPCC. (2018). Summary for Policymakers. In: Global Warming of 1.5°C. An IPCC Special Report on the impacts of global warming of 1.5°C above pre-industrial levels and related global greenhouse gas emission pathways, in the context of strengthening the global response to the threat of climate change, sustainable development, and efforts to eradicate poverty [Masson-Delmotte, V., P. Zhai, H.-O. Pörtner, D. Roberts, J. Skea, P.R. Shukla, A. Pirani, W. Moufouma-Okia, C. Péan, R. Pidcock, S. Connors, J.B.R. Matthews, Y. Chen, X. Zhou, M.I. Gomis, E. Lonnoy, T. Maycock, M. Tignor, and T. Waterfield (eds.)]. In Press. https://www.ipcc.ch/site/assets/uploads/sites/2/2019/06/SR15_Full_Report_High_Res.pdf.

McKenzie, N. (2017). We need tourist to spend more money. *The Tribune*, www.tribune242.com. Retrieved 2 February 2019.

Ministry of Tourism. (2019a). The history of the ministry of tourism. www.tourismtoday.com. Retrieved 2 March 2019.

Ministry of Tourism. (2019b). The history of The Bahamas before 1945. www.tourismtoday.com. Retrieved 2 March 2019.

Mycoo, M. and Donovan, M.G. (2017). *A blue urban agenda: Adapting to climate change in the coastal cities of Caribbean and Pacific small island developing states.* New York and Washington, DC: IDB Monograph. doi: 10.18235/0000690.

Nair, V. (27 September, 2019) Tourism resilience: Bouncing back after hurricanes. The Nassau Guardian. https://thenassauguardian.com/2019/09/27/tourism-resilience-bouncing-back-after-hurricanes/.

Neely, W. (2019) The greatest and deadliest hurricanes to impact The Bahamas. The stories behind the great storms. Bloomington, IN; iUniverse.

Pattullo, P. (1996). *Last resorts: The cost of tourism in the Caribbean.* Kingston: Ian Randle Publishers.

Pine II, J. and Gilmore, J. H. (July–August 1998). Welcome to the Experience Economy. *Harvard Business Review.* https://www.researchgate.net/publication/260917972_The_experience_economy_pastpresent_and_future. Retrieved 15 December 2019.

Rolle, S. et al. (2015). Vision 2040: Situational analysis/the dynamics of family island development. Unpublished document for the National Development Plan 2040. College of The Bahamas, Nassau, The Bahamas.

Rolle, R. (4 November, 2019). New report: Rising seas risk worse than feared. The Tribune. http://www.tribune242.com/news/2019/nov/05/rising-seas-risk-worse-feared/. Retrieved 2 December 2019.

Smith, D. (2012). PLP plan jettison's anchor project. *The Tribune*. 25 April 2012, www.tribune242.com. Retrieved 1 February 2019.

Smith, L. (2007a). Mixed track record of out island resort projects. *The Tribune*. 18 July 2012, www.tribune242.com. Retrieved 2 April 2019.

Smith, L. (2007b). Tourism and anchor projects in The Bahamas. 21 March 2007, www.bahamapundit.com. Retrieved 2 February 2019.

Sullivan-Sealey, K., Cushion, N., Semon, K., & Constantine, S. (2007). Environmental management program for Baker's Bay Club. Great Guana Cay, Abaco, Bahamas. University of Miami.

The Bahamas Investor. (18 September, 2019) Dorian could cost The Bahamas $3-5bn. http://www.thebahamasinvestor.com/2019/dorian-could-cost-bahamas-3-5bn/. Retrieved 5 December 2019.

The Nassau Guardian. (14 August 2015). Anchor projects the 'bane of The Bahamas' Smith Says. The Nassau Guardian. https://thenassauguardian.com/2015/08/14/anchor-projects-the-bane-of-the-bahamas-smith-says/. Retrieved, 22 September 2019.

UNEP/UNWTO. (2005). *Making tourism more sustainable: A guide for policy makers.* France: Division of Technology, Industry and Economics, pp. 8, 9, 10. http//wedocs.unep.org/handle/20.500.11822/8741http://wedocs.unep.org/handle/20.500.11822/8741.

UNWTO. (2008). Climate Change and Tourism – Responding to Global Challenges. World Tourism Organization and United Nations Environment Programme. Madrid, Spain. http://www.unep.fr/shared/publications/pdf/WEBx0142xPAClimateChangeandTourismGlobalChallenges.pdf.

Vision 2040 (2016). State of the nation report: National development plan of The Bahamas. http://www.vision2040bahamas.org/. Retrieved 02 April 2019.

Part I

Development

1   Identities in flux

Psychological acculturation and developing tourism in The Bahamas

Mayuri Deka

A change in the slogan from the famous "It's Better in The Bahamas" to "The Islands of The Bahamas... It Just Keeps Getting Better" in the mid-1990s indicates not only a revision of the marketing strategies designed for the Family Islands but also a shift in the perspective toward the tourism sector in its entirety based on the changing socio-economic trends. Focusing more on possibilities, this slogan encapsulates the selling of wish-fulfillment where tourist is able "to insert his/her own fantasy about a vacation in The Islands of The Bahamas and thereby cover the widest possible range of vacation experiences" (Delancy, 1996).[1] Potential and present tourists are encouraged in viewing this slogan to imagine a destination where not only their fantasies of sun, sand and sea are satisfied but also they can interject their personal version of the perfect Bahamian vacation onto the reality. This is evident in the policy shift in viewing tourism as a mass-marketed industry to attract massive numbers beginning since the 1980s. With an objective of boosting the flailing tourist numbers, the Bahamian government initiated multiple programs within the tourism sector.[2] One of the most prominent campaigns of these governmental initiatives, under the flagship of Clement T. Maynard and the Ministry of Tourism, was aimed at instilling in Bahamians a sense of pride in their role as good hosts to the tourists.

As a means of creating a lasting image of the "fun-loving, eager" Bahamians, this campaign had far-reaching consequences. Presented to the world as such, as Strachan (2003) points out, "the clientele has ingrained images of how the 'natives' ought to behave at all times and how they should treat visitors" (p. 116). The image of the quintessentially smiling Bahamian with a colorful cocktail in hand willing to serve the tourist became ubiquitous with this marketing push. With the increase in visitor numbers combined with these programs promoting a happy servility in the Bahamian population, there has been an increasingly one-sided contact between the "donor" culture and the "recipient" host culture where the acculturative pressure flows in an unbalanced way.[3] While tourists do take home certain aspects of Bahamian culture based on their appreciation of the culture, as is evident from 53.1% of tourists in 2016 indicating that they would return to the islands, the inequality of this influence seems to be only increasing.

This is impacting not only the Bahamian host culture, but also resulting in individuals demonstrating changes in traits and behaviors as a response to this acculturation. As the chapter presents in the next section, there is growing evidence of a biased process where while some Bahamians resisting this influence, many are "borrowing" more from the tourists resulting in acculturation (psychological) stress in the individuals. This impacts not only the effective functioning of individuals in their daily lives, but also their overall skills in dealing with novel situations.

The individual in the social: tourism and acculturation in The Bahamas

But can tourism shape self-perception of Bahamians through its presence? So pervasive and overpowering an industry must – through its physical presence, its economic presence, its social presence, and its media presence – impose itself on the imaginations of Bahamians, i.e., impose itself in such a way that it begins to affect how Bahamians imagine themselves as social beings, and how Bahamians imagine the landscape of their community, country, and world (Strachan, 2003, p. 114).

Within the updated framework of tourism since the 1980s, The Bahamas has become a commodity that sells itself as the "Paradise" – a land drenched in sun, rum and good times. The numbers show the popularity of this myth as the tourists flock to the country. The arrival of tourists in The Bahamas increased to 707.50 thousand in March 2018 from 609.6 thousand in December of 2017 (https://tradingeconomics.com/bahamas/tourist-arrivals). While Caribbean Tourism Organization's Caribbean Tourism Performance Report released in 2018 shows that The Bahamas was not a part of the member countries that recoded the highest percentage of visitor growth in 2017, the increased numbers of tourists do indicate the favorability of The Bahamas as a tourist destination. J.H. Bounds (1978) in his study of the Bahamian tourism sector from the beginning of the tourism sector to the late 1970s pointed out the following:

> The Bahamian people are part of the great triumvirate of tourism: sun, sand, and an amiable people. A nation that can mix these three agreeable proportions into a tourist attracting amenity can languish in a luxurious tourism industry. There is no better combination for attracting tourists and The Bahamas has all three in the most perfect proportions. The Bahamian people are mostly Black with a strong culture related to the Caribbean Black culture with its tendencies toward sleepiness, laziness, strong Christian religion, a slow pace of life, a strong musical rhythm best exemplified in the calypso (Goombay in The Bahamas), a great ability to dance, an interest in living one day at a time, and a social friendliness toward each other and their guests that makes tourists want to meet them.
>
> (pp. 186–187)

The favorable perspective of the likeability of the Bahamian people and its impact in promoting tourism to the country is reminiscent of the sensitizing campaign of the Ministry of Tourism in the 1980s. Individual Bahamians became the target as one of the factors in "the great triumvirate of tourism." Trained to become more welcoming and exhibit all the traits of a "good host," this stress on "service with a smile" was aimed to eradicate or at least diminish the negative connotations of "servility" redolent of the era of slavery. Consistently attempting to anticipate the expectations of the tourists, the Bahamian worker was to happily and willingly cater to the desires of the tourist. The pride in the work as a "good host" they do was intrinsically entwined with fulfilling the tourist's wishes for a perfect holiday in paradise. However, given the country's history in slavery Strachan (2003) points out that "in The Bahamas, as in the rest of the region, there is a line in the minds of the people between 'service' and 'servility'" (p. 116). The consequences of this campaign which while actively trying to emphasize a certain type of Bahamian in the interaction with the tourist become even more crucial when we consider the scope of the tourism sector within the country. According to the Travel and Tourism Economic Impact (2017) report generated by the World Travel and Tourism Council, the direct contribution of Travel and Tourism to GDP in 2016 was BSD 1,773.9 million (19.8% of GDP) (p. 7). This was expected to rise by 3.4% to BSD (1,834.7 million) in 2017. Tourism also generated 53,000 jobs directly in 2016 (27.3% of total employment), and this is projected to increase by 3.3% in 2017 to 55,000 (27.9% of total employment). The scope of these jobs is vast including employment by hotels, travel agents, airlines, and other passenger transportation services (excluding commuter services) along with restaurant and leisure industries directly supported by tourists (p. 8). Given that most Bahamians are employed directly or indirectly in tourism and this sector is the major direct contributor to the GDP of the country, there is an increased contact between tourists and Bahamians who aim to please and fit into the "service with a smile" mold.

Furthermore, there are basic structural changes occurring in the tourism sector where tourists' preferences and behaviors are changing (Alegre & Cladera, 2006). Many people are spending long stretches of time in places with a better climate than their home area (Munar, 2010). Moreover, with increasing developments in travel and communications, there are larger numbers of people traveling to other countries to work and partake in partial-tourism. Brent Symonette, Minister of Immigration, stated in June 2017, "In January 2012 to present some 115,323 permits have been issued... Now, whether they are homeowner's permits, permanent residents, permits to reside, resident spouses or work permits" (Repatriation numbers increasing, 2017) is questionable. In a country where the total population in 2017 was 395,361, residents with permits constitute a significant portion of the total demographic. A portion of these are "residential tourists" who only have permits to reside without the right to work.[4] These groups of people from diverse ethno-racial backgrounds become a part, sometimes permanently, of the consumer base in each tourist area. They have a huge impact on the area where they now live (Casado Díaz, 1999) as these partial-tourists are in constant contact with the host culture and society, which in certain situations can lead to acculturation (Cohen, 1984).[5] Wealthier residential tourists often demand and receive accommodations and services from the host culture that duplicates their lives back home. Within The Bahamas, there are many pockets of residence like Lyford Cay and Paradise Island that cater specifically to the lifestyles of the wealthy foreign residents or residential tourists. The functioning of these spaces is dependent on a workforce that supplies exceptional services with a smile. Considering the paucity of these usually better-paid jobs, there is increasing competition to get and stronger desire to retain the job. In this changing economic climate, there is growing evidence that prestige and authority are based on factors such as personal property, political position, economics, and such rather than on family, age, or religion of the traditional Bahamian culture. While tourism is one of the external factors influencing the change in traditional culture resulting often times in acculturation, it is a major player in the transforming relationships between people and cultures of unequal economic development.

Acculturation is the result of consistent and relentless contact between two cultures where the individuals experience a change to their original cultural patterns (Redfield et al., 1936). As Park et al. (2003) explain, it "is a long-term process in which individuals modify or abandon certain aspects of their original culture as they adopt patterns of the new (adopted) culture" (p. 142). When discussing The Bahamas, especially with the increasing contact and impact of the tourists on the cultural form of the country, it becomes crucial to focus not only on the social outcomes but also on the effect on the individuals. While Sam and Berry (2010) show how group acculturation is at the societal level where changes occur in the group's culture, customs, social institutions, food, clothing, and language, individual (or, psychological) acculturation changes a person's psychological make-up and influences them as a unique entity. Individuals assimilate the value systems of the host culture into their own behavior and lifestyles.

Psychological acculturation is, thus, at the level of the individual and is clearly manifested in the contact between the donor and host cultures. Moreover, the psychological response is linked to each other (Berry, 1988, 1990; Berry & Kim, 1987, 1988). It is possible to detect an individual's response to acculturation resulting from their contact through tourism when it changes their group's original belief system and behavior patterns. Within the Bahamian society there are continuous discussions about the increasing influence of the Americans on the original culture. As early as the 1920s–1930s there was fear of assimilating into foreign systems. G. Saunders (1997), for instance, points out how in that era "tourism, which attracted 'the fun-loving heavy drinking' visitors and made liquor so accessible, had a profound impact on Bahamian drinking habits and the growth of alcoholism" (p. 31).

With more access to liquor and the myth of the paradise where fantasies come true, there was a discernible shift in the Bahamian population who adapted to the new cultural stimulus. While there is a general lowering of the levels of alcohol consumption over the last few years, the normalizing and acceptance of alcohol within Bahamian culture is evident.[6] There has and continues to be increased import of not only goods but also attitudes the longer there is contact with tourists from other cultures. For a developing country like The Bahamas, the nature of this contact is essential. Unlike countries with minimal tourist-host ratios where hosts may influence the behavior of tourists while they are in the host community (Ryan, 1991), in The Bahamas since tourists are mainly Western and wealthier than the average Bahamian, there is more likelihood of "borrowing" from the hosts (Mathieson & Wall, 1982).[7] For instance, given that Americans have constituted most of the tourists in the last few decades, there is a growing awareness of an increased "Americanization" of the core cultural values and behaviors such as the growing stress on individual ownership instead of communal investment. The Ministry of Tourism in listing the advantages and disadvantages of tourism states,

> Some say that Tourism has a negative effect on the Bahamian culture. It has often been said that Bahamians have become too Americanized and have lost their identities as they try to become the tourists (actors/actresses, singers, rappers etc.) they see and admire who come to The Bahamas often.
>
> (p. 2)

As a powerful next-door neighbor with superior technology, America has an increasingly huge impact on the socio-economic and political fabric of the nation which percolates to social and individual cultures. The frequent use of Americanized accents while speaking with visitors has become commonplace in the touristic areas. This is even seen in written documents where Bahamians are increasingly using American English. Gonçalves et al. points out that "a tendency for Postcolonial varieties of English...to prefer American spelling over the British one has been observed, at least, for...The Bahamas, regarding syntax". However, the level of assimilation and amount of change in an individual's value and behavioral system would be dependent on the type of strategy they adopt in interacting with the donor culture.

Lew (1989) points out that there are various ways in which the host society's culture could react to the donor culture. The most basic classifications are innovation diffusion and cultural adaptation. In innovative diffusion, there is an adoption of practices developed by a donor culture depending on the level of similarity or difference between the two groups. The greater the similarity, the larger the chances of assimilation by the host culture. Furthermore, as Kastamu (2015) points out "of particular interest is the receiver group's perception of the innovation in terms of relative advantage, compatibility, complexity, experimentation (ability to try without adopting), and visibility of results" (p. 6). On the other hand, cultural adaptation strategies tend to center on the changes in a host culture that happens as a result of evolving external impulses. Rogers (1983) defines cultural adaptation as "the process of change in response to a change in the physical environment, or a change in internal stimuli, such as demography, economics, and organization" (p. 401). These strategies can take multiple forms where in some cases there is resistance to change and a strong desire to preserve the original cultural patterns. In The Bahamas, with the increasing awareness of the "borrowing" from donor cultures, especially American values and behaviors, there is a growing initiative to conserve the traditional ways of living. For instance, there is a growing stress to promote traditional art forms through the Straw Market. But this strategy compartmentalizes the response to the donor culture – borrowing some while resisting others.

For the individuals in the host country, this group strategy is crucial in determining the response to external stimuli. In the process of acculturation, Berry (2003) posits four categories of response to the cross-cultural contact. These categories consist of assimilation where the donor culture is adopted while discarding the host culture; separation where the donor culture is rejected, and the host culture is preserved; integration where the donor culture is acquired while retaining the host culture; and marginalization where both the donor and host cultures are rejected. Both integration and marginalization employ a selective process of maintenance and/or reject the donor culture. This would result in a moderate level of behavioral changes in an individual. Moreover, while some behavioral and attitudinal changes in the individual can be found among those who have chosen the separation strategy, much larger shifts occur in those who adopt the assimilation strategy. It is the adoption of one of these strategies that determines whether an individual has acculturation (psychological) stress which effects their ability to live optimally within a society and maintain good mental health. However, these negative consequences of acculturation are not inevitable as it is possible to successfully adapt to the donor culture, representing a multicultural attitude.[8] Within the Bahamian society, there are increasing instances of individuals exhibiting symptoms of psychological stress and struggling to respond in a healthy manner to the cross-cultural contact though the expanding commercial tourist sector.

Responding to cross-cultural contact: acculturation and psychological stress

It was a glorious playground, but a very expensive place. The tourists poured money into the colony, but the people, both white and colored, gave a great deal of their character in exchange for it (Burns, 1949, p. 37).

Acculturation (psychological) stress is a consequence of acculturation and arises from the pressures to retain certain aspects of the host culture while being forced to adopt the donor culture's values and behaviors (Rodriguez et al., 2002). This stress does not implicitly have to be a negative experience as it can function as a warning system in the face of impending change where the individual is motivated to formulate and execute an effective response. However, when individuals are torn between having to choose between their group and individual strategies, it is possible to suffer from negative acculturation stress. Accordingly, components of acculturative stress may appear differently onto the different acculturation categories of assimilation, separation, integration, and marginalization. Berry (2003) posits that integration results in the lowest levels of stress, whereas marginalization would be associated with the highest levels of stress. An individual who chooses an integration strategy would have lower levels of personal stress as they adopt or resist the cultural values and behaviors of the host culture as expected by their group's expectations of incorporation. This is seen in the success of individuals working in the Bahamian tourist sector when in contact with visitors (especially Americans) who are more able to project the image of the "good host" with all the expected traits such as enthusiasm, happiness, and so on while speaking with an American accent and projecting American ideals, and who can code-switch to Bahamianese one moment later. These individuals can take certain aspects of the donor culture and retain their own original cultural patterns as is expected by the general Bahamians cultural adaptation strategy. This behavior supports and sustains their sense of self as a Bahamian without devaluing their local language or cultural patterns.

This ability to fit into the group's expectation leads to lower acculturation stress than even if the individuals practiced assimilation or separation strategies. As Kastamu (2015) points out both these strategies are "associated with moderate levels of stress since they imply a selection process that may not be supported or appreciated by the individual's relatives or friends" (p. 7). Individuals who choose to adopt characteristics of the donor culture that are not acceptable to the larger group might feel higher levels of stress. For instance, the younger generation is criticized for being "too opinionated" indicating an American valuing of speaking openly and directly to others. This usually translates to young people clearly articulating their thoughts and opinions in a culture that expects them to "sit small" and to be "seen but not heard." Multiple students in my class (University of The Bahamas) during discussions focused on argumentative strategies have hesitated at first to participate fully as they are socialized to believe that strongly stating thoughts is not welcome and is considered rude. As they become more comfortable to state their ideas over the course of the semester with my encouragement, many of them admit to confrontations with parents leading to stress. These numbers increase going into the Junior and Senior years when students disclose how their relationships with family (especially parents) were suffering because they were now openly stating their thoughts. Moreover, they also admitted that their way of thinking had changed and clashed with the way their larger family thought. While some of this can be attributed to general maturation, the large numbers and the stress on "mouthing off" points to a larger phenomenon of cultural assimilation of American values leading to moderate stress. Within this demographic of university students, however, there are very few students who adopt the separation strategy and reject characteristics of the donor (here American) culture. This can be seen in society more so in the older generation who are forced to adopt certain donor characteristics that they are uncomfortable with. Usually, these are the parents of the students who complain about increasing adoption of foreign values and behaviors. Glinton-Meicholas (2000) in her explanation of the objective for the first conference on Bahamian culture and the Bahamas Association for Cultural Studies (BACUS) focuses on the reason why individuals are being forced to adopt,

> We have no clearly defined, stable ethos, and perhaps this is why many of us become chameleons, soaking up that of any people with whom we come in contact. Where we have nothing in place that we acknowledge and validate, something or someone else will fill the gaps for us. We all know that nature has a problem with voids.
>
> (pp. 104–105)

This tendency to pressurize individuals to adopt characteristics that they do not identify with is extremely harmful to the human psyche. This feeling of distance from the group becomes extreme if the individual adopts the marginalization strategy. When an individual does not identify with either the donor culture or the host culture, they tend to suffer from acculturation stress resulting in serious psychological problems. This is usually indicated by the presence of psychosomatic symptoms, depression and anxiety. With technological development and the expansion of the tourism sector, however, sometimes individuals are given no option but to either accept or resist the donor culture according to the group's acculturation strategy.

The individual's ability to negotiate these pressures which appear with increased tourist-host contact is based on multiple factors. Kastamu (2015) points out that "these factors can be delineated under three separate headings: (1) individual variables prior to acculturation; (2) the individual's experience of acculturation; and (3) individual variables during the acculturation process" (p. 55).[9] These variables strongly determine the ability of the individual to undergo optimal acculturation and maintain mental health. If the individual's experience with the donor culture is positive, the acculturation process that they will undergo would be less stressful. For Bahamians, the lesser the cultural distance to the donor (say American), the more positive the results would be. As Berry (1990) claims, the amount and nature of the contact (pleasant/unpleasant), whether the contact meets the individual's requirements and whether the initial contact was viewed as positive or not, may predict the success or failure for subsequent encounters. A hotel worker who has had a positive experience with the people and culture of the donor and understands the advantages of adopting certain characteristics would be more successful in acculturation and suffer from less psychological stress. Indeed, Ministry of Tourism and Aviation's Bahamian Residents General Public Survey (2008) claims, "For those who would choose to work in the tourism industry, the most popular reason by far (72%) was that they 'enjoyed meeting people'" (p. 11). This enjoyment is only possible if the experience between the host and tourist is positive. Conversely, a worker who has had unpleasant experiences with the people and culture of the donor and does not see any clear benefit to assimilating into the culture would probably suffer from psychological stress if pressurized to adopt these values and behaviors. Higgs (2008) focuses on "the lived experience of women, who on a daily basis are compelled to 'perform' their constructed indigenous identities created through the marketing of The Bahamas to the rest of the world, as the 'ultimate tourist destination'" (p. iii). The forced presentation of themselves as always happy and smiling, for instance, to fit the expectations of the tourists' Bahamian vacation fantasy probably results in an unpleasant experience for the workers if they are not actually feeling cheerfulness. As Higgs (2008) further points out that "this performance is not simply an assumption of identity, but a violently psychological, and contradictory, script to mold identity" (p. 32). This form of acculturation strategy where individuals are being pressured to act out the donor culture's expectations while repressing their own identity can result in severe psychological stress. This might be one of the reasons why the Ministry of Tourism and Aviation's Bahamian Residents General Public Survey (2008) found that there was a decrease to 70% in 2008 from 78% in 2006 in the desire of residents that work in the tourism sector. Thus, some aspects of the host-tourist contact may act as stressors for the individual where it is not the acculturative process itself that is a stressor, rather it is how the individual sees them and what they make out of it to be able to cope with the shifts.[10]

The coping strategies and resources that an individual has will eventually determine the level of stress during the acculturation process. These psychological characteristics of the individual are contextual as not only they are influenced by the individual's appraisal of the acculturation process but also the resources available to them for managing it. The emphasis on context means that the shape of the coping efforts is dependent on the individual and the specific variables in the process. It changes with every individual and situation. Therefore, a hotel worker who has prior experience in dealing with the pressures of acculturation would be better suited to cope with an aggressive assimilation group strategy. If a hotel wants its employees (especially those who identify with Bahamianese as their socio-cultural language) to only speak in "Standard English" and/or "Americanized English" while devaluing Bahamianese, then an individual with good coping strategies and resources would be able to counteract the damage to the internal psyche. However, a person who is unable to cope with this situation would probably suffer from low self-esteem, damaged sense of self and depression. The outcome of experiencing an acculturation process is, therefore, dependent on whether the individual evaluates the encounter to be solved successfully or not.

To a large extent this judgment is also determined by the sense of control and self-efficacy an individual believes they exhibit. If the individual believes that in a stressful situation the events are contingent upon their own behavior rather than external stimuli like luck or fate, they may be more liable to have a successful psychological adjustment. However, if the individual perceives to have less or no control over the situation or especially the outcome, the chances of mood disturbances increase (Dyal, 1984; Sandler & Lakey, 1982). As Tran's (1993) research revealed lower levels of personal efficacy have been found to lead to higher levels of depression, and vice-versa. In the example above of the hotel worker who is forced to speak with a specific diction and language, perceived control and self-efficacy becomes pertinent. If workers fear losing their job for non-compliance with the management's dictates, then there is a lower level of perceived control or self-efficacy leading to stress. However, it is also possible that if the individual perceives the situation to be uncontrollable then it might result in acceptance and lesser stress (Folkman, 1984; Litt, 1988). While there are other factors like the availability of coping resources from the social networks around the individual which supports them to create and sustain a cohesive sense of self and the nature of the host society (collectivist-individualist), the level of control exhibited in the evaluation and the action part of the acculturation process has a profound impact on the lessening or heightening of psychological stress.[11]

Psychological stress, therefore, resulting from an acculturation process where the host culture is pressurized to either accept or reject characteristics of the donor culture is contextual and dependent on the evaluation of the situation by the individual along with the available coping strategies. This process is unique to every individual, especially in a country like The Bahamas which has a high tourist-host ratio, and is economically dependent on America where most of the tourists hail from. However, the stress is not implicitly negative as it can be a warning for increasing cultural changes and allows an individual to prepare strategies to cope. The general objective for every individual to maintain optimal mental health is to assess and act the cross-cultural contact that tourism forces on them in such a way that it sustains their sense of self and does not lead to psychosomatic stress and depression.

Conclusion

The Bahamas is the fantasy of sun, sand, and sea where the potential for better things always exists. This is especially true today in the wake of the devastating Hurricane Dorian that swept the Abaco and Grand Bahama's island in September 2019. While the strength of this storm was unimaginable and the destruction historically unprecedented with damages around

US\$7 billion, the governmental and civil response was thought-provoking. Almost as an organic solution, the rallying cry of the nation for the global eyes watching was that The Bahamas was "open for business," i.e., tourism. There was an intrinsic understanding that the failure of the tourism industry at that point would lead to catastrophic losses that the country could not afford. As of October 25, 2019, very prominently in the "Islands of The Bahamas" webpage is the statement:

> More than a month has passed since Hurricane Dorian made landfall on two northern islands of The Bahamas. Already, Grand Bahama Island is rebounding with many of its hotels and attractions reopened and plans for its airport to resume international service soon. While The Abacos face a longer road to recovery, the country remains resilient and steadfast in its commitment to help the island rebuild by maintaining a healthy flow of tourism – which accounts for half of the country's GDP – to the islands that were not affected by the storm.

The stress on the country and its peoples' pledge to the success of the tourist industry and, therefore, the satisfaction of the tourists is apparent. Indeed, in the wake of the storm the desire for the industry to succeed is even greater. Bahamians within the industry are probably, either through their organization's in/direct pressure or through their own impetus, is even more directed toward the wish-fulfillment of the tourists flocking the shores.

However, this myth-building would further result in increased pressure to not only interact with the donor culture but also adopt their cultural characteristics and behaviors. With the Governmental push to provide "service with a smile," the majority of the Bahamians (who work in the tourism sector) are being forced to adopt strategies of either innovation diffusion or cultural adaptation. However, depending on the individual's evaluation of the acculturation process and coping strategies available to them, the result could either be acceptance or psychological stress. Given the proximity to a major socio-economic influencer (the United States), there are increasing numbers of individual's depression and psychosomatic stress within the Bahamian population. While there might be multiple reasons for the increase in these cases, there is also a clear shift in the Bahamian values and behaviors leading to intra- and inter-personal conflict (p. 12). As individuals struggle to maintain optimal mental health, it becomes crucial not only to promote positive cross-cultural contact and evaluation but also to increase the resources available for coping with the shifts.

Notes

1 This shift in the slogan also publicizes the image of the hardworking Bahamian who is tireless committed to improvement, especially within the tourism sector.
2 In conjunction with the sensitizing campaign, as Strachan points out, there was also an increase in worldwide advertising that exuded the battle cry of the officials in the tourism offices "The Bahamas-Our Pride and Joy" (p. 116).

3 It must be noted that there are other factors such as immigration, economic development, and education that are also leading to an increased contact between Bahamian "hosts" and other "donor" cultures. However, the shift in governmental policy toward tourism has resulted in an influx of visitors which has not only rapidly increased the contact but also changed the nature of the "borrowing."

4 The Bahamas 2010 Census indicates that of the 290,725 Bahamian citizens recorded, 95.6% were born in The Bahamas but collectively 2.9% were born in the United States, Haiti, Jamaica, and Turks and Caicos Islands. Other Commonwealth and Non-Commonwealth countries accounted for the balance. Therefore, 4.4% of Bahamian citizens are foreign-born. Furthermore, the total immigrant population represented 18.4% of the Bahamian population. This could also have an impact on the acculturation process of the country.

5 Bethel (2000) in "Navigations: National Identity and the Archipelago" discusses how, especially, in the out islands long-term visitors and winter-residents have a complex and significant impact on the local population which goes beyond the economic.

6 World Health Organization's Global Alcohol Report on The Bahamas has numbers which indicate the levels of alcohol consumption in The Bahamas since the 1960s to the present day.

7 For an ethno-cultural breakdown of the tourist demographic in The Bahamas, please refer to the Demographic and Psychographic Profile: Islands of The Bahamas.

8 As Berry (1990) points out that acculturation stress is not an unavoidable response to acculturation. There are an assortment of group and individual characteristics that predict whether an individual will be affected by this cross-cultural and the variables that govern the relationship between acculturation and stress.

9 Berry and Kim (1987, 1988) claim that factors such as age, gender, education, religion, and health have an impact on the individual's ability to engage properly with acculturation prior to the process. During acculturation, variables such as socio-economic status, experience of pre-acculturation, and knowledge of the donor's language might impact the individual's ability to accept or reject the process. Also, those with control over their contact with the donor culture tend to have less acculturation stress. Individuals with high mobility and voluntariness of contact may experience less difficulty than those who have no control over the donor-host contact (Berry, 1988, 1990; Berry & Kim, 1987, 1988; Berry et al., 1988).

10 Berry (1990) and Brislin et al. (1986) discuss the importance of the individual's interpretation of the acculturation changes and how that can predict the outcome of whether it will lead to psychological stress.

11 Further discussion on social support can be retrieved from Cohen and Wills (1985) and Wethington and Kessler (1986) who explain the ways these networks can provide resources to an individual while sustaining their sense of stability and well-being. Triandis et al. (1988) and Triandis et al. (1990) focus on the various variables of a collectivist-individualist culture that can impact the acculturation process for an individual.

References

Alegre, J., & Cladera, M. (2006). Repeat visitation in mature sun and sand holiday destinations. *Journal of Travel Research*, 44, 288–297.

Berry, J. W. (1988). Imposed etics-emics-derived ethics: The operationalization of a compelling idea. *International Journal of Psychology*, 24, 721–735.

Berry, J. W. (1990). Psychology of acculturation: Understanding individuals moving between cultures. In R. Brislin (Ed.), *Applied Cross-Cultural Psychology* (pp. 232–253). Newbury Park, London: Sage.

Berry, J. W., & Kim, U. (1987). Comparative studies of acculturative stress. *International Migration Review*, 21, 490–511.

Berry, J. W., & Kim, U. (1988). Acculturation and mental health. In P. R. Dasen, J. W. Berry, & N. Sartorius (Eds.), *Health and Cross-Cultural Psychology: Toward Applications* (pp. 207–236). London: Sage.

Bethel, N. (2000). Navigations: National identity and the archipelago. *Yinna: Journal of the Bahamas Association for Cultural Studies*, 1, 21–38.

Bounds, J. H. (1978). The Bahamas tourism industry: Past, present, and future. *Revista Geografica*, 88. Pan American Institute of Geography and History, 167–219.

Brislin, R., Cushner, K., Cherrie, C., & Yong, M. (1986). *Intercultural Interactions: A Practical Guide.* Newbury Park, London: Sage.

Burns, A. (1949). *Colonial Civil Servant.* London: Allen & Unwin.

Casado Díaz, M. A. (1999). Socio-demographic impacts of residential tourism: A case study of Torrevieja, Spain. *International Journal of Tourism Research*, 1(4), 223–237.

Cohen, E. (1984). The sociology of tourism approaches, issues and findings. *Annual Review of Anthropology*, 10, 373–392.

Cohen, S., & Wills, T. A. (1985). Stress, social support, and the buffering hypothesis. *Psychological Bulletin*, 98, 310–357.

Delancy, G. (1996). Tourism in the islands of The Bahamas. Report prepared for the Planning, Research & Statistics Department, Nassau, The Bahamas.

Folkman, S. (1984). Personal control and stress and coping processes: A theoretical analysis. *Journal of Personality and Social Psychology*, 4, 839–852.

Glinton-Meicholas, P. (2000). Uncovering the Bahamian self. *Yinna: Journal of the Bahamas Association for Cultural Studies*, 1, 104–110.

Gonçalves, B., Loureiro-Porto, L., Ramasco, J. J., & Sánchez, D. (2018). Mapping the Americanization of English in space and time. *PLoS One*, 13. Retrieve from http://journals.plos.org/plosone/article?id=10.1371/journal.pone.0197741

Higgs, D. M. (2008). Behind the smile: Negotiating and transforming the tourism-imposed identity of Bahamian women (Doctoral Dissertation). Retrieved from https://scholarworks.bgsu.edu/acs_diss/35/. DM Higgs – 2008 – Cited by 2 – Related articles.

Kastamu, M. P. (2015). Tourism as acculturation process and a modern leisure activity (Doctoral Dissertation). Retrieved from http://www.academia.edu/14883309/Tourism_as_Acculturation_Process_and_a_Modern_Leisure_Activity

Litt, M. D. (1988). Cognitive mediators of stressful experience: Self-efficacy and perceived experience. *Cognitive, Therapy and Research*, 12, 241–260.

Mathieson, A., & Wall, G. (1982). *Tourism: Economic, Physical and Social Impacts.* New York: Longman Scientific & Technical.

Ministry of Tourism and Aviation. (2008). Bahamian residents general public survey. Retrieved from www.tourismtoday.com/sites/default/files/res_report_2008_gb_website.pdf

Munar, P. A. (Ed). (2010). *Turismo Residencial. Aspectos Económicos y Jurídicos.* Madrid: Ed. Dykinson.

Park, S., Paik, H., Skinner, J. D., Ok, S., & Spindler, A. A. (2003). Mothers' acculturation and eating behaviours of Korean American families in California. *Journal of Nutrition Education and Behaviour*, 35, 142–147.

Redfield, R., Linton, R., & Herskovits, M. J. (1936). Memorandum for the study of acculturation. *American Anthropologist*, 38, 149–152.

Repatriation numbers increasing. (June 22, 2017). *The Nassau Guardian.* Retrieved from https://thenassauguardian.com/2017/06/22/repatriation-numbers-increasing/

Robards, C. (2011). Survey: Alcohol abuse a growing problem in The Bahamas. *The Nassau Guardian*. Retrieved from https://owl.english.purdue.edu/owl/resource/560/10/

Rodriguez, N., Myers, H. F., Mira, C. B., Flores, T., & Garcia-Hernandez, L. (2002). Development of the multidimensional acculturative stress inventory for adults of Mexican origin. *Psychological Assessment*, 14, 451–461.

Sam, D. L., & Berry, J. W. (2010). Acculturation: When individuals and groups of different cultural backgrounds meet. *Perspectives on Psychological Science*, 5(4), 472–481.

Strachan, I. G. (2003). *Paradise and Plantation: Tourism and Culture in the Anglophone Caribbean*. Charlottesville and London: University of Virginia Press.

The Islands of The Bahamas. (2019). Retrieved from https://www.bahamas.com/hurricanestorm-Information.

Tran, T. V. (1993). Psychological traumas and depression in a sample of Vietnamese people in the United States. *Health and Social Work*, 18, 184–194.

Travel and Tourism Economic Impact. (2017). Report prepared by the world travel and TourismCouncil, London, United Kingdom. Retrieved from https://www.wttc.org/-/media/files/reports/economic-impact-research/archived/countries-2017-old/montenegro2017.pdf

Triandis, H. C., Brislin, R., & Hui, C. H. (1988). Cross-cultural training across the individualism- collectivism divide. *International Journal of Intercultural Relations*, 12, 269–289.

Triandis, H. C., McCuster, C., & Hui, C. H. (1990). Multimethod probes of individualism and collectivism. *Journal of Personality and Social Psychology*, 59, 1006–1020.

Wethington, E., & Kessler, R. C. (1986). Perceived support received support, and adjustment to stressful life events. *Journal of Health and Social Behavior*, 27, 78–89.

2 The impact of tourism development on small island communities in The Bahamas

The case of Abaco, Bimini and Exuma

Jessica Minnis, Sophia Rolle and Ian Bethell-Bennett

Tourism has become one of the world's fastest growing industries. Yet many of the destinations experience rapid development and find that within years their resorts have become too limited for the ever-increasing appetite for bigger, newer, more entertaining resorts. Tourism has created a small world of enclosed communities in the Caribbean that often cost the countries more than they deliver in jobs, though employment is one of tourism's biggest offers to local communities. Sheller, (2003), Pantojas-Garcia (2008) and Pattullo (1996), among others, work around the polemics of tourism in the Caribbean and its often-troublesome relationship with the local community. The Bahamas has developed a long lasting, at one-time high-end tourism product that attracted winter residents to their shores. This paradigm shifted in the 1980s and early 1990s to a more mass-marketed approach to massive tourism. This included cruise ships, large-scale resorts with all-inclusive offerings and gated residential communities where gambling and casino life were a draw. The mass approach to tourism has meant that tourists usually spend in the home market as Pattullo (1996) indicates as packages are purchased and paid for in advance of arrival in the destination.

The Bahamas's tourism model has not kept pace with those developments. It has continued to rely on a model where Foreign Direct Investment (FDI) would answer all the prayers of the local communities. However, the offshore industry often shows that companies come in for the period of their tax incentives and leave once the tax holiday ends. This has several negative impacts on the community and the country as well as the economy. The Bahamas has been in the tourism business since the mid-1800s, and its approach to tourism development has seen changes due to modern tourism branding strategies, globalization, climate change, sea level rise and catastrophic hurricanes that have over the years proliferated. As the tourism product evolved, similarly, there have been differing policies regarding the size and types of developments, development incentives and commitment to sustainability of tourism resorts and commitment to sustainability of the lifestyles and culture of the local communities in which these resorts are located.

The Bahamas is an archipelago of 700 islands, cays and rocks, with a population of approximately 390,000, most of which reside on the island of New Providence where the capital city is Nassau. New Providence is one of the small islands in the chain that runs from Florida in the north down to Cuba in the south. The island is 21 miles long by 7 miles wide. Bimini, one of the northern islands, is 53 miles east of Miami, Florida, and is divided into South Bimini and North Bimini. North Bimini, where Alice Town, the capital, is 7 miles long by 700 feet wide. Abaco is another group of islands in the Bahama chain and is made up of Great Abaco, Little Abaco and other Cays. Exuma is further south and is made up of numerous cays, sandbars and the main island of Exuma. This pilot examines the populations and developments on Great Guana Cay, Abaco, North Bimini and the main island of Exuma. Many of the cays have been privately owned for decades and have continued to be bought and sold either as private islands to be enjoyed by families or as resort islands to be enjoyed by the likes of cruise ship passengers on Carnival cruises, for example. Some of the islands/cays were ceded or deeded to minor royals before the covenant of The Bahamas was formed. Many of the latter have continued to be exclusive getaways for the rich and famous. For the most part, these privately owned cays were underpopulated, and so there was no displacement of the local population involved. Historically, too, the islands have been very diverse with the particular settlements in the Abaco boasting a predominantly white population and wanting to secede from The Bahamas, to Exuma boasting a predominantly black population that grew, in part, out of the failed plantation of Lord John Rolle who abandoned the same to his former slaves.

Tourism in The Bahamas grew from a very small industry in the 19th century, when Americans came to improve their health in the warmer climates and British would take extended leaves from the cold and damp of the United Kingdom or for medical reasons, to a multi-million-dollar industry in the 21st century. Built on the design implemented by Sir Stafford Sands in the early 20th century, tourism has remained a FDI-focused industry. Sands encouraged large hotel, steamer, and tourism companies to come to The Bahamas through legislation such as the Hotels Encouragement Act, which in part was responsible for the development of three of the early major hotels: the British Colonial, the Royal Victoria and the Montague Beach, the latter two have since been demolished. Tourism grew from other sources of income such as plantations, sponging and fishing, that mostly failed due to bad soil and disease, and rum running and wrecking. The Sands model of FDI has not been altered, in fact, it has been expanded; major hotel chains own the development and provide Bahamians with jobs. This was moderately different during the late 1960s through the early 1990s while the Progressive Liberal Party (PLP), the first majority government that pushed for and achieved independence under the banner of black equality and Bahamianization, was in power. In 1992 this protective legislation began to weaken as government acts such as The Immovable Property Act were repealed by the International Persons

Landholding Act (1993). The former was meant to provide the local population with first choice on land purchases and included them in business development. Since then, it has become possible for foreign companies to establish a presence in The Bahamas without having a local partner, as was required previously. This shift in the power dynamics has created less equality in economic empowerment. However, the push has been to promote tourism, especially as banking – the country's second economic pillar – began to erode.

Governments have been warned of the perils of relying solely on tourism but have chosen to ignore these warnings. One of the early warnings came from the famed *Moyne Report* (1938) that argued that governments should not put all their eggs in the tourism basket. Today, this has been displaced by a focus on tourism at the expense of all other industries in The Bahamas (Saunders, 2003). Agriculture and Industry were pushed out by tourism's glitz and glamour and the allure of less hard work for more money; being a maid or a bartender was easier than working in the fields, and these offered a more 'sustainable' income. Generations were brought up on this belief as The Bahamas moved from a winter tourist industry to a year-round industry after the 1959 Cuban Revolution. Tourism, as Jamaica Kincaid (1988) points out in *A Small Place*, creates disparate worlds: one inhabited by tourists where glamour, pleasure and enjoyment rule, and the other where locals reside that is unglamorous and arduous, what Frantz Fanon (1967), referred to as the native quarter, where poverty, crime and violence dominate. This native quarter was echoed recently by a Member of Parliament who argued that tourist areas needed to be protected more than 'the native quarters', where more policing and control were essential. What has been underscored by studies and the passing of time is that tourism creates many types of social problems that grow with increased tourism development. Many communities that have had tourism for a longer period as Hall and Page (2014) indicate are less happy with it than are communities where tourism is newer.

Tourism has often been a leading driver in the rush to development, but this pilot study examined the kinds of development that were being experienced. Of late, notwithstanding the international literature on tourism and its tendency towards growth but not necessarily development, there have been a number of regional events that have given pause to reflect on the role of tourism in small island communities as well as the role of government in tourism development. Development should encompass all aspects of a nation's fabric from the economic to the industrial and the human capital. For the purposes of this study, one of the most informative statements that has emerged from a discussion around tourism's impact on small island communities is an obiter dicta statement by Justice Carroll in the Save Guana Cay case in the Supreme Court of The Bahamas. In the legal decision Carroll underscores that his observations are not law, nor are the issues they raise justiciable, but he sees them as going to the heart of the matter in these small town communities where large-scale investors come in and remove the land from the commons, and thereby exclude most locals from its enjoyment.

In 2002, the PLP government implemented its Anchor Investment Policy which was intended to promote large-scale developments on each of the occupied Family Islands. This policy saw the development of projects on islands like Mayaguana, Abaco and Grand Bahama which was intended to have the "trickledown effect that would positively impact" other sectors (*Bahama Journal*, August 8, 2006). This concept leads to some misconceptions, and the study will show how the longer-term tourism development projects begin to see the problems inherent in trickledown effect.

In 2007, the Free National Movement (FNM) indicated that it did not intend to continue this policy (*Bahama Journal*, June 14, 2007) but noted its intention to "favour a model that better suits the country's environment." The model, since 2007, has not been altered, notwithstanding the party's pre-election promise and their performance while in office.

Tourism development, no matter what scale, has the potential to impact the lives of island residents and requires a commitment from national governments. Governments are obliged to provide infrastructural developments such as roads and electricity production and piped-water facilities. There must also be access to potable water, schools and clinics. While residents have benefited from increased jobs and increased income, they have been plagued with infrastructural challenges like the sustained provision of electricity, access to medical clinics, increased illegal immigration and adequate school facilities. The best case study on this in the Caribbean was in the mid-1990s with the expansion of El Conquistador Resort development in Puerto Rico where the community would go without water and often without electricity as well when the hotel was booked full, given the strain on the local resources. Similar occurrences have become commonplace in Nassau, with The Bahamas Electricity Corporation, now Bahamas Power and Light, after its semi-privatization and sale, arguing that they had adequately updated their facilities to meet the increasing demand and then in the summer of 2014 having black and brown outs island wide because there is too much demand for the infrastructure. The fear was that Bahamas Electricity Corporation (BEC) will be crippled by the coming online of the new resort Baha Mar in late 2014 (Brown, 2014). In 2018 and 2019, this proves to be warranted with daily power outages in the capital.

Recently, there have been several occurrences on local Family Islands which bring to bear the question of whether tourism development of any kind is firstly needed and secondly wanted by residents of those communities. In 2005, residents of Guana Cay, Abaco, organized themselves into an association intended to fight developers as they felt there would be a "... rape and destruction of the environment, as they have done in Bimini and elsewhere" (The Grand Bahama info Newsletter, 2007).

In December 2007, when the government and the developments of Resorts World on Bimini announced that they would be creating a gated community where residents would have to request permission to enter, local residents rioted. A local columnist attributed this to residents being frustrated as they are confined to one-third of the island. An elected island official also noted that

> ...anchor projects are almost self-sufficient where everything that is needed for the visitor is going to be made available for them right there...so the spin off benefit for the local residents and local merchants doesn't seem to be as glorious (Figure 2.1).

Exuma experienced an increase in major crimes, a challenged housing market and increased cost of real estate in the wake of the introduction of the anchor projects. This island also saw an outbreak of malaria, which is transmitted by the *Anopheles* mosquito which is not endemic to The Bahamas. This prompted speculation that the mosquito-borne disease could have been imported by one of the many visitors to the island or imported by the island's growing illegal immigrant population, yet another impact of tourism on small island communities.

Moreover, the mega resort located on the island has been criticized as not benefiting Bahamians. The President of the local Chamber of Commerce stated "...let's begin to develop Exuma along the lines of small guest houses owned by Bahamians" (Bahamas B2B, 2006). Despite this recommendation, the government created one of the largest resorts outside of the capital. Exuma's tourism was further challenged by the fact that the mega resort located on the island, which is currently one of its major employers, was up for sale. The Four Seasons resort, which had developed the property initially, experienced too many labour-related issues as well as the high cost of labour, and

Figure 2.1 Image of Resort World development. Photograph courtesy of Ian Bethell-Bennett.

so opted to sell out. The property was purchased by the Caribbean-based company Sandals. As with the Four Seasons, the Sandals is an all-inclusive property. When a sale was concluded, there were still forbearing questions as to how the change in ownership would impact employment and the lives of people in the community.

Small island nations, especially in the Caribbean, are beginning to experience unprecedented growth in the development of tourism and tourist resorts. The Turks and Caicos Islands have seen developments in Providenciales as well as South and North Caicos. Similarly, in 1994, St. Vincent and the Grenadines embarked on a $108 million tourism development project. Sandals bought two major properties in Barbados and St. Lucia, and abandoned the one on Barbados on the former Paradise Beach Resort, after felling all the mahogany trees thereon, despite legal regulations against the same.

The United Nations Environment Programme (2006) notes that "while tourism development can be crucial to the economic development and poverty alleviation of SIDS [Small Island States], this development can have serious and, in some cases, irreversible environmental and social impacts." It continues "it is thus extremely important to develop rational and objective methods for measuring any negative environmental and related social impacts." It is hoped that this study will work to illustrate the need for true measurement of the impact on small communities. Government has been remiss to do such measurements.

Despite having developed a tourism product that has sustained its economy since independence, The Bahamas has yet to complete a national tourism impact study. Many of the studies conducted in tourism relate to quality control/standards and planning for its development and sustainability (e.g. Hospitality Human Resources Needs Assessment (Rolle, et al., 2005), sponsored by the Bahamas Hotel Association). A policy relating to the impact of tourism on small island communities has yet to be developed. More critically, such a policy should be evidence based and must be shared with practitioners and the community at large. The United Nations Environment Programme states:

> The chosen destinations provide a unique venue for developing models for sustainable planning and management of tourism. Implementation, monitoring and evaluation of pilot projects dealing with sustainable tourism development in these destinations can lead to valid models applicable in a second stage in more complex economic systems. An assessment model can be developed based on sustainable tourism principles, incorporating state-of-the-art instruments to assess and measure tourism's positive effects and negative impacts on sustainable development. This can then guide decision-making processes on the development of the tourism sector by governmental authorities in SIDS.
>
> https://www.unwto.org/sustainable-development

Given this observation, the development of a national tourism development policy tailored to small island developing states should be encouraged. Such policy development in The Bahamas should be developed around primarily local data. In addition to policy development, such primary data can determine areas where tourism may need further study and attention. To date, there has only been one study conducted on the impact of tourism on local communities. There has been one study conducted on the impact of large-scale resort development on small island communities, the results of which were not released. The government and Ministry of Tourism have held the results close to their chests.

This study has piloted its work initially in three island communities: Exuma, Abaco and Bimini. The populations of these islands vary. Abaco is the more densely populated than Exuma; however, the density of the population is no indicator of the size of the same. Bimini is also very densely populated, especially given the size of the island. All of these islands have small and often declining populations. This pilot hopes to take all of this into consideration when it asks how residents feel about the impact of tourism development on their lives and their communities.

Methodology

A self-administered questionnaire was used to solicit local resident's attitudes toward the impact of tourism and tourism development in the islands of Bimini, Abaco and Exuma, The Bahamas. The survey examined the impact of tourism and development from economic, social/cultural, environmental and development perspectives.

The survey was divided into five sections. The first section contained demographic questions; the second section contained 21 questions that examined the economic impact (positive and negative); the third section contained 18 questions related to the social/cultural impact (positive and negative); the fourth section contained 10 questions that addressed environmental impact (positive and negative); and finally, the fifth section contained 4 questions that focused on developmental issues. The questions used in the survey were ones that have been used in similar research and adjusted to country context (Golzardi et al., 2012; Shariff & Abidin, 2013; Wang et al., 2006). The response format was a Likert scale (1 = strongly disagree, 2 = disagree, 3 = neutral, 4 = agree, 5 = strongly agree).

The sample size was determined using The Bahamas Census Data produced by the Department of Statistics on the three islands – Bimini, Abaco and Exuma – based on their population size, 100 participants from each of the islands were to be surveyed for the study.

The survey was administered during the months of May and June 2014 with the assistance of two trained staff members of the Ministry of Tourism Office in each of the islands. Prior to administering the survey, each respondent was given a Consent form that stated the purpose of the study, indicating that their involvement was voluntary, assurance of confidentiality and anonymity of their responses. Data was collected using a random sampling in the islands in order to achieve representation from a wide section of the islands as possible to obtain a broad range of attitudes. Out of 300, 249 surveys represented an 83% response rate for the study.

On completion of the data collection, the surveys were checked for completeness and consistency. The data were entered using the Statistical Package for the Social Sciences (SPSS). Kruskal-Wallis test and cross tabulation were used in analysing the data. During data entry, reverse scoring of negative values regarding some aspects of tourism in each of the four sections was recorded in order to correspond to the same scaling. Cronbach's Alpha was calculated for the four sections (economy, social/cultural, environment and development) to test for reliability and consistency of each scale. The Cronbach's alpha coefficient for all four sections ranged from 0.07 to 0.04 for reliability for basic research. The low score of 0.04 on the development scale is attributed to the small number of items in the scale and expected to be lower.

Research findings

Demographic background

The majority (67.6%) of the respondents in the study were female, 32.3% were male. The modal age group of the respondents were between the ages of 35–49 (34.6%), followed by 26–34 (27.3%) age group. The majority (48.5%) of the respondents were single, 42.4% were married, 4.8% were divorced and 3.2% were widowed. In terms of nationality, 94.3% were Bahamian, 3.2% were Haitian-Bahamian and 2.4% were Jamaican and American. The highest level of education attained by the majority (47.3%) of the respondents was 10th–12th grade, while 19% had completed college. 70.8% of the respondents were employed, 16.5% were self-employed, 10.9% were unemployed and 1.6% were retired. The majority (62.1%) of the respondents were employed in the private sector and 37.8% in the public sector.

Tourism's impact: an economic perspective

Research questions

1   What are the perceived major myths of tourism development in small island developing states?
2   What is the economic trickledown effect of tourism development in small island developing states?
3   Has tourism development helped or hurt small islands within the archipelagic nation of The Bahamas, specifically the Abacos, Bimini and Exuma?
4   Do residents in the islands perceive tourism development to be sustainable or unsustainable?

Doxey (1975) has been able to capture the evolving sentiments of local people who have lived with tourism expansions that have occupied greater proportions of local economies over time. This author notes that there are four main stages to consider in the assessment of local feelings toward the tourism industry. These are as follows:

Euphoria – Locals welcome tourists, and there is little or no control or planning at this stage;

Apathy – The tourists are taken for granted while the relationship between both groups becoming more formal;

Annoyance – Residents experience misgivings as the tourism industry saturates the community;

Antagonism – Locals express open irritation towards tourists and tourism. Planning at this stage is considered remedial even though there is increased promotion of the destination. Doxey (1975) contends that this is done in an effort to offset a growing deterioration in the reputation of the destination.

Evan Hyde, a Black Power leader in Belize in the early 1970s, suggested that 'Tourism is whorism', Erisman (1983) comments, which seems to further reflect the claims that tourism tends to lead to conflict between locals and hosts. Britton (1977) goes further in suggesting that local cultural expressions have been bastardized in order to be more comprehensible and therefore more saleable to mass tourism. This fragmentation of cultures seems to occur at many levels within destinations. The most notable evidence of this is expressed in forms of prostitution and crime; the erosion of languages in favour of more international dialects; the erosion of traditions, either forgotten or modified for tourists; changes to local art forms, foods, dress, religion and even family relationships (Hamilton, 2003; Pattullo, 1996; Ryan, 1991). Recently, there have been several occurrences on local Out Islands that raise the question of whether tourism development of any kind is firstly needed and secondly wanted by residents.

People residing in small island developing states must however come to grips with reality and understand that there are several myths as well as some realities associated with tourism development. As far as the realities, not all of them always bring about economic independence or elevated standards of living for the masses. One of the myths that is far too often attached to tourism development period as indicated by Sola-Fayos et al. (2014) is that the type of activities will bring about strong sustainable development. The contrary truism however is that it is not so much the development itself as it is the de facto policies, strategies and programmes that can be measured overall in the discussion of tourism development. The myth about tourism development bringing economic relief is almost always fuelled by governments, and key stakeholders who will ultimately share in the spoils (pun intended) of the development. The myth is also promulgated by international organizations concerned with tourism policy and good practice, as well as some multilateral agencies whose job is to promote good development.

The trickledown effect is yet another myth about tourism development. As far as economies of scales, tourism development in and of itself cannot produce the economic trickledown effect necessary to grow an economy. The net effect of growth in tourism businesses and the amount of income producing jobs created as a result of investments (mostly foreign) drives economies and produces income on multiple levels. Generally, the tourism businesses that are generated as a result of the investment are almost always those required by the visitor to the destination. Ultimately the cycle of supply and demand for businesses by the visitor benefits the locals in small island communities. When asked specifically across the island's surveys, only 22.6% of respondents in Bimini strongly agreed that tourism development had led to more spending in their communities. This perhaps could be directly tied to the fact that Bimini is presently in the midst of large-scale tourism development, and while the development is seen by developers and politicians as having a major economic impact on the economy of the island, when questioned, residents in fact contradicted this claim. The results were even less favourable in the other two islands. When we drilled down even deeper into the settlements in each island, results were similar with 23.8% of residents in Exuma, 21.0% of Biminites and 14.0% of residents in Abaco strongly agreeing with the notion that tourism development increased spending in their settlement.

When questioned on the veracity of tourism in the three islands, residents overwhelmingly disagreed that tourism development had either brought better opportunities to the islands, 50% in Bimini, 38.6% in Abaco and 23.8% in Exuma, or had somewhat increased the value of their property or even had caused the level of employment to decrease in the traditional service sectors. Some 58.1% of residents in Bimini were particularly strong in their disagreement that property prices had somewhat increased because of tourism development. This kind of feedback from residents paints a very clear picture for future developers and governments alike who sometimes become confused about the neoliberal concepts that suggest that the placement of static developments in small communities like Bimini, The Bahamas, is seen as good improvement that is desirable for everyone.

When questioned about the impact of tourism on the natural environment, surprisingly, 47.5% of residents in Bimini strongly disagreed that the impact was negative. Conversely, 24.6% of them strongly agreed that in fact the types of tourism development were causing some harm. These results came as somewhat of a surprise to us as we expected that the outcome would have revealed something different. Residents in Exuma (43.5%), on the other, agreed that tourism development served to destroy mangroves, native plants and beaches in their island. 21.8% of Abaconians strongly felt the same way. We concluded that these results were consistent with the fact that both Abaco and Exuma had a longer history of conservation and both have more residents living on the island.

Results about the built environment were also interesting. 64.5% of residents in Bimini indicated that tourism development had changed the island's landscape (buildings, topography; sea-view), while only 37.6% of residents in Abaco and 29.0% in Exuma felt this way. Again, one might conclude that the built environment is new to Bimini, as well as it is the smallest of the three islands examined. Naturally it would stand to reason that the effects of any type of development on this tiny island will be felt by all.

Social and cultural impact

In addition to the economic impact of tourism and tourism development in the islands of Abaco, Bimini and Exuma discussed above, the study sought to ascertain what the local residents thought about the various anchor resort developments in their islands, and what impact, if any, they had on the culture of their settlements and island specifically.

With the expansion of the different anchor resorts on the island's residents they were able to expand their opportunities to showcase their culture. Through the assistance of the government, via the Ministry of Tourism, craft markets were erected for artisans to sell their products, many local historical sites were restored either by the government agencies or by the locals for visitors to see, restaurants serving local cuisine also expanded to include tourists interested in sampling local foods. Various festivals such as Goombay Summer, Pineapple Festival and Regattas were also promoted as activities of interest. Air and sea linkages between the various islands afforded the tourist the opportunity to experience the various cultural offerings of each island. However, the information capturing this aspect of tourism and tourism development in The Bahamas is minimal. Understanding local resident attitudes toward tourism development is important for future growth and success in the islands. This is supported by Ismail and Turner (2008) in their research on small island states in Malaysia. That research indicated that economic gain with social and environmental factors will influence resident's attitudes of tourism and their support for tourism development.

Further, research conducted in other countries found that tourism in a positive way promotes cultural exchanges and creates avenues through which local artisans can display their art and handicrafts, and perform their music and dance (Brida et al., 2011; Munhurrun, & Naidoo, 2011; Khan, 2013). Tourism also enables local residents to meet new people and learn about new cultures and life styles (Brida et al., 2011; Munhurrun, & Naidoo, 2011) and the preservation of culture and historical sites (Ismail & Turner, 2008; Vounatsou, Laloumis, & Pappas, 2005), and encourage locals to stay at home (Vounatsou, M., Laloumis, & Pappas, 2005; Khan, 2013). Further, tourism provides recreational opportunities for residents and tourists (Brida et al., 2011;

Figure 2.2 Photograph of an anchor project in Exuma, The Bahamas. Photograph
courtesy of Ian Bethell-Bennett.

Abas, & Hanafial, 2014). On the other hand, research also found that
tourism and tourism development have contributed to various negative
socio-cultural impacts such as value/moral transformations (Pattullo, 1996;
Vounatsou et al., 2005); dilution of culture (Khan, 2013); increase in crime
levels (Abas & Hanafial, 2014; Abdool, 2002; Blunt, & Semley, 2010); the rise
in prices of land, services and cost of living (Ismail & Turner, 2008; Brida,
et al., 2011; Khan, 2013).

Therefore, the impact of tourism and tourism development also comprise the social and cultural factors to preserve and benefit residents and
culture, and at the same time improve and maintain the well-being of the
local population.

Participants were asked to respond to several statements related to the social and cultural impact of tourism and tourism development in the islands
using a five-point ordinal response category ranking from strongly disagree
to strongly agree. The responses were analysed by island.

Interacting with tourist

Findings in Table 2.1 indicate that overall, the three islands, Abaco, Bimini and Exuma agreed that interaction with tourists is a positive experience (Abaco: 54.5%, Bimini: 54.1%, Exuma: 51.4%). However, the
level of agreement varied, Abaco and Exuma stated they agreed with the
statement, 54.5% and 51.4%, respectively. Bimini respondents strongly
agreed with the statement. This could be attributed to the opening of the
Resorts World, Bimini Casino and Marina on the island in 2013 as well
as the island's reputation as a big game fishing destination. Abaco and
Exuma have had a long history as established destinations among the
Bahamian islands. Similar findings were reported in Folgaria, Italy by
Brida et al. (2011).

Table 2.1 Interaction with tourists a positive experience for locals

	Abaco (%)	Bimini (%)	Exuma (%)
1. Strongly disagree	2.0	0.0	1.4
2. Disagree	3.0	1.6	1.4
3. Neutral	25.3	4.9	25.7
4. Agree	54.5	39.3	51.4
5. Strongly agree	15.2	54.1	20.0
Total (n = 230)	100	100	100

Table 2.2 Tourism development encourages residents to showcase culture

	Abaco (%)	Bimini (%)	Exuma (%)
1. Strongly disagree	1.0	1.7	2.9
2. Disagree	8.9	16.7	1.4
3. Neutral	24.8	26.7	28.6
4. Agree	45.5	45.0	47.1
5. Strongly agree	19.8	10.0	20.0
Total (n = 230)	100	100	100

Tourism development encourages residents to showcase their culture

About the statement "tourism development encourages local residents to showcase their culture," findings in Table 2.2 show that respondents in all three islands (Abaco, Bimini and Exuma) agreed with the statement, 45%, 45% and 47%, respectively. This could be attributed to the fact that residents perform various cultural forms such as Junkanoo and display local arts and crafts for the tourists visiting the islands as a means of demonstrating a cultural identity and pride in the country (Cleare, 2007).

Similar findings were also observed when participants indicated that tourism development strengthens cultural events. Respondents in the three islands agreed with this statement: Abaco 49%, Bimini 48% and Exuma 44%. This could be attributed to the constant flow of tourists to the islands annually. This encourages locals to enhance the tourist experience with entertainment reflecting the culture of the islands as well as recreate aspects of Bahamian culture-regattas and big game fishing (Cleare, 2007). Similar findings were also noted by Brida et al., (2011).

Tourism development encourages residents to preserve their culture

With regard to the statement "Tourism development encourages residents to preserve their culture," participants agreed with this statement. However, Bimini respondents strongly agreed (64%) with this statement compared to

Abaco and Exuma respondents who agreed with the statement (45% and 40%, respectively). Bimini's response may be attributed, in great measure, to the new resort development that has brought approximately 119,00+ visitors to the island for the past few years. So, they may see the need to maintain and preserve their island culture and heritage.

Local recreational programmes improved due to tourism development on the Island

Table 2.3 shows the frequencies of participants' responses to the statement "Recreational programmes have been expanded due to the influx of tourists to the island." Responses to the statement varied in and between the islands. In Abaco, 39% agreed and 28% disagreed with the statement. In Bimini, 39% of the respondents also agreed and 26% disagreed with the statement. However, in Exuma, 53% of the respondents were neutral regarding the statement. The differences in responses could be due to the fact that for respondents who disagreed knew local residents had long established recreational programmes such as nightclubs, sports clubs and water sports, and therefore did not have to rely solely on tourists to provide recreational activities on the island. For those who agreed, their response could be due to observing new activities introduced in the islands such as skateboarding, canoeing and jet skiing by locals and resorts that also provide activities for guest recreation. These findings are also supported by Munhurrun (2011) in his research in Mauritius.

Local recreational programmes in settlements improved due to tourism development on the Island

Regarding local recreational programmes being expanded because of the influx of tourism development in their settlements, the responses were varied between the islands. 30% of the respondents in Abaco agreed, and 34% disagreed with this statement. In Bimini, 58% of the respondents agreed compared to 11% who disagreed. 53% of the respondents in Exuma gave a neutral response to this statement. Exuma's neutral responses may be attributed to settlements having a combination of activities and tourists events to not make distinctions. Participant's large positive response in Bimini may be due to a group of frequent

Table 2.3 Local recreation programmes improved due to tourism development in my island

	Abaco (%)	Bimini (%)	Exuma (%)
1. Strongly disagree	8.2	11.9	4.9
2. Disagree	21.6	15.3	17.3
3. Neutral	24.7	15.3	53.1
4. Agree	39.2	39	19.8
5. Strongly agree	6.2	18.6	4.9
Total (n = 237)	100	100	100

visitors to the island who had donated to their settlement, a new basketball court. The distance between the settlements in Bimini are not far compared to those in Abaco or Exuma. Also, many of the residents are employed to perform at the new Resorts World development recently established on the island.

Incentives to stay on the island

Participants were asked if tourism development provides incentives for residents to stay on the island. The responses between islands varied. In Bimini, 63% of the respondents agreed compared to 21% who were neutral on this statement. In Abaco, 49% of the respondents agreed compared to 32% who were neutral on this statement. In Exuma, the agreed and neutral responses were similar, 42% and 40%, respectively. Abaco and Exuma's neutral responses may be due to the fact they have other activities for example diving, farming and fishing in addition to tourism that may keep them on the island. Bimini's positive response could be due to the employment opportunities compared to the other islands that Bimini is currently experiencing due to the Resort World development. This may reduce the need for residents to relocate to New Providence island for employment. Other possible incentives to stay on the islands may be due to post-disaster regeneration due to FDI and the government's commitment to the country's long-range development. This finding was also noted in a study of socioeconomic impact of tourism in Kashmir by Khan (2013).

Conservation of historical, cultural and traditional buildings

Participants were also asked if tourism development provided incentives for the conservation of historical, cultural and traditional buildings in the island. Responses indicated differences between the islands. In Abaco, 41% of the respondents agreed, and 35% were neutral to this statement. In Exuma, 44% of the respondents were neutral and 35% agreed with this statement. In Bimini, the responses were reversed, 65% of the respondents agreed compared to 23% who were neutral. Again Bimini's responses could be due to the influx of tourists to the island in part due to the recently opened Resorts World resort inclusive of its cruise ship passengers and the local residents wishing to showcase the various historical and cultural attractions the island has to offer, since Bimini was mainly noted for their big game fishing. Long-established tourist destinations like Abaco and Exuma will have gone through these activities because of their noted history of Loyalists settlements and Slave plantations (Craton & Saunders, 1999). This preservation of historical sites was a similar finding by Munhurrun & Naidoo, (2011), in their research on perceived tourism benefits in Mauritius.

Conservation of historical, cultural and traditional buildings in the settlement

Similar responses were found at the level of the settlement. In Abaco, 36% of the respondents agreed and 32% disagreed with this statement. In Exuma,

Figure 2.3 Photograph of Rolle Slave Plantation, Exuma, The Bahamas. Photograph courtesy of Ian Bethell-Bennett.

43% were neutral and 36% agreed with this statement. Bimini was the exception with 53% of the respondents agreeing with this statement. Abaco and Exuma have a longer history of consistent big anchor resort projects and tourism development (Smith, 2007); their historical buildings dating from the Loyalist period in Abaco and the Slave plantations in different parts of Exuma will have been preserved or restored compared to Bimini who is currently experiencing a boom in tourism development. This may provide incentives for the residents to restore and preserve their historical and cultural buildings in the island. These findings were also mentioned in similar studies by other researchers (Figure 2.3).

Migration and international corporations and benefits to foreign entities

As was highlighted in the introduction and the other parts, tourism has generally been constructed as an FDI-focused industry, only using the local environment for the actual product, but divorcing the resort from that environment as much as possible, without losing the local flavour. Of course, the best discussion can be gleaned from Resorts World on Bimini, where the interviews and the surveys, although positive, revealed an acute awareness among the local population of the unbalanced nature of employment in the resort. While most persons were extremely positive about the development on Bimini, they were quick to say that they understood the negative impact that tourism could have on their community. They were sensitive to the fact that the company brought in both low-end labourers and high-end executives. The problem was compounded by the fact that there had been a great deal of outward migration from Bimini because of few employment prospects, but also they were aware that there was preferential treatment of foreign workers. Lower-end construction workers were willing to work longer hours and harder than local workers. Many of the workers were imported from Asia and/or Latin America. The executives were imported from other areas. This raised grave concern among local, but they were still happy to have jobs. Interviews, though, revealed far more than the surveys managed to capture. The information from interviews, coupled with newspaper articles that covered the concerns of locals that their community was being swamped by foreign workers and then could not hope to hold their own because of a small workforce, spoke directly to these facts. Again, while many Biminites were pleased for the jobs and the progress, they were concerned about how it was being done. They did not see Bimini benefiting sufficiently from the resort. Those who were not in the resort area, but rather in Alice Town, appreciated the business the boat and the resort brought but noted that once the last trolley returned, that was it, all tourists returned to the ferry back to Miami or to the resort; there was no real sustainable business. They were happy when persons ventured to town as the shops on the resort offered them all they needed, which often translated into tourists not leaving the resort. Further, when the weather was bad, there was no business. Ironically, out of all the islands, Bimini was the happiest with tourism development but also the most aware of the problems inherent in the development and the least willing to allow the land to be taken away that was under them. On such a small island, this is a key issue. Government has ignored the cries, except to provide employment. People on all the islands are quick to point out, however, that even though employment has increased, the kinds of jobs they have access to do not compare to those foreign workers or expatriates can access.

At the same time, all the communities complained about the impact of Haitians on their ability to earn. They felt that organizations were quick to hire Haitian labour because they worked harder and longer, and they did not require the same treatment as did Bahamian low and semi-skilled labourers. This was a common, loud concern of all persons surveyed as well as interviewed. Haitian migration is a common trend in The Bahamas and is not necessarily tied to employment, though they do look for work. Haitians are therefore capable of provoking massive emotional reactions among many Bahamians. This was most evident on Guana Cay, because it was a predominantly white/brown community, the Haitians who had come in search of work stood out. This created acrimony among the locals and the Haitians, but this was worsened by the push down of the Americans coming into the higher positions as well as those Americans, who were buying up their land. On Guana they insisted that initially relations were good with tourists or Americans, but later, once they had acquired what they needed or wanted, they no longer mingled with the local community as they no longer needed anything from them. While this way of thinking may seem sceptical, according to the Abaconians, it was the way things were. This was especially true for one interviewee. The pressures are huge, she noted.

Moreover, the lack of willingness to do hard work changed the dynamic of the community. According to some, especially on Guana Cay, given that tourism was light work for high pay, people, especially the young fellows, were unwilling to do traditional work such as fishing and small plot farming. They were also less willing to work hard. This meant that when things slowed down, the youth would be seen sitting under trees consuming alcohol.

Crime was another major concern. Many people noted that in their community they had never locked doors but now they needed to as there were too many strangers around. Also, resentment grew, and people were less willing to work together. It was, as Justice Carroll noted in the introduction, almost impossible to make a living through traditional means because their lands were now closed off to them. The land had become a part of the gated community to which they were not allowed access. While residents on Guana Cay did protest, they were not as vehement as the residents on Bimini, who refused to allow Resorts World to close off 'their' end of the island. The residents and the older foreign owners had enjoyed decades of good relations, they claimed, that were only changed when Resorts World bought the land.

Crime from prostitution to rape had risen but was not spoken of too much because of ideas that speaking of it too much would make it come to pass. There was, though, an idea that tourism promoted a certain kind of life. Persons were aware that prostitution was a part of the tourist product. Guana Cay experienced its first murder in 2014, a fact they were not happy about. Biminites were no strangers to crime and hardship given that the drug trade went through Bimini in the early 1980s to Miami.

A few points were clear from the discussion everywhere: Tourism increased the price of land; Tourism created social 'problems' such as prostitution and drugs because these were what tourists wanted; large-scale development meant that people would try to undermine local communities; balance between locals and outsiders was set off because of the apparent 'easy money' tourism created. Crime such as petty theft and sexual assault rose due to tourism.

Conclusion

Two factors emerge from the findings on the social and cultural impacts of tourism and tourism in the islands of Abaco, Bimini and Exuma. One was the overall perception by the respondents in the islands, and the second was the level of agreement between the islands.

With regard to the first factor, findings show that all respondents agreed that interaction with tourists was a positive experience. Respondents also agreed that tourism and tourism development afforded residents the opportunity to showcase, strengthen and preserve their culture. This is so because employment opportunities in the community and various resorts are available for artisans, musicians and handicraft persons to display and sell souvenirs, which enhances the tourism product and visitor's experience. Respondents also agreed that this cultural preservation also caused residents to preserve their historical and cultural sites. These sites might have been lost, considered not relevant or of little interest because of the influences of images from other countries. In the same vein, respondents agreed that local recreational programmes were improved due in part to interactions with tourists and resort activities. Over the years, special efforts have been made by the government's Ministry of Tourism to develop sports tourism in the islands to further enhance the tourism experience. These findings are similar to ones conducted in other countries.

The second factor is related to the level of agreement between the islands. The island of Bimini stands out in terms of level of agreement to the social and cultural impacts of tourism and tourism development compared to Abaco and Exuma. This is attributed to the fact that Bimini is currently experiencing revitalization in tourism in the island due to the recent opening of a mega resort and casino plus a cruise ship that visits the island daily. This has brought new and enhanced employment opportunities for the residents in all areas of the tourism industry. This revitalization has also stemmed local emigration to New Providence and other islands because of the available employment opportunities. Abaco (7,646) and Exuma (6,928) with larger populations and long-established successful resorts, as well as other opportunities that complement the tourism industry, do not need to rely heavily on tourism and development compared to Bimini (1,988) with its small population.

In sum, the views of the respondents can be considered a positive reflection of the tourism industry of The Bahamas, and the efforts and success of the government through the Ministry of Tourism to promote the islands of The Bahamas as a favourable tourist destination. However, the impact of migration, both low-skilled workers and highly trained expatriates, was cause for great concern. Further, the segregation of the tourists from the local communities was another marker of difference and created tensions. The longer the community had been exposed to tourism and the more development there was, the more complicated the relationship became between them. Labour relations became fraught with tensions, and people complained that foreign workers were brought in because locals would not work for long hours. The pilot ultimately shows that the information gathered is valuable and the study should be expanded to include the other islands that are now faced with anchor projects. Further studies are also needed in the area of tourism development and resilience post-hurricanes and other natural disasters.

References

Abas, S., & Hanafial, M. (2014). Local community attitudes towards tourism development in Tioman Island. *Tourism, Leisure and Global Change, 1,* TOC-135–147

Abdool, A. (2002). Resident' Perception of Tourism: A comparative study of two Caribbean communities. A thesis submitted in fulfilment of the requirements of Bournemouth University. A thesis submitted in fulfilment of the requirements of Bournemouth University for the degree of Doctor of Philosophy. Retrieved from http://eprints.bournemouth.ac.uk/458/1/Abdool%2C_Afzal_Ph.D_2002.pdf

Bahamasb2b. Bahamas News Archive. (2006). *Emerald bay anchor project threatened.* http://www.bahamasb2b.com/news/wmview.php?ArtID=9350.

Blunt, P., & Semley, N (2010). Community responses to tourism and crime. Crime Prevention and Community Safety 12(1):42-57. DOI:10.1057/cpcs.2009.7. Retrieved from, https://www.researchgate.net/publication/248877010_Community_responses_to_tourism_and_crime

Brown, S. (29 August, 2014). Baha Mar may cripple B.E.C. The Tribune. Retrieved from www.tribune242.com

Brida, J., Disegna, M., & Osti, L. (2011). Residents' perceptions of tourism impacts and attitudes towards tourism policies in a small mountain community. http://dx.doi.org/10.2139/ssrn.1839244. Retrieved 31 July 2018.

Britton, S. G. (1977). Making tourism more supportive of small-state development: The case of St. Vincent. *Annals of Tourism Research, 4*(5), 268–278.

Caribbean Update. (February, 1994) *St. Vincent & the grenadines: $108 million tourism development project.* http://www.gpa.unep.org/documents/tourism_and_sids_english.pdf. Retrieved 21 June 2018.

Cleare, A. (2007). History of tourism in The Bahamas: A global perspective. Philadelphia, PA: Xlibris.

Craton, M., & Saunders G. (1999. Islanders in the stream. A history of Bahamian people Volume I. Athens, GA: University of Georgia Press.

Culmer, D. *The Bahama Journal.* (July 16th, 2007). *Mixed views on change in anchor policy.* https://ufdc.ufl.edu/UF00084249/02939 Retrieved 10 June 2018.

Dames, C. *The Bahama Journal.* (June 14th, 2007). *Malaria outbreak.* http://www.jonesbahamas.com/?c=45&a=9093. Retrieved 10 June 2018.

Doxey, G. V. (1975). *A causation theory of visitor-resident irritants: Methodology and research inferences.* Paper presented at the TTRA Conferences, San Diego, CA, pp. 195–198.

Erisman, H. M. (1983). Tourism and culture dependency in the West Indies. *Annals of Tourism Research, 10*(3), 337–361.

Fanon, F. (1967). *Black skin, white masks.* New York: Grove Press.

Golzardi, F., Shabnam, S., Kamal, S., & Sarvaramini, M. (2012). Residents attitudes towards tourism development: A case study of Niasar, Iran. *Research Journal of Applied Sciences, Engineering and Technology, 4*(8), 863–868.

Hall, C. M., & Page, S. J. (2014). *The geography of tourism and recreation: Environment, place and space.* 4th ed. London: Routledge.

Hamilton, L. (2003). *Sustainable tourism: Practices, risks and challenges faced by Caribbean firms.* Mayagüez: University of Puerto Rico-Mayagüez.

Ismail, F., & Turner, L. (2008). *Host and tourist perceptions on small island tourism: A case study of Perhentian and Redang Islands, Malaysia.* International Conference on Applied Economics. ICOAE, pp. 401–410. http://vuir.vu.edu.au/30065/1/Fathilah%20Ismail_Part1.pdf Retrieved 31 July 2018.

Khan, F. (2013). *Socioeconomic impacts of tourism on the rural people of Azad Kashmir: A case study of Rawalakot & Banjonsa in Azad Kashmir.* MA Thesis. Swedish University of Agricultural Sciences. http://stud.epsilon.slu.se/. Retrieved 30 July 2018.

Kincaid, J. (1988). *A small place.* New York: Farrar, Straus and Giroux.

Lundy, T. *The Bahama Journal.* (July 14th, 2006). *Anchor project policy creates dilemma.* http://www.jonesbahamas.com/?c=47&a=9503. Retrieved 5th June 2018.

Moyne Report (The West India Royal Commission Report). (1939). Her majesty stationary office. London: Darling & Sons.

Munhurrun, R. (2011). Resident's attitude toward perceived tourism benefits. *International Journal of Management & Marketing Research, 4*(3), 45–56.

Pantojas, G. E. (January–June, 2008). Economic integration and Caribbean identity: Convergencies and divergencies. *Caribbean Studies, 36*(1), 53–74.

Parker, Q. *The Bahama Journal.* (August 8th, 2012). *Anchor projects under scrutiny.* http://jonesbahamas.com/2012/08/. Retrieved 15 July 2017.

Rolle, S. et al. (2005). Hospitality industry human resources needs assessment. Principal writer-Chapter 3 Overview of issues in hospitality and tourism. Project contract by The Bahamas Ministry of Tourism and The Bahamas Hotel Association.

Pattullo, P. (1996). *Last resorts: The cost of tourism in the Caribbean.* Kingston: Ian Randle Publishers.

Ryan, C. (1991). *Recreational tourism: A social science perspective.* New York: Routledge.

Saunders, G. (2003). *Bahamian society after emancipation.* 2nd Ed. Kingston, Jamaica: Ian Randall Publishers.

Shariff, N., & Abidin, A. (June, 2013). Community attitude towards tourism impacts: Developing a standard instrument in the Malaysian context. *Proceeding of the International Conference on Social Science Research*, ICSSR 2013 (e-ISBN 978-967-11768-1-8). pp. 4–5. Penang, MALAYSIA. Organized by WorldConferences.net. Retrieved 31 July 2018.

Sheller, M. (2003). *Consuming the Caribbean: From Arawaks to Zombies.* London: Routledge.

Smith, L. (2007). Mixed track record of out island resort projects. The Tribune, 28 March, 2007. https://www.bahamapundit.com/2007/03/by_larry_smith_.html Retrieved 2 April, 2019.

Sola-Fayos, E., Alvarez, M. D., & Cooper, C. (2014). *Bridging tourism theory and practice (Vol. 5). Tourism as an instrument for development: A theoretical and practical study.* pp. x–xiii. Turkey: Emerald Group Publishing Ltd.

The Grand Bahama info Newsletter. (October 4th, 2007). *Save Guana Cay issues new case against developers and local government.* http://grandbahamianinfo.com/articles/gb-1004-07/saveguana-10-04-07.htm. Retrieved 15 June 2018.

The Islands of The Bahamas. (Undated). Ministry of tourism http://www.bahamas.com/bahamas/about/general.aspx?sectionid=23080&level=2. Retrieved 20 May 2018.

The United Nations Environment Programme. (October, 2006). Planning instruments for sustainable tourism development in Small Island Developing States (SIDS). http://www.gpa.unep.org/documents/tourism_and_sids_english.pdf. Retrieved 20 June 2018.

Vounatsou, M., Laloumis, D., & Pappas, N. (2005). Social impacts of tourism: Perceptions of Mykonos City residents. *Journal of Travel Research, 36*(2), 1–19.

Wang, Y., Pfister, R., & Morais, B. (2006). Residents' attitudes toward tourism development: A case study of Washington, NC. *Proceedings of the 2006 Northeastern Recreation Research Symposium GTR-NRS-P-14.* www.nrs.fs.fed.us/pubs/gtr/gtr_nrs-p-14/54-wang-p-14.pdf. Retrieved 31 July 2018.

3   Living on islands

Tourism and quality of life on the islands of Abaco, Bimini and Exuma, The Bahamas a case study

Jessica Minnis and Margo Blackwell

Introduction

In this chapter, we examine tourism and tourism development on the quality of life of residents in the Family islands of Abaco, Bimini and the Exuma in The Bahamas. Few studies have examined the effects of tourism and tourism development on the quality of life of residents in The Bahamas especially since 2002 when anchor projects (large tourist resorts) as a government developmental policy and strategy were implemented on the various Family Islands.

According to Aref (2011) indicators of quality of life, such as the physical, environmental, economic, social and other factors that impact daily living, can give information on how well a country or government is doing compared to other countries or consecutive governments within a country. The use of these quality of life indicators provides support for governments, when making decisions about outcomes and when evaluating strategic decisions which can impact the quality of life of people.

According to World Travel and Tourism Council (2019), the travel and tourism sector is an important economic activity in most countries around the world. Travel and tourism account for 10.4% of global GDP and 10% of total employment in 2018. Tourism is closely linked to development and growth in many countries, and there are a growing number of new destinations (Statista, 2018). Tourism and tourism development also have an impact on the natural and built environments and on the well-being and culture of host populations (UNWTO, 2005).

Studies outside The Bahamas have examined residents' perceptions regarding the economic, social, cultural and environmental impacts of tourism (Ismail & Turner, 2008; Aref, 2011). The studies found tourism to have a positive effect on the quality of life of residents with regard to employment, water quality, environmental protection, infrastructural development and good for local business (Aref, 2011; Nkemngu, 2015; Zeinali et al., 2015). While studies did find these favourable aspects of tourism, there are several studies which have found tourism and its related products had a negative impact on residents (Teye et al., 2002; Mbaiwa, 2003).

Tourism has played a significant role in the development of The Bahamas since the mid-1800s when the islands were the place to recover from health issues and then the destination for sun, sand and sea (Cleare, 2007). Over the years, The Bahamas has successfully maintained a robust tourism product inclusive of different tourism developments despite its location in a hurricane zone. Despite this, the geographical location of The Bahamas to the North, Central and South America and the Caribbean has made it a popular tourist destination.

Tourism's contribution to employment regardless of the impact on quality of life of residents cannot be underestimated. Tourism together with tourism-related industries accounts for approximately 70% of The Bahamas' GDP, and directly or indirectly, employs half of the country's labour force (Moody's Analytic, 2019).

Driven by the need for employment and to support development of the family of islands, in 2002, the Government of The Bahamas initiated an Anchor Investment Policy. This was a part of a larger Foreign Direct Investment policy that looked at large-scale industrial development inclusive of tourism development (Smith, 2018). The tourist policy, as initiated by the government to create employment on each of the large Family Islands in the archipelago, was to establish large hotel resorts to be called "anchor projects" (Christie, 1984).

Over the past three decades, the Governments of The Bahamas all have supported different development incentives, commitment to sustainability of tourism resorts and commitment to the sustainability of the quality of life and cultures of the islands in which these resorts are located (Smith, 2005; Smith, 2013; Christie, 2016).

Since 2002, a number of anchor projects were developed on several of the major islands of The Bahamas: On Abaco – Bakers Bay and Schooner Bay, Bimini – Resorts World, Exuma – Sandals, San Salvador – Club Med, Grand Bahama – Grand Lucaya and New Providence – Baha Mar and Atlantis (Smith, 2012; Black, 2015).

Over the years however, the anchor projects have received mixed reviews from Bahamians impacted by the projects. Some residents supported the projects indicating they were good for the islands and economy (Smith, 2008), others disagreed highlighting the environmental damage caused by the various developments (Duncombe, 2008; Alexander, 2014; Bethell-Bennett, 2017), or the projects were too large for some of the islands infrastructure and population, (Hartnell, 2013a) or the government needed to diversify the economy and not rely solely on tourism and anchor projects (Bahamas Local, 2015; Gibson, 2016).

It is within this context that we examine Family Island residents' perceptions regarding tourism and tourism development in their islands. More specifically, we explore the impact of these anchor projects on the residents of Abaco, Bimini and Exuma, and how they perceive that their quality of life had improved as a result of tourism and the anchor projects located in their islands.

Definition of quality of life

Quality of life is a concept that describes the living conditions of the individual. In this chapter, the quality of life refers to the well-being of people and the environment in which they live (Das, 2008). It takes into consideration the physical, environmental, economic, social and other factors that impact daily living, the degree to which peoples' needs are met or satisfied and the experiences positive or negative of people in the environment in which they live (Diener & Suh, 1997; Das, 2008). In addition to the above quality of life definition, we also include Aref's (2011) definition that embraces government outcomes and decision making about quality of life of people.

Study site: The Bahamas

The population of The Bahamas is about 351,500 (Department of Statistics, 2012). 85% of the country's population reside in the most urbanized islands of New Providence (Nassau) and Grand Bahama (Freeport), and 15% reside in the Family islands. In the islands under study, Abaco is a 120-mile-long chain of islands; the capital, Marsh Harbour, is located on Great Abaco Island; Abaco is a renowned boating centre. The residents are employed in areas such as banking, boatbuilding and fishing. Bimini is one of the northern islands and is located 53 miles east of Miami, Florida. Bimini is divided into South Bimini and North Bimini. North Bimini is 7 miles long and 700 feet wide, and contains the capital Alice Town. Bimini is noted for its big game fishing and cultural history. Exuma is in the southern part of the archipelago and comprises two main islands – Great Exuma, with the capital George Town, and Little Exuma and approximately 365 cays. Exuma is noted for its Marine Park, farming and diving (www.the-bahama-islands. com, www.myoutislands.com).

Context: quality of life in family islands

The last Bahamas Living Condition's Survey was done in 2001. It highlighted the difficulty of servicing all the residents of The Bahamas evenly due to the archipelagic nature of the country's uneven population distribution. For example, 72 residents in Ragged Island, and 277 residents in Mayaguana compared to 246,329 in New Providence. The population distribution also impacted the cost-effectiveness of social services thereby posing a challenge for policy planners to not marginalize any group while trying to meet the needs of the poorest sections of the country (Department of Statistics, 2004).

According to Rolle et al. (2015), most public services are concentrated in urban centres of Nassau and Freeport, because of the concentration of infrastructural development there (Nassau, the capital and Freeport, the second city); the Family Islands are under-served due to the high cost per capita of developing each Family Island collectively. After independence in 1973, the Government invested heavily in infrastructural development across the islands. For example, in 1992, tens of millions of dollars were spent to improve major roadways, medical facilities and water systems, upgrading the airports in the Islands, maintaining the docks and extensive electrification and telecommunication systems (Interknowledge Corp, 1996; Black, 2013).

Notwithstanding the improvements to the Family Island infrastructure, the islands are still challenged by transportation issues between the various settlements and islands, healthcare facilities, roads, employment, goods and services (Bahamas Local, 2015). For instance, mail boats are still utilized to transport mail, dry goods, vehicles, live-stock, building materials among other things between the islands (Rolle et al., 2015; www.sustainabledevel-opment.un.org, July 2018).

Added to the structural challenges, The Bahamas experience hurricanes. Situated in the hurricane zone, the islands over the years have endured direct or indirect impacts from hurricanes such as environmental damage, infrastructure, loss of employment and revenue and losses in tourism sectors (Rolle et al., 2015; UWI, 2017; ECLAC, 2018). Annually, residents prepare to protect life and property; some move to shelters, some remain home and some take a "wait and see" philosophy (Ward, 2019).

Most infrastructural assets such as housing, roads, ports and tourist facilities are located on or close to the shorelines; thus, residents experience hurricane damage, storm surges, power outages and, in some cases, destruction to the overall environment as evidenced by Hurricane Dorian in September 2019 (ECLAC, 2018; IADB, 2019).

For the island residents, the recovery process takes time because supplies and equipment must be shipped from the capital (Nassau) (Rolle et al., 2015). Additionally, limited and stretched resources, loss of visitors, extensive and costly damages overall to infrastructure and environment and, at times, a

Figure 3.1 Photograph showing road and dock Guana Cay Abaco, The Bahamas. Photograph courtesy of Ian Bethell-Bennett.

slow economic recovery prevent a quick revitalization. For example, cumulative hurricanes (Joaquin, 2015; Irma, 2016; and Matthew, 2017) caused damages and losses of approximately $678 million (Smith, 2018). Dorian compounded the recovery process with damages estimated at $3 billion, and recovery from Dorian will take years (IADB, 2019). Nevertheless, Bahamians proved resilient, regrouping to rebuild and finding ways to make a living. The Government has successfully marketed the islands to boost tourism (Cooper, 2018; The Tribune, September 2019; Knowles, 2019) and attract foreign investments through anchor projects despite the hurricanes and competition from other tourist destinations (Christie, 2016; www.tourismtoday.com, 2019).

Methodology

This chapter utilized data from a study that examined the impact of tourism and tourism development on three Islands in The Bahamas: Abaco, Bimini and Exuma conducted during May–June 2014. Totally, 300 surveys were distributed: 100 per island; 249 surveys were obtained representing 83% response.

Demographic background

The majority (67.6%) of respondents in the study were female, and 32.3% were male. The modal age group of respondents was 35–49 (34.6%), followed by the 26–34 (27.3%) age group. Marital status is as follows: 48.5% were single, 42.4% were married, 4.8% were divorced and 3.2% were widowed. In terms of nationality, 94.3% were Bahamian, 3.2% were Haitian-Bahamian and 2.4% were Jamaican or American. The highest level of education attained was 10th–12th grade (47.3%), while 19% had completed college. With regard to employment, 70.8% were employed, 16.5% were self-employed, 10.9% were unemployed and 1.6% was retired. Most of the respondents (62.1%) were employed in the private sector and 37.8% in the public sector.

Findings and discussion of the study

In the Family Islands, the tourist stopover increased from 837,273 in 2001 to 2,173,606 in 2018 (Ministry of Tourism, 2019) due to tourism promotions and anchor projects such as Sandals, Baker's Bay and Resorts World – Bimini implemented by the government and gave the islands more employment opportunities. Considering the impact of several severe hurricanes notably during 2016–2019 in the islands (Smith, 2018; Darville, 2019) the initial study questions did not directly address the respondent's perception of hurricanes and how these impacted tourism and tourism development and the quality of their lives. However, based on the above, we wanted to know how the respondents perceived tourism and tourism development affected the quality of their lives. The findings will be discussed under two subheadings: tourism and tourism development.

Tourism

Stated previously, tourism employs half the labour force directly and in-directly and accounts for about 60%–70% of the Gross Domestic Product (GDP). The participants were asked to respond to several statements related to the economic impact of tourism (Table 3.1). Most of the respondents agreed with the following questions.

Table 3.1 Percent of respondents agreed on economic benefits of tourism (n = 249)

Questions	Total (%)	Abaco (%)	Bimini (%)	Exuma (%)
Tourism increases employment opportunities	74.3	65.4	88.3	75
Tourism has given economic benefits to local people and small businesses	70.8	68.3	85.3	63.1
Tourism contributes to income and standard of living	81.4	72.3	90.3	85.7

Table 3.1 shows that the respondents from the three islands agreed that tourism increases employment opportunities. Today, The Bahamas earn almost $2 billion from tourism – money which pays the wages of some 40,000 Bahamians in hotels, shops, tour companies, restaurants and other services. So, tourism produces a full spectrum of employment opportunities – from unskilled, semi-skilled to professional (Department of Statistics, 2016; www.cia.com; Smith, 2007).

When questioned about tourist spending benefitting the local community and businesses, most of the respondents (70%) agreed (Table 3.1) that tourist spending benefited local businesses on the islands such as diving companies, restaurants, tour companies and car rentals. For instance, the mean total expenditure spent per trip to a Family Island was $1,058 by domestic tourists alone (Ministry of Tourism & Aviation, 2008). It was estimated that second homeowners contributed millions of dollars to the Family Island economy through their various purchases (Robinson-Blair, 2011) and international divers spend approximately $80 million a year in the islands (Alexander, 2014).

Many of the islands received electricity, and improved roads and water throughout the islands post-1992 (www.bahamasinvestor.com; Black, 2013). Recently the Government completed upgrades to the airport facilities and a mini hospital was completed in Abaco and Exuma (Bahamas Investor, 2015).

When asked if public utilities and infrastructure were improved because of tourism, most of the respondents (39.8%) agreed and the same percentage among the islands (Table 3.2).

Table 3.2 Tourism improves public utilities and infrastructure (schools, clinics, roads, electricity)

	Total (%)	Abaco (%)	Bimini (%)	Exuma (%)
1. Disagree	29.7	46.5	14.8	20.3
2. Agree	39.8	31.7	57.3	37
Total (n = 246)				

Their responses are understandable seeing that infrastructure improvements to the islands that were meant to improve their quality of life were usually presented by the Government within the context of tourism and anchor projects on the islands (Christie, 2016).

Prices of goods and services

Respondents had mixed views regarding the increase in prices of goods and services because of tourism. Many respondents agreed and disagreed (32% and 33.3%, respectively) with this statement, and the three islands responded in like manner (Table 3.3).

Table 3.3 The prices of goods and services in the area have increased because of tourism

	Total (%)	Abaco (%)	Bimini (%)	Exuma (%)
1. Disagree	33.3	37.6	41.9	28.6
3. Neutral	34.6	23.8	40.3	43.4
4. Agree	32.1	38.6	17.7	35
N = 246				

Their responses may be linked to the fact that the cost of living is high in The Bahamas (fourth most expensive country in the world) and not because of tourism (Dimitropoulou, 2019). Residents pay various government taxes and import duty on all goods (Dupuch Publications, 2011; Alexander, 2018), plus freight costs to the islands (Hartnell, 2015). Moreover, value added tax of 7% was imposed by the Government for all goods and services which was increased to 12% in 2018 that further increased the cost of living for Family Island residents (McKenzie, 2013; Carey, 2018).

All the islands disagreed that shopping opportunities were better because of tourism. The islands do not have a large variety of shops like those found in New Providence. Family Islanders either shop in Nassau or in the United States (especially Florida) because of its proximity to The Bahamas, to purchase household goods, food, clothing, etc. Items purchased in Nassau or Florida are then shipped via the mail boat services to their respective Family Islands (Rolle et al., 2015). While shops do exist for tourists who may purchase souvenirs as reminders of their trip, the islands are "home" to locals who require basic amenities. Shopping is not tourism dependent for residents of these islands.

When asked if tourism increased their standard of living, the findings show disagreement among the respondents; 39.9% of the total respondents agreed compared to 24.6% who disagreed (Table 3.4).

Table 3.4 My standard of living has increased considerably because of tourism

	Total (%)	Abaco (%)	Bimini (%)	Exuma (%)
1. Disagree	24.6	46.1	8.1	22.6
3. Neutral	35.5	33.3	29.0	42.9
4. Agree	39.9	30.4	62.9	34.5
N = 248				

A study conducted by the Ministry of Tourism & Aviation (2008) in the is-lands under study (among others) supports the findings of the respondents who agreed that tourism increased their standard of living; 52% of the respondents work in the tourism industry, 10% in construction and 5% in domestic services. Likewise, the different annual home-coming festivals and regattas, in Abaco, Bimini and Exuma, attract local and foreign visitors and made it possible for the residents to benefit economically (Cooper, 2018). The anchor projects also provided employment which meant many residents did not have to migrate to Nassau or Freeport for employment (Christie, 1984). These factors referenced could have had some influence on the respondents' positive answer regarding their standard of living improving due to tourism.

On the other hand, the respondents (24.6%) who disagreed that their standard of living improved because of tourism could be ascribed to other industries that offset tourism in the islands such as farming and fishing (Du-puch Publications, 2011). Similarly, some persons were employed in govern-ment agencies or in the private sector, hence do not consider their standard of living being directly associated with tourism.

There was also variation in responses between the islands; Bimini's respond-ents (62.9%) agreed that their standard of living improved due to tourism. This could be attributed to the Resorts World development (coming on the heels of Hurricane Sandy in 2012) on the island adding more jobs for residents such as a casino, and tourist attractions resulting in more tourists to the island (Baha-maspress.com, 2014). According to the then Prime Minister Christie, in 2013, Resorts World increased seaplane flights to Bimini with 2500 flights carrying over 7,000 passengers, making it the busiest seaplane route in the Caribbean (Vedrine, 2015). However, 46.1% of Abaco's participants disagreed. Some res-idents in Abaco are employed in the private sectors, such as fishing, banking, real estate and beauty salons, so may not equate their standard of living di-rectly to tourism because they cater to both locals and tourists alike (Ministry of Tourism & Aviation, 2008; Carroll & Brown, 2017). It is interesting to note that 35.5% were neutral regarding whether tourism increased their standard of living. This could be attributed to respondents being employed in other activ-ities indirectly associated with tourism such as fishing, domestic services and private businesses. This needs to be further investigated.

Tourism development: social and environmental impact findings

Social

As mentioned earlier, since 2002, several anchor projects were established on the large Islands, e.g. Abaco, Bimini and Exuma (Smith, 2013). The aim was sustainability of the islands and an improved quality of life for Family Islanders (Christie, 1984; Bahamas Information Services, 2003) especially too, since they often experienced some damage due to hurricanes, e.g. Irma and Matthew. The participants responded to several questions regarding the impact of tourism development in their islands (Table 3.5). All respondents agreed with the following questions.

Table 3.5 Respondents that agreed to the following questions

Question	Total (%)	Abaco (%)	Bimini (%)	Exuma (%)
More important benefits of tourism development are how it can improve the local resident's standard of living	55.2	51.6	73.8	54.1
Tourism development provides incentives for residents to stay in the island	60.5	56.4	77.4	51.5
Tourism development has changed the islands landscape (buildings, topography, sea-view	50.4	45.5	75.8	34.8
The government must provide incentives to residents of the island in order to encourage local tourism development	68.7	60	88.5	63.7

Respondents were asked whether more important benefits of tourism development were that tourism development improved residents' standard of living (Table 3.5). Many respondents (55%) agreed with the question. Their responses can be attributed to the recent economic improvements in the islands as a result of the anchor projects and the second homeowners. The two combined provided jobs in such areas as construction, 10%; local entertainment and restaurants, 18%; and domestic services, 5% (Department of Statistics, 2016). They also invested and purchased goods and services in the islands, hence local incomes increased, thus sustaining the islands economies (Smith, 2005; Robinson-Blair, 2011; Alexander, 2014; Bahamasinvestors.com, 2015).

The respondents also agreed (60.5%) that tourism development provided incentives for residents to stay in the islands (Table 3.5). Residents were employed because of the anchor projects and services that accompanied the developments. Further, the need to migrate particularly to Nassau for employment would be reduced (Smith, 2008; Robinson-Blair, 2011; Bahamas Press, 2014). Two statements by residents substantiated this

Job creation is another major economic benefit of the resort. In the past, a vast majority of Biminites had to move to Nassau or Freeport to find jobs. To date, the resort has 180 Bahamians employed and 75 more jobs are currently available (Smith, 2008).

"major expansion at the Resort (Resorts World) saw many openings for well-paying careers that will likely bring many Biminites back home and keep others from leaving" (Bahamaspress.com, 2014).

When asked if tourism development changed the landscape of the island (buildings, sea-view, topography), 50% of the respondents agreed (Table 3.5). The responses may be linked to the developers restructuring the land to accommodate large hotels, marinas and golf courses. For example, Sandals, a luxury all-inclusive resort in the Exumas, included a "George Norman" designed golf course and deep-water marina (Robinson-Blair, 2011).

Between the islands, Bimini responses stood out; 76% agreed their landscape changed because of the Resorts World project. A resident at a town-hall meeting highlights this point, "It (Resorts World project) is designed with tourists in mind; with architecture that is different from local architecture and situated outside the township housing the local residents" (Rolle et al., 2015). As Hartnell (2013b) opined (it) shows the dilemma when job creation pressures result in projects that potentially alter an islands character, the very thing that attracts tourists in the first place.

Respondents overwhelmingly agreed (68.7%) the government must provide incentives for islands residents to participate in tourism development. The developers were given concessions by the government to establish resorts on the islands. Local entrepreneurs felt they too should be given similar opportunities to participate in the tourism market (Cooper, 2011; McKenzie, 2014). Comments from local residents addressed this concern: "Government was not doing sufficient to ensure that Bahamians are trained to take positions held by foreigners"; " ....the Government is relying on our two pronged economy-tourism and financial services, ... rather than developing its human capital where one can become an entrepreneur" (Bahamas Local, 2015; Gibson, 2016).

Many respondents (79%) indicated it was important to develop plans to manage growth of tourism in the islands. Their response was understandable because most of the planning for development was done by the government and developers in Nassau and projects then imposed on the islanders, sometimes without taking into consideration the size of the population and infrastructure in relation to the project (Hartnell, 2013a). As opined by two residents at a town-hall meeting in Bimini, "Family Islanders tend to feel like outsiders in the decisions made about development" (Rolle et al., 2015). "Resorts (Resorts World) do not consult with local council; they came in with the master plan and showed them (residents) their plan, they had no input" (Smith, 2008; Rolle et al., 2015); so, government officials in Nassau determine how the islands will be developed and when (Hartnell, 2013b).

Many respondents (54.7%) disagreed with the question that tourism development reduced the quality of outdoor recreational opportunities in their islands. Locals have their own traditional activities such as regattas, fishing tournaments and festivals (Dupuch Publication, 1995; Alexander, 2018). Further, with the Ministry of Tourism over the years, marketing the Family Island and their activities, the islands have seen an increase in local and international visitors (Cooper, 2018; Robinson-Blair, 2011; Alexander 2018). Concomitantly, residents are sports enthusiast and participate in various tournaments – football, softball, track and field etc. – which are not associated with tourism development (Dupuch Publication, 1995).

Environment

There were mixed responses to questions related to development affecting traditional sectors (fishing and farming), overcrowding of public space, whether development negatively impacted the natural environment of the islands and if benefits of tourism development outweighed the negative impacts.

In terms of overcrowding in the islands, Bimini stands out with 75.8% of the respondents agreeing to the overcrowding. Bimini, particularly North Bimini where most of the development is located, is 11 square miles, with a population density of 180 persons per square mile compared to Abaco, 649 square miles with a population density of 27 persons per square mile, and Exuma, 112 square miles with a population density of 62 persons per square mile (Department of Statistics, 2012). Because Abaco and Exuma are larger islands and their resorts are interspersed over the islands, residents do not experience the overcrowding like Bimini. It is understandable that Biminites would feel the overcrowding when tourists and large developments are added to the island. On Guana Cay, one of the Bimini islands with the large resort, Bakers Bay, the residents felt the resort will negatively impact the islands with already strained infrastructure and amenities in the future (Reynolds, 2010). Comments by some Biminites addressed this, "the population doubled in three years"; "no space"; and "population of 1,600, now all hotels are filled with 3,000 people" (Alexander, 2014; Rolle et al., 2015).

Respondents were also mixed regarding the question about tourism development and its negative impact on the natural environment: 45% disagreed and 27% agreed with this question. One explanation for respondents' disagreement could be that despite the dredging for a marina, loss of mangroves due to construction and golf course, destruction of coral reefs among other environmental issues (Alexander, 2014; Rolle et al., 2015; Darville, 2019), respondents did not see a decline in tourism and tourism development; thus, their quality of life was not negatively impacted. This view was found to be the case in a study in Abaco by Carroll and Brown (2017). For one Biminite, the developments were a means of protecting the economic future of their children (Smith, 2008). Another resident opined,

> I'm not an expert on the environment but, I know Bimini people are going to benefit tremendously (Alexander, 2014). Three hundred people from Bimini petitioned the government in support of Resorts World development. They saw it as the lifeblood of the Family Island's struggling economy.
>
> (Smith, 2008)

Not addressed specifically in the survey but may be considered because of the rebuilding after the damage by Hurricanes, Irma and Matthew for example, tourism development helped them financially.

Conversely, 27% of respondents agreed the developments negatively impacted residents' quality of life. Their responses may be ascribed to some protests by local and international environmentalists, who spoke out and demonstrated against the destruction of the mangroves, local reefs, grouper, conchs and turtle habitats because of the scale of construction taking place on the islands by tourism development (Duncombe, 2008; Reynolds, 2010; Alexander, 2014). A Guana Cay resident opposed the developments because the development's footprint was too large and destructive for the small island, whose economy relies on small-scale tourism and fishing (notesfromtheroad.com). According to the president of Save Guana Cay Reefs, "we are absolutely not opposed to development, we just want the developments to be better planned, the impacts monitored and most importantly, environmentally safe for the surrounding reefs."

Regarding the question concerning the benefits of tourism development outweighing the negative impacts, the responses were also mixed, 45% agreed and 27% disagreed. For those who agreed, this may be linked to the economic benefits and the increase of visitors to the islands over the past several years. New jobs were created because of the resort developments and second homeowners in the islands, which led to improved incomes for the residents (Bahamas Information Services, 2003; Robinson-Blair, 2011; Bahamas Press, 2014). Moreover, as highlighted by Carroll and Brown (2017), the concern of the environment is important to Bahamians, but currently, does not appear to be extremely important, mainly because the influx of tourists has not declined and the islands always showed resilience after a hurricane (Sachs, 2019). This view was expressed by a spokesperson for the Bimini Blue Coalition(an environmental group), who said "people understand the importance of tourism and welcome new investments as long as they display a basic respect and understanding of what has established Bimini as an attractive tourist destination for the last several decades" (Alexander, 2014). Among the islands, Abaco and Exuma respondents, despite experiencing environmental problems inclusive of the annual hurricanes, also viewed development in their islands as positive. For one thing, their islands are large enough to accommodate the big developments compared to Bimini. They were not overwhelmed by tourists and second homeowners who contributed to the economy in numerous ways; these outweighed the negative impacts (Smith, 2005). Another consideration, the developments provided jobs in a depressed economy after a hurricane damage.

Conversely, 66% of Bimini respondents disagreed that tourism development outweighed the negative impacts. Biminites response may be related to a few factors. One, most of the large resorts are located on North Bimini, a small and narrow island. At times tourists outnumbered the residents (Rolle et al., 2015). There was much environmental degradation (loss of mangroves, reefs) as a result of the construction (Reynolds, 2010; Alexander, 2014). Another factor, some residents were "locked out" of the construction jobs and entrepreneurial job opportunities (Hartnell, 2013b). Most of the work was being done by foreign workers, and few Bahamians were employed in the Bimini Bay Casino (Hartnell, 2013b). Another factor, passengers arriving at the airport in South Bimini were ferried to a private dock at Bimini Bay, rather than the public dock in Alice Town, thus reducing the economic benefits for Biminites (Hartnell, 2013b).

Most respondents disagreed (64%) to the question that tourism development had a negative impact on the quality of their life. This may be attributed to the fact that The Bahamas has a long history in tourism (Cleare, 2007). Over the past several years, The Bahamas generally and Family Islands specifically have experienced an increase in tourism and tourism development (Cooper, 2018; Ministry of Tourism, 2019). For instance, Travel and Tourism contribution to the GDP of The Bahamas was 47% ($4,343 million) in 2017 and expected to rise to 59% of the GDP in 2028 (www.wtt.com; Hartnell, 2017). Further, many Family Islands see tourism and tourism development benefitting them in the long run (Alexander, 2014; Bahamas Press, 2014). As a Biminite opined, "the Bimini Bay Resort has invested in a reverse osmosis plant that not only supplies water to the development, but also provides potable water to local residents and businesses, making the resort the water supplier for the entire island" (Smith, 2008). Over the years, Abaco, Bimini and Exuma have seen improvements to their airports, telecommunications, new business enterprises and health facilities supplied by the government (The Bahamas Investor, 2015; Parker 2016). These improvements may also be indirectly related to needed improvements due to hurricane damage and now being addressed by the government. Within this context, tourism development positively contributed to their quality of life.

Summary

In summary, most of the respondents believe that tourism and tourism development improved their quality of life even though they recognized the environmental costs associated with the developments. Employment because of resort developments and second homeowners boosting the economy in the islands played a major factor in their outlook. Moreover, the respondents thought it was important for residents to be involved in the planning of tourist developments in their islands as opposed to decisions being made in Nassau by the government and developers. By so doing, developments would complement the size, infrastructure and population capacity of the islands. Furthermore, residents wanted to be given an opportunity to develop their own plans to manage tourism in the islands because of their experiences with the mega resorts and knew what they wanted development to look like. Residents "knew" their island. In their mind, if residents were allowed input into the developments, then, residents will not need to migrate to Nassau in search of employment.

The respondents although aware and concerned about the degradation of their natural environment, it took a backseat to the employment opportunities that tourism and tourism development brings which provided them with a good quality of life however they defined it. With the continued increase of tourists and their spending in the islands over the past several years, the islands will embrace the goose that lays the golden egg.

Recommendations

Further research needs to be conducted on the quality of life and tourism and tourism development in other Family Islands to make comparisons and to better inform policy on future scale of anchor projects in the islands. Additionally, future research must address the impact of natural disasters and sea level rise on tourism and tourism development and the quality of life of Family Island residents, particularly since research has indicated that The Bahamas may be affected by sea level rise in the future (Rolle, 2019).

References

Alexander, C. (July 2018). Abaco's unparalleled tourism landscape. Destination Abaco, The Bahamas Exeuprint Ltd; Marsh Harbour, Abaco, The Bahamas.

Alexander, H. (6 July 2014). Islanders in the stream: The battle for the soul of Bimini. *The Telegraph*. www.telegraph.co.uk. Retrieved, 14 February 2019.

Aref, F. (2011). The effects of tourism on quality of life: A case study of Shiraz, Iran. *Life Science Journal*, Volume 8, Issue 2, pp. 26–30. www.lifesciencesite.com. Retrieved, 28 March 2019.

Bahamas Information Services. (2003). PM opens casino at Emerald Bay. www.exumamap.com. Retrieved, 28 March 2019.

Bahamas Local. (6 May 2015). Sands: Family Islands need more than 'Anchor projects.' *Bahamas Local*. www.bahamaslocal.com. Retrieved, 28 March 2019.

Bahamas Press. (5 June 2014). More jobs are opening for Bahamians at Resorts World Bimini. www.bahamaspress.com. Retrieved, 23 March 2019.

Black, A. (15 January 2013). Luxury resorts, improved infrastructure aimed at spreading prosperity across the Archipelago. *The Bahamas Investor Magazine*. www.bahamasinvestor.com. Retrieved, 23 March 2019.

Blanchet, P. (15 November, 2019). Damages and other impacts on Bahamas by hurricane Dorian estimated at $3.4 billion: Report. News Release. https://www.iadb.org/en/damages-and-other-impacts-bahamas-hurricane-dorian-estimated-34-billion-report. Retrieved, 5 November 2019.

Bethell-Bennett, I. (10 November 2017). Tourism and anchor projects: The Bahamian panacea. *The Nassau Guardian*. www.thenassauguardian.com. Retrieved, 23 March 2019.

Carey, T. (30 May 2018). Budget: VAT to rise from 7.5 percent to 12 percent. *The Tribune*. www.tribune242.com. Retrieved, 15 September 2019.

Carroll, J., & Brown, M. O. (2017). An assessment of tourism sustainability in Abaco, Bahamas. *Journal of Tourism Insights*, Volume 8, Issue 1, Article 2. https://doi.org/10.9707/2328-0824.1073.

Christie, P. (1984). Tourism and its effects on the individual and society. *International Journal of Bahamian Studies*, Volume 5. doi:10.15362/ijbs.v5i0.83. Retrieved, 23 March 2019.

Christie, P. (6 June 2016). P. M. Opens Resorts World Bimini Hilton hotel. *The Bahamas Investor*. www.thebshsmssinvestor.com. Retrieved, 30 December 2019.

Cleare, A. (2007). *History of tourism in The Bahamas: A global perspective*. Xlibris Corporation; Philadelphia.

Cooper, R. (16 December 2011). Brasilia, a development model for the Family Islands. *The Nassau Guardian*. www.thenassauguardian.com. Retrieved, 22 March 2019.

Cooper, A. (15 March 2018). Branding campaigns expected to boost tourism numbers. *The Freeport News*. www.thefreeportnews.com.

Darville, F. (24 September 2019). Face to face: The long history of hurricanes in The Bahamas. The Tribune. www.tribune242.com. Retrieved, 29 December 2019.

Das, D. (2008). Urban quality of life: A case study of Guwahati. *Social Indicators Research*, Volume 88, pp. 297–310. doi:10.1007/s11205-007-9191-6.

Department of Statistics. (2004). Bahamas living conditions survey 2001. www.bahamas.gov.bs

Department of Statistics. (2012).*The Bahamas in figures 2012*. Napco Printing Services; Nassau, The Bahamas.

Department of Statistics. (May 2016). Labour force and household survey report. Nassau. *The Bahamas*. https://www.bahamas.gov.bs/wps/wcm/connect/83b2d95e-e52c-4086-a25f-c1c536011af4/Labour+Force+Report+May2016_for+website.pdf?MOD=AJPERES. Retrieved. 13 April 2019.

Department of Statistics. (2016). *Household expenditure survey 2013 report*. www.bahamas.gov.bs. Retrieved, 15 October 2019.

Diener, E., & Suh, E. (1997). Measuring quality of life: Economic, social and subjective indicators. *Social Indicators Research*, Volume 40, pp. 189–216.

Dimitropoulou, A. (22 January 2019). Most expensive countries in the world to live in, 2019. *CEOWORLD Magazine*. https://ceoworld.biz/2020/02/03/most-expensive-countries-in-the-world-to-live-in-2020/ Retrieved, 15 December 2019.

Duncombe, S. (2008). Unsustainable development, not bad press is creating "black mark on Bimini's future." www.ReEarth.org. Retrieved, 1 April 2019.

Dupuch Publications. (1995). *The sporting life*. Bahamas Handbook. Etienne Dupuch Jr. Publications Ltd; Nassau, The Bahamas.

Dupuch Publications. (2011). *Bahamas Handbook*. Nassau, The Bahamas, Etienne Dupuch Jr. Publications Ltd.

ECLAC. (January–March 2018). Irma & Maria by the numbers, pp. 6–7. www.eclac.org/portofspain.

Gibson, A. (4 February 2016). A young man's view: Signing away The Bahamas. *The Tribune*. www.tribune242.com. Retrieved, 23 March 2019.

Hartnell, N. (25 October 2013a). 2/3 of Biminites don't want more visitor arrivals. *The Tribune*. www.tribune242.com. Retrieved, 25 March 2019.

Hartnell, N. (3 September 2013b). Bimini suffers its "worst state ever". *The Tribune*. www.tribune242.com. Retrieved, 25 March 2019.

Hartnell, N. (30 January 2015). Out Islands pay "3 times" Nassau shipping costs. *The Tribune*. www.tribune242.com. Retrieved, 25 March 2019.

Hartnell, N. (12 April 2017). Vacation rentals 'explosion' threat to hotel business. *The Tribune*. www.tribune242. Retrieved, 5 May 2019.

Interknowledge Corp. (1996). Infrastructure of The Bahamas equipped for economic progress.www.geographia.com. Retrieved, 10 September 2019.

Ismail, F., & Turner, L. (2008). Host and tourist perceptions on small island tourism: A case study of Perhentian and Redang Islands Malaysia. Paper presented at International Conference on Applied Economics ICOAE (pp. 401–410). http://www.kastoria.teikoz.gr/iocae2/wordpress/wp-content/uploads. Retrieved, 10 September 2019.

IADB-Inter-American Development Bank. (2019). Damages and other impacts on Bahamas by Hurricane Dorian estimated at $3.4 billion: Report. www.iadb.org. Retrieved, 30 December 2019.

Knowles, R. (21 March 2019). Historic tourist arrivals in 2018. *The Nassau Guardian*. www.thenassauguardian.com. Retrieved, 29 December 2019.

Maycock,D.(11June2018).$2.5billioninVatincome-Yetdebtwentup.*TheTribune*.http://www.tribune242.com/news/2018/jun/11/25bn-vat- income-yet-debt-went/. Retrieved 15 December 2019.

Mbaiwa, J. (2003). The socio-economic & developmental impacts of tourism development on the Okavango Delta, north-western Botswana. *Journal of Arid Environments*, Volume 54, pp. 447–467. doi:10.1006/jare.2002.1101. Retrieved, 1 April 2019.

McKenzie, N. (10 October 2013). VAT impact "three times a severe" for Out Islands. *The Tribune*. www.tribune242.com. Retrieved, 1 April 2019.

McKenzie, N. (14 April 2014). Gov't urged to "level investments incentives." *The Tribune*. www.tribune242.com. Retrieved, 1 April 2019.

Ministry of Tourism & Aviation. (1–22 November 2008). Bahamian Resident's general public survey. Family Islands. http://www.tourismtoday.com/sites/default/files/res_report_2008_gb_website.pdf. Retrieved 29 December 2019.

Ministry of Tourism. (2018). Stopover visitors Islands in The Bahamas. www.tourismtoday.com. Retrieved, 29 December, 2019.

Ministry of Tourism. (2019). Foreign arrivals to The Bahamas by air, sea landed and cruise1998–2019. www.tourismtoday.com. Retrieved, 21 December 2019.

Moody's Analytic. (9 October 2019). *Economic indicators: Bahamas*. www.economy.com. Retrieved, 29 December 2019.

Nkemngu, A. P. (2015). Quality of life and tourism impacts: A community perspective. *African Journal of Hospitality, Tourism and Leisure*, Volume 4, Issue 1. http://www.ajhtl.com/uploads/7/1/6/3/7163688/article_11_vol_4_1_2015_jan-june.pdf Retrieved 25 April 2019.

Parker, Q. (23 September 2016). PM: Register Abaco second homes and rental villas. *The Nassau Guardian*. www.thenassauguardian.com. Retrieved, 25 April 2019.

Pine II, J. and Gilmore, J. H. (July–August 1998). Welcome to the Experience Economy. *Harvard Business Review*. https://www.researchgate.net/publication/260917972_The_experience_economy_pastpresent_and_uture. Retrieved 15 December 2019.

Reynolds, M. (28 October 2010). Abaco residents urged protest two proposed Developments. *The Tribune*. www.tribune242.com. Retrieved, 21 March 2019.

Robinson-Blair, T. (2011). *Foreign homeowners spread their wealth*. Dupuch Publications; Nassau, The Bahamas.

Rolle, R. (4 November 2019). New report: Rising seas risk worse than feared. *The Tribune*. www.tribune242.com. Retrieved, 22 December 2019.

Rolle, S., Bethell-Bennett, I., Thomas, A., Edwards, M., Bethel, N., Minnis, J., & Blackwell, M. (2015). *Vision 2040. Situational analysis: The dynamics of Family Island development.* Unpublished report. The College of The Bahamas.

Sachs, A. (8 November 2019). In The Bahamas, a hard-hit island beckon again. *The Philadelphia Inquirer.* www.inquirer.com. Retrieved, 22 December 2019.

Smith, L. (27 November 2005). Will development kill The Bahamas? *Nassau, The Bahamas, Bahama Pundit.* https://bahamapundit.typepad.com/bahama_pundit/2005/11/will_developmen.html.

Smith, L. (21 March 2007). Tourism and anchor projects in The Bahamas. *The Tribune.* www.tribune242.com. Retrieved, 23 March 2019.

Smith, R. (10 June 2008). Biminites show support for Bimini Bay. *The Nassau Guardian.* www.nasguard.com. Retrieved, 31 March 2019.

Smith, L. (8 July 2012). Mixed track record of Out Island resort projects. *The Tribune.* www.tribune242.com. Retrieved, 30 March 2019.

Smith, D. (6 August 2013). Master plan for the Family Islands. *The Tribune.* www.tribune242.com. Retrieved, 23 March 2019.

Smith, F. (23 November 2018). Freeport, the original anchor project. *The Nassau Guardian.* https://thenassauguardian.com/2018/11/23/freeport-the-original-anchor-project/.

Smith, X. (19 January, 2018). Palacious: Between 2015 and 2017 hurricanes cost 4678 mil. in losses. The Nassau Guardian. https://thenassauguardian.com/2018/01/19/palacious-between-2015-and-2017-hurricanes-cost-678-mil-in-losses/

Statista Research Department. (21 August 2018). Global travel and tourism industry-statistics and facts. *Statista.* www.statista.com. Retrieved, 29 December 2019.

Teye, V., Sonmez, S., & Sirakaya, E. (2002). Residents' attitudes towards tourism development. *Annals of Tourism Research*, Volume 29, Issue 3, pp. 668–688.

The Bahamas Investor. (26 October 2015). PM address Exuma business Outlook. *The Bahamas Investor.* www.bahamasinvestor.com. Retrieved, 24 March 2019.

The Bahamas Voluntary National Review on the Sustainable Development Goals to the High Level Political Forum of the United Nations Economic and Social Government of the Bahamas. (July 2018). www.sustainabledevelopment.un.org/memberstates/bahamas.

The Tribune (30, September 2019). Tourism tells Canada: We're open for business. *The Tribune.* Retrieved, 8 December, 2019). http://www.tribune242.com/news/2019/sep/30/tourism-tells-canada-were-ope

The University of the West Indies. (2017). Hurricane Irma 2017. www.uwi.edu/ekacdm/.

United Nations Environmental Programme and World Tourism Organization. (2005). *Making tourism more sustainable. A guide for policy makers.* www.world-tourism.org. Retrieved, 3 March 2019.

Vedrine, B. (30 January 2015). Significant gains in tourism in 2014. *Bahamas Information Services.* www.bahamas.gov.bs. Retrieved, 14 March 2019.

Ward, J. (30 August 2019). On alert. *The Nassau Guardian.* www.thenassauguardian.com. Retrieved, 30 December 2019.

World Travel and Tourism Council. (March 2019). Economic impact 2019. www.wttc.org. Retrieved, 10 October 2019.

Zeinali, B., Jafarpour, M., Omidi, E., Tahmasbi, N., & Dorangard, S. (2015). Will tourism development improve the quality of life in Hashtpar city? An analysis of local resident's attitudes. *International Journal of Economy, Management and Social Sciences*, Volume 4, Issue 3, pp. 293–300.

4   Vacation rental market in The Bahamas

Jay Jones-Mills

In The Bahamas, the concept of vacation rentals (VRs) is not new (Moyle, 2018). The VR properties are throughout The Bahamas and are a combination of foreign-owned second homes, and Bahamian owner occupied or stand-alone properties. In an article on foreign second homeowners in The Bahamas by Robinson-Blair (2011), she indicated that second homeowners would place their homes in an income-generating rental pool when they returned to their country. They stay in their homes for a period and then rent them for the rest of the year. This is very prevalent on the islands of Eleuthera and Abaco. However, in New Providence and Paradise Island, they usually closed their homes and went away (Robinson-Blair, 2011).

A home rental ranged from $3,500 to $10,000 per week depending on the location especially if there was a beach (Hartnell, 2017a; Moyle, 2018). According to Moyle (2018), for decades VRs were handled by local real estate agents and they tended to revolve around the higher end of the market especially in Family Islands like Abaco, Exuma and Eleuthera. Now the owner does his/her own marketing or uses a property manager (Robinson-Blair, 2011).

Moyle (2018) also mentioned that the VRs were not exclusive, but it was assumed that the homeowner had to have an amazing expensive property to participate. Moyle also pointed out that the online VR sites such as Airbnb have enabled persons with an Internet connection to market and rent their properties or living space to anyone globally. Because of this technology, Airbnb and others are empowering Bahamians to participate in the tourism sector in positive ways. According to the Minister of Tourism, traditionally, the Bahamian VR market has been dominated by non-Bahamians; however, in today's market there is an increasing number of Bahamians participating in this lucrative sector (Airbnbcitizen, 2017).

The VRs were gaining in popularity among the tourists, because they had the opportunity to see The Bahamas at its best and at a fraction of the cost of a hotel (Bain, 2015). Hotels and guest houses began to view VRs as competition to their businesses because the VRs were not paying hotel taxes or surcharges on their room rentals and they were impacting hotel occupancy rates (Robinson-Blair, 2011; The Nassau Guardian, 2017a). There were others who saw VRs boosting the Bahamian economy, providing employment and creating entrepreneurs (Bain, 2015; Hartnell, 2017b; The Nassau Guardian, 2017).

Legislation was introduced into the Hotel Act of 2009 whereby foreign homeowners would have to license their property as "owner occupied" and pay a 6% guest tax of their rental income to the Government. The question became for the Government, how was this legislation to be enforced (Robinson-Blair, 2011). So, the VRs flourished unchecked and unregulated for several years (The Nassau Guardian, 2017). They came under scrutiny by the Government during the implementation of Value Added Tax (VAT) in the country by the Government in 2015. The Government realized VRs as a potential revenue-generating source (Parker, 2016). As noted by the Minister of Tourism, the VRs were making a contribution to the economy, but operated without taxation (McKenzie, 2017). When VAT was implemented, the Prime Minister indicated that all VR properties in the country should be licensed and other commercial entities such as hotels pay license fees and taxes to The Bahamas treasury. VRs were also to register with the Ministry of Tourism (Parker, 2016). In compliance, the Ministry of Tourism established a Hotel Licensing Department. The Department was tasked to set up rules and establish legislation to monitor and regulate this sector. Thus there was a section within the Department, to specifically monitor and regulate VRs. As the Minister of Tourism pointed out, this (VR) is a part of the tourism industry and the country's "brand" reputation is at stake (Jones, 2017).

A VR registration drive was launched in 2016 (McKenzie, 2017). Since then, there was an increase in the number of individuals registering with the Ministry (McKenzie, 2017). However, no formal legislation was enacted; thus VR's remained unregulated (Jones, 2017). During this time, a concern arose around the popular VRs and the fear of VAT was being implemented by the Government in 2015. Property Management firms were concerned VAT will cost them their businesses by driving visitors to book VRs through other foreign sources to avoid the tax (The Tribune, 2014).

The Government again realizing it was missing out on significant tax revenue from VRs because payments were remitted to landlords outside The Bahamas and not to the Bahamian treasury, the Ministry of Tourism "felt it prudent to enter a relationship with Airbnb to govern the terms by which people could rent their vacation homes in The Bahamas" (Hartnell, 2007b). So, in 2016 a Memorandum of Understanding (MOU) was signed with Airbnb (Jones, 2017). According to the Minister of Tourism, the MOU will only become a full agreement once new VR tax was implemented (Hartnell, 2017b).

It is against this backdrop this chapter examines the impact of Airbnb on the tourism market in The Bahamas

VR-Airbnb

Airbnb is a free online VR platform, part of the growing Internet "sharing economies." Travellers connect with hosts via their website and rent the "space" of their choice: a tree house, an apartment, a home or even a boat, and enjoy a specific experience at a fraction of the cost of a hotel (Salter, 2012). Airbnb was started in 2007/8 and since then has grown into a billion dollar online business having over 6 million listings, 2.9 million hosts and 150 million users, and in over 191 countries (Smith, 2019; Airbnb Press Room, 2019). Airbnb promotes connecting people with places and culture, and facilitating memorable stays, in a personalized and sustainable way at an affordable price (Salter, 2012; Airbnb Press Room, 2019). They have created a marketplace that links prospective guests with hosts willing to share their space and culture via an online site and managed by Airbnb. This arrangement has made vacation travel much easier. Feedback about Airbnb has been positive as their statistics show.

There is, though, a negative view of Airbnb held by some people in business circles. Matt Kurtz (2014) in his article, "In Focus: Airbnb's Inroads into The Hotel Industry," refers to it as a "disruptive service" that is "a platform which through its innovation disrupts the established way of doing business in a given industry." He further expounds that Airbnb has done just this with the lodging industry. It owns no physical structures but has managed to garner millions of units of lodging internationally and, because of their available supply, can now compete for the business of the travelling public with the long well-established hotel chains. The result of this could be a decrease in prices for the hotel industry. Kurtz believes that "its rapid rise and expansion make Airbnb a serious competitor for the traditional hotel industry." His suggestion is to acknowledge Airbnb's presence, monitor them and perhaps list some of their hotel rooms with Airbnb.

Information on Airbnb in The Bahamas is limited. Information on them was obtained from articles written in the local newspapers, i.e. *The Tribune*, *The Nassau Guardian* and *The Bahama Journal*, and from interviews with officials in the tourism industry and local VR hosts. Consequently, I have found that it is only one of the online agencies of the VR sector popular in The Bahamas. Other sites used were Flipkey and VRBO (The Nassau Guardian, 2017).

From its inception in 2007/8, Airbnb has become a leader in the VR market with a presence in 191 countries inclusive of some Caribbean islands such as Jamaica, Dominica and Antigua (Caribbean 360, 2017; CTO News, 2017). Airbnb seems to have also become the leader in the VR market in The Bahamas (Moyle, 2018; Neely, 2019). Airbnb's Shawn Sullivan, Public Policy leader for Central America and the Caribbean, and Carlos Munoz, Public Policy and Government Affairs met with officials of the Ministry of Tourism and signed an MOU with The Bahamas Government (Thompson, 2017). This MOU outlined the expectations for their mutual operation in the country, including exchanging of information, and will pave the way for Airbnb "to collect all due taxes and fees associated with The Bahamas based vacation rentals listed on its website and ensure those landlords are in full compliance with local rules and regulations" (Hartnell, 2017b). Additionally, the MOU will function as an integral part of the country's tourism sector (Jones, 2017). According to Mr. Sullivan's Airbnb numbers, there are 1,900 active listings and 1,200 active hosts (Jones, 2017). Airbnb considers The Bahamas an important location and is quoted as saying,

> Our average host makes about $6,000 per year through Airbnb. Most people who use Airbnb to come to The Bahamas come from the United States, Europe and parts of Latin America. This is an important market for Airbnb. I think that The Bahamas has a lot to offer.
>
> (McKenzie, 2017)

The Government has yet to decide on the tax since the signing of the MOU (McKenzie, 2019a): Who is to be taxed and how much should they be taxed? The Minister of Tourism initially mentioned that VAT would not be applicable for Airbnb providers given that most homeowners do not meet the minimum requirements of $100,000 needed to pay the 7.5% tax; however, a tax will be imposed (Robards, 2018). According to the Minister of Tourism, although the fees and amount of taxation must be decided, the taxation will level the playing field in the accommodations sector (McKenzie, 2017; Nassau Guardian, 2017). To implement the regularization, process, the Ministry of Tourism reached out to the VR-occupied homeowners via the local realtors and local media asking them to advise the Ministry of Tourism of their existence (Parker, 2016). The request revealed 1,900 active properties listed on Airbnb (The Nassau Guardian, 2017). Presently some 1,700 properties have been identified on Airbnb alone (Robards, 2019).

Since the signing of the MOU with Airbnb, there have mainly been positive and some negative reactions from some constituents in the tourism sector. On the positive side, the VR sector is increasing in popularity and attributed to Airbnb activity (McKenzie, 2019a; Neely, 2019; Robards, 2019). Promoting VRs via Airbnb is being recognized as a viable option for the average Bahamian to participate in the tourism industry and benefit, and the benefits can be all encompassing. The visitor can see The Bahamas at its best and at a fraction of the cost of a hotel. The host supplements his/her income, the money stays at home so the economy is boosted and the country is promoted (McKenzie, 2014; Bain, 2015; The Nassau Guardian, 2017). Further, in 2018, visitors to The Bahamas were able to access more than 2,900 VRs throughout The Bahamas. Income received by a host was approximately US$7,500, and Airbnb hosts welcomed around 59,000 guests (Neely, 2019). Additionally, some advocated for VR regulations because they were "eating" into the hotel occupancy and businesses and should be taxed (The Nassau Guardian, 2017; The Nassau Guardian, 2017b), and some also suggested prohibitive zoning on VRs

(McKenzie, 2019b). A hotel union was concerned about the number of tourists choosing VRs over hotels and resorts and was trying to get them to opt for hotels (McCartney, 2018). On the other hand, a few felt the taxation may scare the visitors away and deter possible Bahamian entrepreneurs (Hartnell, 2017d). One private VR owner opined why worry about taxes, VRs already pay VAT through their varied purchases in the country (Hartnell, 2017c).

Of note, even with the annual hurricanes that indirectly or directly impact The Bahamas, VRs were and are still popular and thriving. People were and are still willing to invest in or rent VRs. According to Williams (2017) and Christie (2019), veteran real estate agents, their experiences have taught them that hurricanes positively affected the Bahamian real estate market in that they had received inquiries soon after a hurricane. According to Williams (2017), shortly after a hurricane, some people take advantage of the disaster to invest in properties, others vacation to escape the cold weather for warmer temperatures, "thoughts of hurricanes become a distant memory." Additionally, after hurricanes and particularly Dorian (2019), many people were displaced which meant they needed accommodations. Those who could afford to rent, rented houses or condominiums (Christie, 2019). As stated by Christie (2019) "helping a buyer or seller (or renter) in the aftermath of a hurricane is the next chapter in rebuilding the affected islands, more so Abaco and Grand Bahama after Dorian's devastation".

From my conversations with people in the tourism industry, I surmised that there are constant inquiries about participating in the VR business and someone expressed their desire to open their own version of a Bahamian Airbnb.

Airbnb has made a good impact on VRs and the tourism sector. It appears to have contributed to the economic development of the country (McKenzie, 2019a). So far, there have been very good reviews about the VRs in The Bahamas. The future looks promising for the sector despite natural disasters and regularization with proposed VAT in the upcoming 2019–2020 budget (McKenzie, 2019a) and should bode well for all, in the long run.

Limitations of the study

The effects of hurricanes on the VR market in The Bahamas were not considered in the research for this study. This is attributed in part to the fact that hurricanes are the norms, a part of life for Bahamians including the author so can become a second thought. As expressed by an islander "We have survived through all of the hurricanes that are major, including Floyd, and none of us has had to evacuate" (Ward, 2019). The islands have always rebounded, rebuilt and attracted visitors after a hurricane. Because of this, sometimes hurricanes have inadvertently been overlooked when conducting tourism-related research, as was in this case. With the frequency in severe storms inclusive of Dorian in 2019 happening annually, these forces of nature have become more real and will now have to be taken onto consideration when conducting tourism research in The Bahamas.

Input from local VR hosts and Airbnb members/affiliates

Several Bahamian VR hosts were interviewed to ascertain their views of the online VRs, and their involvement in the business and to what extent the local VRs are impacting the hotel business. Most of the hosts interviewed spoke so on condition of anonymity thus, I refer to them numerically.

VR host 1

My first host is a retired lecturer who got into the business about three years ago for economic reasons. It was a way to increase his income and consistently maintain and enhance his home at the same time.

This host currently uses Airbnb and seems to prefer them as there is less "bureaucracy" and is cheaper. In the past he has used Home Away and VRBO. The host's home is a one level property located in a pleasant, quiet, residential area about a five-minute walk to the beach and the local bus stop, from where his guests can take a short scenic, non-stop ride to down-town Nassau. He has two complete one-bedroom units within his house which he prefers renting to couples. Rental is year-round. His guests stay between four and seven days, and he has a small percentage of repeat visitors.

According to the host, the guests are looking for an experience outside of the hotel. They are looking for "things Bahamian." They want to participate in the local culture. The guests want to be with a Bahamian host in a Bahamian environment. They want to visit the other Family Islands, go to beaches frequented by Bahamians, eat the Bahamian foods and simply experience the Bahamian culture firsthand. He sees his role as being the discreet, unobtrusive host: not necessarily volunteering his services but available if requested. He prefers to give them as much freedom and privacy as possible.

The host does not see the VR sector becoming a threat to the hotel market. He feels that the markets cater to different types of people. VR guests do not want to stay in hotels. They choose to stay locally. The tourism market is simply providing a third choice to travellers: hotel, cruise and now VRs. He says, "it's like comparing people who choose between a skiing vacation in Vail and a speedboat adventure in Exuma, Bahamas."

According to the host, the VR is self-regulating, and he is not in agreement with the Ministry of Tourism's move to regularize it. He feels that being a fledgling market introducing regulations will upset the market. In essence, a negative review about a VR would reflect badly on The Bahamas as today's traveller is experienced and discerning. Moreover, the market is injecting funds into the local economy. The hosts receive money which supplements their income. In turn, these funds are spent locally and used to employ people for property repair/construction using locally purchased materials.

VR host 2

The second host is a veteran in the VR's market. She has been a participant host for several years and views it as a business that is rewarding to both host and guest but should be done properly, not haphazardly.

This host ventured into the general rental market for economic reasons. She was on her own with a large five-bedroom home which she decided to divide making one portion a monthly rental unit. This was not as successful as anticipated so she turned to the emerging VR market being popularized by the Internet.

VRBO now a subsidiary of Home Away was her first-choice carrier, and she dealt with them for several years. She has now enrolled with Airbnb. The host's property, like the other previous one, is in a middle-class, residential neighbourhood, and approximately 15 minutes from the beach and from the bus route to down-town Nassau. Most of her guests come from the USA and Canada, and a small number from elsewhere. Her take on the host's duties differs from that of the previous one. She embodies a Bahamian touristic ambassador and a businesswoman, and it has netted her just rewards, monetarily, by the many repeat visitors; in her own words, "I under promise and over deliver." For example, outside of the arrival hall at the airport, a specially engaged and uniformed taxi-driver, with welcoming signage, collects her guests and gives them a tour in route to her home. This sets the stage for further business for the taxi-driver and makes for a warm welcome to the island.

As a VR host, she has advised many people on how to get into the business and prepare property for rental. She is in contact with other hosts, and they have contemplated forming an association, but so far, has not materialized. She opines perhaps when the market was regularized. She does not seem averse to regularization but feels that concessions should be tagged to them.

VR host 3

Another host (anonymous) has been in the VRs business since 2006 and has used various online platforms such as VRBO, TripAdvisor, Flipkey, Home Away and Bed and Bath simultaneously to rent her two cottages. The cottages are self-sufficient and situated near the beach on Exuma Island, about an hour in flight from Nassau. She prefers to accommodate families of four including children or separate couples. This host lives in Nassau, and the idea of a VR property stemmed from the desire to have a second home on Exuma for personal use and to have added income. Currently, she rents the cottages herself via her own website. The reason for this was that the last company used, suggested short-term rentals of two to three days and a low rental cost relative to the accommodation and amenities that would be provided. Given the fact that she lives in Nassau and must travel back and forth to prepare the properties for rental, see to the maintenance and decide on guest arrival and departure, their suggested rental was not compensatory. She opined that if the properties were situated in the capital, Nassau, it might prove cost-effective. She now rents longer term, and currently, the properties are engaged for one year.

She indicated that there are several foreign-owned second home VRs as well as other Bahamian-owned ones in Exuma. She feels that the foreign-owned ones may fare better due to their networking. Now regulations are being drawn up to govern the market, and she will be expected to fall in line.

She feels that the VR's market does present competition for the traditional hotel simply because it provides cheaper accommodation. Airbnb is popular because they are less expensive. From her experience, cheaper rentals can be found with Airbnb while the higher end properties seem to be found with VRBO and Home Away.

Other guest hosts were interviewed, and they all expressed similar views regarding the VR and hotel sector in the islands.

Views of tourism professionals

Several professionals in the tourism sector were interviewed, on condition of anonymity, to give their views on the status of hotels and VRs in the country. From their responses, there seems to be shared views among the professionals I was able to interview regarding the hotels and VR properties dynamics in the country. The opinions are personal and do not reflect an official position of their organizations. They have been derived from their interaction with hoteliers over time and in the absence of statistical research.

Looking first at the traditional hotels, these are struggling, growth is stagnant and there have been closures. There seems to be a variety of reasons for this. These include consistent low occupancy due to increased overseas competition from other destinations like Mexico, The Dominican Republic and Cuba, particularly since tourists can travel there more easily now, and the demand for all-inclusive is increasing. Further, investments in new hotels have decreased. Some investors feel that it is too costly, time-consuming and challenging to do business in The Bahamas. They can obtain value for money elsewhere relative to the costs of operation which include high labour, utilities and low productivity. Other reasons include insufficient or lack of cultural activities for guests, inefficient transportation and insufficient native eateries for The Bahamas in general. Particularly, with respect to the Family Islands, there seems to be challenges with inadequate air lift and infrastructure. Add to this is the emerging VR market.

Small hotels, more so the Bahamian-owned ones, seem to be the ones most affected by the VR sector though there may be some general impact on the market. The foreign-owned ones fare better, perhaps because of their marketing strategy. The complaint to authorities is simply that this new market is taking their business and it is difficult for them to compete. Now the VRs are unregulated, pay no taxes or fees and have no overhead costs like staffing or utilities. This gives them the flexibility of being able to offer their guests a fully furnished property with amenities all in inclusive packages at low nightly or weekly rates or demand higher rates for the same property. Sometimes, too, the VR host discounts a week's rental by offering the seventh night free. They can also open their property seasonally unlike a hotel that has to remain open year-round. Moreover, there is a new type of guest. Vacationing is changing. Tourists are looking for a home away from home where they can have all the amenities of a hotel in a relaxed environment, at a slower pace, unstructured, doing what they want, when they want and how they want.

Survival of the small hotel, it would seem, depends on regulation of the VR sector. This will ensure that they pay taxes like the hotels. Lowering annual licensing fees, promotional costs and utilities costs would help. Another thought was for hotels to help themselves by standing out from the crowd. Differentiate their hotel by enhancing their product offering, e.g. more amenities, a better quality of service. The VRs are here to stay. Airbnb is the giant in this sector and continues to grow, venturing further into different countries.

Recommendations

Because VR's and Airbnb have made inroads into the Bahamian tourist market and are competing with the long-established and popular hotels in The Bahamas, future research needs to assess what type of impact VRs and Airbnb are having on the hotel industry in The Bahamas.

Also, the Government intends to tax and regulate VRs and Airbnb operating within The Bahamas. Because of this, future research needs to examine what impact this will have on tourism and the Bahamian economy.

Conclusion

The VR market has made all the other players on the tourism stage sit up and take notice. The entrepreneurs see a new avenue to supplement their incomes and become stakeholders in an area previously not easily accessible to them. Professional associations are respecting their presence and encouraging their members to do the same. The Ministry of Tourism has a new possible avenue for revenue as soon as the tax laws are passed. The online bookings agencies, particularly Airbnb, see The Bahamas as a prime target for business so will continue to facilitate the growth of this market. The accommodation sector, namely, the hotel industry, is reluctantly realizing that VRs here to stay and is already making great strides in some places. So, yes, the VR's market is impacting tourism. And, yes, the market is impacting the hotel industry.

In The Bahamas today, hotels and VRs share a market space that seemingly tends to favour the VRs. Hotels have not yet been made obsolete, but they cannot continue doing business as usual, if they want to stay competitive and relevant, so the onus is on the hotels to be proactive and initiate change, but they do need help. The enactment of the pending legislation regulating the VRs is a step in the right direction. If seen as fair to both parties, it should level the playing field and bring some balance and harmony to a developing competition for tourist visitors. Hopefully, the legislation when implemented will allow them to co-exist successfully economically.

References

Airbnbcitizen. (2017). The Bahamas and Airbnb begin tourism promotion and policy collaboration. Airbnbcitizen, 10 August 2017. www.airbnbcitizen.com/the-bahamas-mou/. Retrieved, 2 May 2019.

Airbnb Press Room. (2019). About us. https://news.airbnb.com/ Retrieved, 30 April 2019.

Bain, T. (2015). Home away from home-Why vacation rentals are growing in popularity. *The Tribune*, 4 August 2015. www.tribune242.com. Retrieved, 30 April 2019.

Caribbean 360. (2017). Grenada signs MOU with Airbnb. Caribbean360, 10 June 2017. www.caribbean360.com. Retrieved, 30 May 2019.

Christie, J. (17 September, 2019). Hurricane Dorian: Future of real estate in The Bahamas. www.hgchristie.com. Retrieved, 30 December 2019.

CTO News. (2017). CTO signs MOU with Airbnb. CTO, 7 February 2017. www.onecaribbean.org. Retrieved, 2 May 2019.

Dupuch Jr. Publications Ltd. (1995). *The sporting life.* Nassau, The Bahamas: Etienne Dupuch Jr. Publications Ltd.

Hartnell, N. (2017a). Vacation rentals 'explosion' threat to hotel business. *The Tribune*, 12 April 2017. www.tribune242.com. Retrieved, 5 May 2019.

Hartnell, N. (2017b). No Vat in Govt's vacation rental deal with Airbnb. *The Tribune*, 16 June 2017. www.tribune242.com. Retrieved, 25 April 2019.

Hartnell, N. (2017c). Gov't plans threaten to 'kill' vacation rentals. *The Tribune*, 22 August 2017. www.tribune242.com. Retrieved, 5 May 2019.

Hartnell, N. (2017d). Taxation focus "could scare" vacation rentals. *The Tribune*, 23 August 2017. www.tribune242.com. Retrieved, 5 May 2019.

Jones, W. (2017). Tourism signs MOU with Airbnb. *The Bahama Journal*, 10 August 2017. www.jonesbahamas.com. Retrieved, 30 April 2019.

Kurtz, M. (2014). In focus: Airbnb's inroads into the hotel industry. HVS Houston: Houston, Texas. www.hvs.com. Retrieved, 30 April 2019.

McCartney, P. (2018). Hotel union boss says increased vacation home rentals bad for hotels. *The Nassau Guardian*, 10 August 2018. www.thenassauguardian.com. Retrieved, 30 April 2019.

McKenzie, N. (2014). "Lucrative opportunity" in vacation home rental market. *The Tribune*, 25 April 2014. www.tribune242.com. Retrieved, 30 April 2019.

McKenzie, N. (2017). Taxation to hit vacation home rental sector. *The Tribune*, Thursday, 10 August 2017. www.tribune242.com. Retrieved, 2 May 2019.

McKenzie, N. (2019a). Vacation rental Vat targeted for budget. *The Tribune*, Thursday, 14 February 2019. www.tribune242.com. Retrieved, 2 May 2019.

McKenzie, N. (2019b). Hotelier demands "prohibitive zoning" on vacation rentals. *The Tribune*, 27 March 2019. www.tribune242.com. Retrieved, 7 April 2019.

Moyle, M. (2018). Out with the old and in with Airbnb. Out Island Life The Bahamas. www.outislandlifebahamas.com. Retrieved, 2 May 2019.

Neely, T. (2019). Airbnb hosts in The Bahamas welcomed 59,000 guests in 2018. *The Bahamas Weekly*, 13 February 2019. www.thebahamasweekly.com. Retrieved, 30 April 2019.

Parker, Q. (2016). PM: Register Abaco second homes and rental villas. *The Nassau Guardian*, 23 September 2016. www.thenassauguardian.com. Retrieved, 24 April 2019.

Robards, C. (2018). Gov't to inform vacation rental owners of their obligations soon. *The Nassau Guardian*, 29 May 2018. www.thenassauguardian.com. Retrieved, 17 April 2019.

Robards, C. (2019). Second home purchases up following tourism boom. *The Nassau Guardian*, 29 April 2019. www.thenassauguardian.com. Retrieved, 17 April 2019.

Robinson-Blair, T. (2011). *Foreign homeowners spread their wealth*. Nassau, The Bahamas: Etienne Dupuch Jr. Publications Ltd.

Salter, J. (2012). Airbnb: The story behind the $1.3bn room-letting website. *The Telegraph*, 7 September 2012. www.telegraph.co.uk. Retrieved, 20 April 2019.

Smith, C. (2019). 105 Airbnb statistics and facts/ by the numbers. www.expandedrumblings.com. Retrieved, 18 May 2019.

The Nassau Guardian. (2017a). Tourism committee to look at benefits regulations of vacation home rental sector. *The Nassau Guardian*, 30 January 2017. https://thenassauguardian.com/2017/01/30/tourism-committee-to-look-at-benefits-regulation-of-vacation-home-rental-sector/ Retrieved, 30 April 2019.

The Nassau Guardian. (2017b). Chamber CEO: Vacation rental sector in need of regulation. *The Nassau Guardian*, 10 May 2017. www.thenassauguardian.com. Retrieved, 30 April 2019.

The Nassau Guardian. (2017c). Minnis: Appropriate tax soon for vacation home rentals to level the playing field. *The Nassau Guardian*, 6 June 2017. www.thenassauguardian.com. Retrieved, 29 April 2019.

The Nassau Guardian. (2017d). Bahamas signs tax collection MOU with Airbnb. *The Nassau Guardian*, 10 August 2017. https://thenassauguardian.com/2017/08/10/bahamas-signs-tax-collection-mou-with-airbnb/. Retrieved, 30 April 2019.

The Nassau Guardian. (2017e). Airbnb to trigger economic growth. *The Nassau Guardian*, 22 August 2017. www.thenassauguardian.com. Retrieved, 30 April 2019.

The Tribune. (2014). Vacation rental managers fear VAT business loss. *The Tribune*, 24 November 2014. www.tribune242.com. Retrieved, 16 April 2019.

Thompson, L. (2017). Tourism sign MOU with Airbnb to regularize vacation home rentals. Bahamas Information Services, 10 August 2017. www.bahamas.gov.bs. Retrieved, 2 May 2019.

Ward, J. (30 August, 2019). On alert. *The Nassau Guardian*. www.thenassauguardian.com. Retrieved, 30 December, 2019.

Williams, J. (14 September, 2017). How hurricanes affect the real estate market. www.hgchristie.com. Retrieved, 30 December 2019.

5   Case study on Bahamian Carnival

Ian Bethell-Bennett

Traditional masquerade that saw goat skin drums beaten by masqueraders done up in what was available from sponges to newspaper and then to fringing of paper and it being pasted onto old clothes with a mixture of flour and water was slowly changing. The continual creolisation of the performance is significant. It must be noted too that when, for example, there was a blight in the sponges, those were no longer as readily available as they had been so their use as part of the costuming was reduced and whatever material was available would replace the sponges. Bethel and Bethel give an interesting synopsis of the importance of the parade in the late 19th century.

> The black Bahamians of the 1890s faced oppression on all fronts -a ruling white merchant class above them, and unbroken poverty all around. With employment scarce and money short, Christmas for them was little more than a time to express their frustration. It is no wonder, then, that the Junkanoo parades of this period began to resemble mock brawls rather than seasonal celebrations.
>
> (Bethel and Bethel 1991, 37)

Bethel and Bethel (1991) goes on to discuss the struggles and aggressions of this period and the controls put in place by government to control the disorderly behaviour of the parade participants who used it as a time to blow off steam.

> In 1899, a new Act, the Street Nuisance Prohibition Act, came into effect. As its name implies, its purpose was to banish "nuisances" from the streets for most of the year. In order to allow time for legitimate parades, however, the rules of the Act were waived four times a year... The Government was formalising a tradition which had until then been simply customary – the practice of holding Junkanoo parades in the early morning.
>
> (Bethel and Bethel 1991, 37)

Of course, many persons of the early 20th century did not appreciate the "grotesque masqueraders" as an editorial in 3rd January 1913s *Tribune* argued. According to Bethel and Bethel (1991), in their chapter on the reorganisation of Junkanoo between 1948 and 1960, "what was wanted once more was a spectacle for tourists. No longer, therefore, could the masqueraders be permitted to 'rush' anyway they chose; rules were imposed and the parade civilised" (76). Perhaps it must be stressed that Junkanoo provided, what I might refer to as, an escape valve in a hostile environment where Black Bahamians were severely constrained by the white Bahamian mercantile elite. In some ways, government condoned this behaviour, as was pointed out by Powles (1888) and when they decided to clamp down on it as they did in 1923 when they chose not to suspend the Nuisance laws that allowed the masqueraders to congregate in the streets. Bethel and Bethel (1991) along with Craton and Saunders (2000) work through the tensions that the mid-20th century would witness in The Bahamas. Traditional mas, as discussed above, has been all but completely replaced by a commercialised parade where people are no longer performing to evoke fear in their opponents or to let off steam and frustration, but rather to demonstrate the beauty of their costumes and the sweetness of their music and to win prize money. The shift in style has been more about appearance and less about meaning or content.

The nationalist agenda requires a sacred commitment from Bahamians not to stand in the way of progress. The community is committed to tourism/progress ever since the late 19th century. Caribbean dependence on tourism but arguable awareness of its fickle nature as well, as deepened in the few years since Angelique Nixon's essay was published, the reality has changed greatly. This is nowhere more obvious, I do not believe, than in The Bahamas. Nixon surmised that:

> This erasure and forgetting is perpetuated through the tourist industry that appears as "the benign blight that is tourism can infect all of those island nations." Walcott warns that tourism (seen as harmless) can all too quickly take over: "until each rock is whitened by the guano of white-winged hotels, the arc and descent of progress."
>
> (Nixon 2011, p. 17)

Arguably what Nixon sees as erasure and forgetting, has moved into third gear as governments "fight" for tourist dollars. They must position themselves so that tourists will spend their much-desired dollars in the paradise engineered by Atlantis to attract them to the islands, once British, now Bahamian, but always deeply influenced by the United States. Government has upped the ante in selling its product to a world market as ministers become the first points of meeting/entry. It has also been clearer that large-scale tourist resorts will potentially fail. The Bahamas heads the case study in this field with two major noteworthy failures over the last few years, the closure of the Four Seasons property at Emerald Bay on Exuma and the yet unopened Baha Mar resort on New Providence.

The Bahamas Carnival Model

The new carnival product seeks to make money. It also seeks to import costumes from China where they are made cheaply and can be resold at a good profit. Carnival does not offer locally made costumes nor does it offer a market for making/creating local costumes. This is a shift that ultimately removes the level of cultural agency from within the local community and sends it offshore to China, which is where most carnival costumers source materials, if not the complete costume package.

In the meantime, the current government has decided to seek cultural tourists:

> Just months after admitting that The Bahamas has dropped the ball on cultural tourism, a greater emphasis is being placed in the sector, according to Tourism Minister Obie Wilchcombe.
>
> In a recent interview with Guardian Business, Wilchcombe unveiled some of the ministry's plans to embrace Bahamian culture and market it to visitors over the course of 2014. This move, he said, will help The Bahamas to be the destination of choice among tourists.
>
> (Bahamas Local, 2014)

So, with the government's announcement came an understanding that the country would be embarking on a Nine-million-dollar journey into Carnival. While culture has been deployed as an attraction, it is not an indigenous culture, if such a term can be used in this context, but rather an international model that will be used. Indigenous culture will be dropped much like the ball mentioned by the newspaper story. However, it is important to explore the use of culture in this context. The minister has already established that his ministry will be focussing on cultural tourism; it has now to be established what culture and how this focus will be achieved.

Tourism is our culture, declared Wilchcombe, Minister of Tourism (2nd February 2015). In his battle with leader of the Opposition over Bahamas Junkanoo Carnival where Minister Minnis stated,

> "Our culture is Junkanoo and we should not be trying to sell other individuals' culture. We should put more money into Junkanoo," Minnis said.
>
> "Let us continue to expand it so that Junkanoo becomes associated with The Bahamas, so that other artists, like reggae artists, can incorporate it into their music."
>
> (Cartwright-Carroll, *The Nassau Guardian* 3 February 2015)

The 11-million-dollar enterprise went ahead and has "changed" the cultural landscape of the country. Ironically, the minister also sees the "natural" beauty of the country as its money-making asset.

> "Our greatest asset is what God has given us, and we are going to do all we possibly can to protect it and that is a mandate from the leader of

our country, a mandate from the people of our country, and we are not going to in any way breach that," he added

While placating the worries of some civic organisations, the Minister continued his campaign for carnival.

"This is all in an effort to promote who we are for people to understand our culture and to appreciate that we are not just sun, sand and sea. Once we can get that presented to the world, we will be able to be an even stronger destination," he said.

In another article from the February 2015 press fury, the minister's position becomes clear:

Tourism Minister Wilchombe declared that the number one aim of the inaugural Bahamas Junkanoo Carnival is to promote the "true identity of Bahamian culture". He said he is "not at all concerned" with any negative issues surrounding the festival.

(Wells 2 February 2015)

It is significant that Wilchcombe sees Junkanoo Carnival as the "true identity of Bahamian culture" and this further obviates the point that tourism takes over cultural production and that tourism and culture have become synonymous with Junkanoo Carnival. Nixon argues that

[t]he performance of Caribbean festivals for the tourist market has great significance because such cultural performances are part of the process of forging national/cultural/regional identity, but we must question this process because tourism deeply affects culture and identity.

(Nixon 2015, p. 23)

Minster Wilchcombe sees the Carnival as being on a scale with the Olympics and foresees that The Bahamas can compete with the other destinations to lure tourists, notwithstanding:

Junkanoo Carnival has in recent weeks come under a lot of scrutiny. Last week, it was revealed that the members of the Carnival Commission were seeking to pay American pop star Janet Jackson $1.9 million to perform during the week of activities, a proposal that was rejected by the government.

Three members of the Carnival Commission recently resigned; two of them, Ed Fields and Freddie Munnings, reportedly left the commission due to issues with the government and the other, Inga Bowleg, reportedly needed more time to devote to her career.

(Ricardo Wells *The Tribune* 2 February 2015)

The discussion in the press shows how tenuous Junkanoo Carnival is as well as the government energy devoted to creating a new cultural product. While the minister argues that "We want to get every recording artist that we have on stage. We want to get our people out there. We want people to see how good our people are" (Ricardo Wells *The Tribune* 2 February 2015).

He seemed to be positioning for international artists to be featured as much or more than Bahamians. He also said, 'despite recent assertions by anti-Carnival groups, the government is working to build a platform to display true "Bahamianism" because that is what will separate The Bahamas' tourism product from competitors'.

Ironically, in the government's speeches, the first thing that always came out was that The Bahamas is a Christian nation, a fact that is at odds with the Carnival image the government was so eager to promote. *The Tribune* story also discusses:

> Then came news that the Bahamas Christian Council would not support the "immodest" costumes for the planned event, saying the scant attire could lead to "fornication, promiscuity, rape incest" and other "sins of the flesh."
>
> That led Mr. Wilchcombe to defend the festival, stressing that the celebration would encourage "Bahamianism" and not "sins of the flesh." Mr. Wilchcombe added the Bahamas Junkanoo Carnival Commission would take "into consideration" all concerns voiced by the Christian Council.
>
> (Ricardo Wells *The Tribune* 2nd February 2015)

Nevertheless, The Carnival committee seemed to be directed in many different directions. There is a slogan to promote Bahamian culture; to show the world who we are and to showcase Bahamian Artists. At the same time, though, the organisers are seeking acts from everywhere. The event actually went over budget, people failed to realise the financial goals and gains set by the Committee as some people actually lost revenue because of a poorly thought out event map that saw some vendors removed from the actual festivities which translated into no foot traffic nor car traffic. The other complaint was that there were too many foreign acts, which tended to dominate the event. There were far more refusals to work with the event than the leaders discussed in the story, and the fallout has been ongoing.

Tourism as agent of cultural change

The transformative impact of tourism is clearly evident in work from The Bahamas, especially on Guana Cay with the advent of Baker's Bay resort and also the earlier work of Historian Gail Saunders (1997), who underscored how tourism works to change culture, which would include speech patterns and language use, for example. In her study of Bahamian culture,

Saunders argues that, it was certainly changed by tourism's impact. Further, Freitag offers:

> When tourism is introduced into an area, the industry and the tourist inevitably become a part of the ecosystem and the region will transform itself in response to new opportunities and negative costs.
>
> (Freitag 1996, p. 228)

The traditional or rural form of Rake and Scrape have explained what this is somewhere earlier/ can't recall seeing it produced in Bahamian communities on Cat Island, for example, where wash tubs and saws were pressed into service as instruments of noise, became less a marker of culture and a way of life, particularly for young people and more of something to be seen at festivities. Rake and Scrape music would have formed the basis of Junkanoo. Prior to the shift in Junkanoo to a spectator event, it had produced music and art for the community. While the art was temporary and transient as costumes were used for one parade and abandoned, left on the side of the road. The music, though, was local and vibrant. Rommen (2011) explores the loss of Bahamian music through tourism exposure and change. In *Funky Nassau: Roots, Routes, and Representation in Bahamian Popular Music* Rommen emphasises that:

> throughout the two-decade period between 1945 and 1965, the night-clubs, restaurants and taxi drivers of Nassau were doing booming business. By the end of the 1960s, however, many of the Over-The-Hill nightclubs were beginning to struggle and fail, and by the middle of the 1970s it was clear that the foundation for sustaining live entertainment was on the decline throughout The Bahamas.... Hotels employ only a very few local musicians to perform in public areas in full.
>
> (Rommen, 2011, p. 20)

What Rommen (2011) describes is an assumption that the process of the death of public performances of Bahamian music and social life is due in part to the increase of mass tourism. Ironically, in the early days of tourism in The Bahamas, Bahamian music was instrumental in bringing tourists to the islands. By the 1970s, it had all but disappeared as tourism created its own culture. Just as desegregation occurred, so too did the death of Over-The-Hill, as Bahamians could now go into hotels and enjoy the sounds and sights with the tourists. The only hotel that really encouraged this comingling of locals and tourists, though, was the Nassau Beach Hotel on Cable Beach, owned by the Crothers family, it was a hotspot for local music through the 1980s and performance in the Out-Island room. This also came to an end. It is not insignificant, however, that as the population gained acceptability, Bahamian culture through popular music and public performance began to die off. This trend is like what has been witnessed in the rise of tourist culture that has been delineated at the beginning of the chapter and the shift towards Carnival. Carnival becomes a signifier of greater cultural focus, but at the risk of losing indigenous culture. This needs to be further developed.

Clifford (1988) understands the importance of no longer seeing national cultures as bound by tradition; they are always constantly changing. So, the adoption of carnival in The Bahamas could be one manifestation of this change. Cultural transformation is normal especially in the sociocultural context of tourism where contact and movement are constant. While Rommen (2011) may see a loss of Bahamian music through the "touristscape", the migration and emigration of people and ideas into and around The Bahamas is particularly important because the country is so small and its borders so porous, the cultural forms will necessarily change. R&B and Reggae, among other world forms, have infused Bahamian music, as have elements of Haitian music, though, this shall not be discussed by locals given their fraught relationship with Haiti, Haitians and the cultural influence resultant from heavy migration flows. So, tourism provides one level or type of cultural change, on the one hand, and migration, often drawn in by the existence of the tourism industry exacts another level of cultural transformation, on the other hand. Clifford argues that

> twentieth-century identities no longer presuppose continuous cultures or traditions.... individuals and groups improvise local performances from (re)collected pasts, drawing on foreign media, symbols and language.
>
> (Clifford 1988, p. 14)

Perhaps it is constructive to posit that culture is discontinuous from its past. As Bethel and Bethel (1991) indicate, tourism has a profoundly changing effect on the landscape and so on culture. The linkage between landscape and culture means that when one is transformed the other follows. This is articulated clearly by Glissant in *Caribbean Discourse* (1989). As the landscape changes, the identity, the relationships between person and land, the performance of identity, of culture for the consumption of those in a position of power/privilege becomes cultural and not the canned culture put on for performance. Over time, the traditional culture shifts to a new packaged culture.

DeLoughrey et al. (2005) put it thus: "the 'international standardization of consumption' by which local economies, cultures, and ecologies are sacrificed for the sake of neo-colonial gain". In such cases, "the market-driven force, so typical of tourism, would blindly convert all islands into a 'Mini-Miami'".

As cited above, Glissant (1989) holds a telling view of the relationship between Caribbean inhabitants and the land: "The relationship with the land is one that is even more threatened because the community is alienated from that land" (Glissant 1989, p. 105).

So, as relationships change, culture changes and the relationship between the folk and the land changes. Ultimately, tourism becomes its own culture as the Minister of Tourism desired. There may be an insidious under-recognised impact of tourism's cultural change though, especially as Carnival is introduced as if it were a part of the local culture. In theory, identity is fluid, but it is not as fluid as there is an anchor to keep some connection to a past. When alienation becomes all but complete, then the citizen can barely recognise his or her place in the new cultural milieu.

This is underscored by Hall's assertion that "we may know or suspect that these identities are representations constructed by others, but nonetheless we invest in the particular position, recognize ourselves in it, and identify with it" (Hall 1997, p. 98). The above can be demonstrated here by Carnival as engineered to be local culture, which is like the reshaping or tropicalisation Thompson critiques. This investment in these identities becomes a project directed by government, who are only interested in the bottom line.

The Junkanoo of the folk, once open to mass participation, now closed off by barriers and bleachers, has been shifted to Carnival. The produced and managed or sanitised culture of tourism, of orderliness and tropicality wins. Again, tropicalness refers to the rendering of local culture in a frame that pleases the tourist gaze. As Higgs (2008) posits in her work, the bodies are always inferior. Boyce-Davies (1994) does this in very interesting ways in *Black women, Writing, Identity: Migrations of the Subject* when she discusses the exoticised black woman. Higgs underscores the lack of identity or agency allowed to these women, especially those who work in tourism as straw vendors, for example, as their identity is presupposed by the tourists' gaze that imbricates them within the paradise myth where nothing is real, and people are all there to serve the tourist dream. The authenticity of a group is eroded when such cultural shifts are undergone.

While there is an element of authenticity to Trinidad carnival in Trinidad, it must be understood too that the ontological perception of carnival is one of engineered culture that shifted after the middle class saw it as acceptable to *win' up* in the streets, which is a huge leap from the working class origins praxis of carnival as working class space. This cultural transformation along exotic lines, the lines of hybridity as Young (1995) would argue, the sanitisation of culture, so that it becomes a safe space for foreign or tourism consumption, is significant.

Tropicalisation dates to the "creation" of the tropics/Caribbean through the colonial experience. As Fanon (1967) offers and Naipaul carries on, the postcolonial government differs little from the colonial government except in skin colour, though many people do not see this. All government sees is a class difference and their ability to use their position of power/privilege to create a tourist culture that imbricates the folk in an ontological paradigm which is of exploitable difference, and exoticism. Thus, the world can be changed to suit those who see themselves as the drivers.

Freitag (1996) underscores that in the small coastal community of Luperón in the Dominican Republic, some residents have benefited from tourism, but

> on the other hand, all residents have had to readjust their lifeways to accommodate the new face of Luperón as its economic focus shifted from a quiet rural agricultural service center to a destination for international mass tourism. The cultural ecology of the region has been transformed by tourism, and for those *luperonenses* not directly employed in the tourist trade, including the majority of the poorest community members, this shift has meant additional hardships and obstacles to endure.
>
> (Freitag, 1996, p. 249)

Freitag shows the epistemic violence strong tourism focus could have as people are changed by a culture of transnational tourism that "wants" festivals like Carnival for its development and heightened enjoyment. The space is radically changed to offer a service. Thompson (2007) creates, what we could refer to as the most complete examination of the visual commodification another underpinning concept which needed earlier introduction and deeper exploration of the Bahamian landscape in *An Eye for the Tropics*. Her framework shows the intentional making of a culture to be consumed by tourists. This arguably lends well to a reading of cultural work undertaken by Higgs where she examines relations of power imbalance imposed by tourism and the local government and shows how these play out in the straw markets in The Bahamas. Higgs points this out in her thesis "Behind the Smile: Negotiating and Transforming the Tourism-Imposed Identity of Bahamian Women":

> Tourism marketing is but one strand of contemporary society, a society dominated by historical, social, economic and cultural relationships which favor groups and perspectives. At the same time, it is a product of those very relationships – the essence of consensual marketing. People and places thus become constructed through limited and circumscribed representations to appeal to groups.
>
> (Higgs 2008, p. 76)

As is the case in Luperón, the cultural reality in The Bahamas has shifted. Perhaps it is more nuanced because of government's focus on "canned" culture or tropicality. Sure, the live music of Junkanoo and the performance of an indigenous culture may still exist in December, but the focus on Carnival and canned music is significant. Marina Village offers on-demand Junkanoo performances for the tourists; these pay the performers to display the culture in a safe, sanitised space engineered to these ends. The cultural space of Bay Street and the significance is removed. This is more along the lines of a non-local Carnival product that may appear to have local currency but offers an imagined and exotic product to be consumed as are the local bodies. Bodies and locations are consumed as a part of tourism culture.

In fact, culture has usually been left out of the equation. Historically, the islands which were a mishmash of "no culture", but the Culture is often then used as a vehicle for forwarding a nationalist agenda within strictures that may not embrace the multiplicity of influences in the country. When Sylvia Wynter (2014) argued that we should sit down together to talk a little culture, she probably did not envisage a culture of nationalism and limitation. She evidences perhaps had an idea of culture that embraced the people, the folk as Nettleford might argue. However, the folk are being removed from national culture and replaced in a stark space of engineered culture as Thompson (2007) and Bethel and Bethel (1991) discuss earlier in this chapter. The Edenic garden Saunders discusses in her 1997 article is increasingly transformed to an Atlantis-styled resort where all culture is performed. In that regard, The Bahamas offers an interesting understanding of culture, cultural manifestation and identity.

Conclusion

So, carnival as a cultural icon is normalised into being through a very determined government project. Just as the Christian Council has embraced a missionary imposed ideal of Christianity that disempowers the locals and dispossess them simultaneously, so too have the government, tourism management and marketing consultants and firms. Complaints about the lack of real local empowerment have continued to mar Carnival as each event is showcased by international talent, such as Destra or Marshal. These figures, though Caribbean, do not lend any credence to the discussion of Junkanoo Carnival being about Bahamian cultural identity, but rather, they further reinforce that tropicalisation and reproduction of a cultural product for tourism.

What is salient and illustrative of another level of epistemic violence evidence is the government's drive to implement a culture of Carnival that goes in tandem with its efforts to make tourism Bahamian culture, from the downplaying of the Africanness of the culture to highlighting the organised performance of fun and celebration. The Christian council stridently criticised the debauchery that carnival would create citing as an example, a video of Kids Carnival where a little girl drops down on the road and simulates torqueing. Torqueing is the gyrating and "wining up" of the body. The idea is that the society will be lost to sinfulness. However, this has already occurred in the shift into high-tourism gear.

As carnival explodes onto the local cultural scene and becomes a part of the tourist culture of the country, the image and imagining created to sell a destination become normalised as a part of the psyche of that place and space and as the identity of the people. Notwithstanding the massive financial loss of over two million dollars as stated in the Bahamas Junkanoo

Carnival Report (2015) that carnival inflicted on the country, the government 2015 Managements estimates state:

> Total Government Subsidy $11,364,678
> Direct Revenue $1,582,973
> Tax Revenue $6,689,127
> Foreign Expenditures: $1,768,754.58 excluded from economic impact assessment.
> Local Economic Activity: Vendor Sales, Employment, Ticket Sales, Bar Sales, Costume Sales
> Tourist Related Economic Activity: Hotel Sales, Stopover Tourist Expenditure, Cruise Pax Expenditure, Car Rentals.
>
> (BNJC Report 2015)

That international expenditure is excluded from the impact is significant as well as the inclusion of costumes in local activity as they would have had to be bought internationally and resold locally. The figures are not flattering, especially when the short fall on tourists appears so significant, despite the large amount of capital outlaid and discussion as to why carnival is so important to the local economy. International artists benefited more than Bahamian artists from carnival as did the actual infrastructural and lighting/ sound providers.

The folk will be encouraged to embrace it as a manifestation of their culture and identity, which, as Fanon (1967) (was quick to point out and S. Hall date pressed to underscore), will replace the inconvenient aspects of local identity that were not condoned by marketing masters and colonial officers. The white rhythms, Antonio Benitez-Rojo (1992) argues, assert their legitimating presence over the polyrhythm of the Peoples of the Sea: they are now deployed by the government and the culture of Junkanoo of resistance has become one of engineered cultural product to create a stronger more "authentic" tourist product. The Bahamas has become carnival and the culture has become tourism, yet it is all international culture. The plantation has been replaced by paradise and the workers are happy to perform their culture for the tourists' enjoyment.

References

Bahamas National Festival Commission Report. Retrieved http://bahamasjunka-noocarnival.com/wp-content/uploads/2014/08/2015-BNFC-Report_28.7.15.pdf
Benítez-Rojo. A. (1992). *The Repeating Island: The Caribbean and the Postmodern Perspective*. Duke University Press, Durham.
Bethel, E. C. and Bethel, N. (1991). *Junkanoo: Festival of the Bahamas*. MacMillan, London.
Boyce-Davies, C. (1994). *Black Women, Writing and Identity: Migration of the Subject*. Routledge, New York.

Clifford, J. (1988). The Predicament of Culture: Twentieth-Century Ethnography, Literature, and Art. Harvard University Press, Cambridge, MA.

Craton, M. and Saunders, G. (2000). *Islanders in the Stream: A History of the Bahamian People: Volume Two: From the Ending of Slavery to the Twenty-first Century*. University of Georgia Press, Athens.

DeLoughrey, E. M., Gosson, R. K. and Handley, G. B. eds. (2005). *Caribbean Literature and the Environment: Between Nature and Culture*. University Virginia Press, Charlottesville.

Fanon, F. (1967). *Black Skin, White Masks*. Grove Press, New York.

Freitag, T. (1996). Tourism and the transformation of a Dominican coastal community. Urban Anthropology and Studies of Cultural Systems and World Economic Development Vol. 25, No. 3, pp. 225–258

Glissant, E. (1989). *Caribbean Discourse: Selected Essays*. Translation and introduction by J. Michael Dash. University of Virginia Press, Charlottesville.

Hall, S. (1997). *Representation: Cultural Representations and Signifying Practices*. Sage Publications, London.

Higgs, D. (2008). 'Behind the Smile: Negotiating and Transforming the Tourism-imposed Identity of Bahamian Women'. Ph.D. thesis Graduate College of Bowling Green State University.

Nixon, A. (2011). 'Imaginings in/of Paradise: Bahamian Literature and the Culture of a Tourist Economy' *Anthurium: A Caribbean Studies Journal*, vol. 8, pp. 1–21, Retrieved 1 October 2018. http://scholarlyrepository.miami.edu/cgi/viewcontent.cgi?article=1044&context-anthurium

———. (2015). *Resisting Paradise: Tourism, Diaspora and Sexuality in Caribbean Culture*. University of Mississippi Press, Jackson.

Powles, L. D. (1996). *The Land of the Pink Pearl* (1888). University of Michigan Library/Media Publishing, London/Nassau.

Rommen, T. (2011). *Funky Nassau: Roots, Routes, and Representation in Bahamian Popular Music*. University of California Press, Berkley.

Saunders, G. (1997). 'The Changing Face of Nassau: The Impact of Tourism on Bahamian Society in the 1920s and 1930s'. *New West Indian Guide/Nieuwe West-Indische Gids*, vol. 71, nos. 1 & 2, pp. 21–42.

Thompson, K. (2007). *An Eye for the Tropics: Tourism, Photography, and Framing the Caribbean Picturesque*. Duke University Press, Durham.

Wells, R. (2015). 'Wilchcombe Aims to Promote the "True Identity" of Bahamian Culture in Carnival' *The Tribune*, 2 February 2015, Retrieved 15 October 2018. http://www.tribune242.com/news/2015/feb/02/wilchcombe-aims-promote-true-identity-bahamian-cul/

Wynter, S. (2014). *We Must Learn to Sit Down Together to Talk a Little Culture: Decolonizing Essays 1967–1984*. Peepal Tree Press, Leeds.

Young, R. C. J. (1995). *Colonial Desire: Hybridity in Theory, Culture and Race*. Routledge, New York.

6 Junkanoo Carnival, Bahamas as a strategy for tourism development

Ian Bethell-Bennett

Introduction

The growth of, what could be referred to as transculturated tradition in The Bahamas is alluded to in *The land of the pink pearl* (1888) by L.D. Powles when he observes:

> About Christmas time they seem to march about day and night with lanterns and bands of music, and they fire off crackers everywhere. This is a terrible nuisance, but the custom has the sanction of antiquity, though no doubt it would have been put down long ago if the white young gentlemen had not exhibited a taste for the same amusement.

This is/was Junkanoo in The Bahamas, though each island has its unique manifestation of it, it tended to be about drumming and 'marching about'. In the 21st-century culture created for tourist consumption, a focus on Carnival is replacing the traditional emphasis on Christmas-time Junkanoo: this goes hand in hand with a rescaping of the Bahamian space, so that it resembles a tropical paradise where nothing is natural, but all is idyllically created to fit into an image of paradise and so sell the destination. With this physical rescaping, the traditional performances of transcultural festivities have been utterly changed on each island and especially in the capital, where, unlike the new performance of Junkanoo Carnival, tourists were not included in the festivities and, until the 1940s, it was 'predominantly a pastime of working-class blacks; middle-class Bahamians, no matter what their colour, together with upper-class whites, had very little to do with the event' (Bethel and Bethel 1991, ix). Perhaps the importance of Junkanoo in expressing the cultural specificity of the folk was partly due to the rigid class and racial structure imposed on working-class black communities especially in the capital where there was well-entrenched legal racial segregation. Bay Street was white, ruling-class space where blacks could work but not live, but could celebrate at Christmas time. This contested nature of Bay Street and the importance of performing Junkanoo on Bay Street are perhaps captured by Martin and Storr (2009) in 'Bay Street as contested space'. The invent of Carnival has deconstructed the power and racial hierarchy and ethos in Junkanoo and engineered a festival that never existed in the Bahamian context before, but the change in Junkanoo has signalled a changing cultural ethos as well. While Carnival is important for luring tourists, the importance of Junkanoo, as well as the changes that occurred to it, is underscored by Bethel and Bethel, 1991.

> The festival of Junkanoo is a symbolic occasion in more ways than one. For years, it represented the temporary freedom of the black Bahamian to dance, sing and make 'noise' on Bay Street, the very heart of the whites' power. Since the organisation and subsequent victory of the black voters, however, that aspect of its symbolism has been lost as evidenced by the recent unpopular proposal to shift the site of the annual parades from Bay Street to the Queen Elizabeth Sports Centre.

Festivals have been an important part of Caribbean life since the arrival of enslaved Africans, perhaps even before (Figure 6.1). Bethel and Bethel (1991) argues that what this chapter will call deculturation or commodification of the festival/culture has been evidenced in Junkanoo. 'For years too, Junkanoo has provided links with The Bahamas's unique African heritage; its

Figure 6.1 Photograph of a Junkanoo costume, Nassau, The Bahamas. Photograph courtesy of Ian Bethell-Bennett.

very survival has indicated that it cannot be viewed as being simply an off-shoot of the more well-researched Jamaican John Canoe' (Bethel and Bethel 1991, ix). In the meantime, Carnival is being developed through the region as a way of attracting tourism dollars.

In *Caribbean Festival Arts* Nunley, Betthelheim & Bridges (1988) explore the histories of festivals in the Caribbean; much like the work done by Bethel and Bethel (1991) in *Junkanoo,* the importance of the former enslaved Africans in creating festivals in the new world is significant notwithstanding the original efforts by colonial powers to curtail and/or control the enslaved people's expressions and to erase the culture that they saw as inferior and unacceptable. In *The Repeating Island* Antonio Benítze-Rojo (1992) discusses this struggle for voice and power insisted on by the colonised and former enslaved. He talks about the self-legitimising white rhythms that claim to be the best rhythms ever. Carnival, Benítez-Rojo contends, is a part of the polyrhythm of the Caribbean people, the people of the Sea, which repeats itself across time and space. He underscores the struggle between European culture and Caribbean transculturated culture that arises from the encounter between all the cultures that make up the Caribbean. Carnival, although usually legitimised by the official discourse of governmental power after its early cultural beginnings, has become a staple across the region. The question arises, then, if Carnival is a part of the expression of the oppressed, the former enslaved, who expressed themselves through the participatory street parade Junkanoo in The Bahamas or whether it has become co-opted and so engineered by the official structure to become a legitimised tourist attraction? The shift from 'Junkanoo … as a public symbol of the Bahamian's Africanness, [that] could provide clues to the meaning of other Caribbean festivals rather than vice versa' (Bethel and Bethel 1991, ix) to their further observation that:

> In recent years, however, it seems that Junkanoo, while growing in beauty and cost, has been losing its distinctive character. The development of tourism and the zeal for cultural advancement have resulted in the imposition of numerous rules on the parade and have thus led to its distancing from the ordinary Bahamian.

This juncture is precisely where The Bahamas embraces the engineering of carnival, or what would then become vexingly known as Junkanoo Carnival. Perhaps there is a natural process of deculturation that is coupled with a project to engineer cultural tourism in the package of Carnival. This chapter cannot answer that question, but it seeks to underscore the governmental push for carnival as a cultural tourism product, notwithstanding the possible coupling with the process of globalisation and natural deculturation.

In this engineering, culture becomes a scene reserved for tourism where everything is made to feel local but not to resemble anything traditionally local. This is what Thompson (2007) refers to as the tropicalisation of the tropics. It is the stripping of identity and indigenous culture from place and/

or space. There is then a replanting of a culture of tourism that embraces international standards and mega resorts where global acts are imported and local art of a type that segregates tourism from the local community and exoticises the once indigenous space making it more like Miami. Cultural engineering as demonstrated with the special re-engineering creates a cultural product that is more easily consumed by tourists and is more in keeping with the idea of the Caribbean as a fun-loving exotic festive place. Carnival fulfils this idea of culture as performed for tourist consumption.

This chapter examines the above-mentioned ideas from Bethel and Bethel (1991) and others with the understanding that there is an existent Bahamian culture that is embodied in aspects such as Junkanoo, oral literature, cookery, 'talk', a way of life that includes commercial fishing on some islands that is quickly being deculturated and replaced by engineered culture for tourist consumption. Because these aspects of Bahamian culture were always under threat given the focus on European epistemology and praxis as well as the lack of support for black or African culture, the latter has been somewhat less entrenched and just added on, as Bethel & Bethel indicates with Junkanoo. So, the living culture of the country is disparaged by the people and/or the state and an imported, engineered culture fit for mass tourism is developed in its place. Tourism encourages this kind of focus on created culture over existent culture. The general thrust is that the state has encouraged the whitening or whitewashing of culture through creating a focus on tourism production, a culture that does not exist but focusses on tourism first; culture unfolds making the tourist feel welcome and unthreatened. The state then encourages a certain kind of living that focusses more on the service and less on the being, the becoming and the national discourse centres around how best to serve tourists. The culture of Carnival serves to develop further a destination that attracts more tourists per year and works in tandem with the physical re-engineering of the space to resemble a tropical paradise created to sell islands to tourists who in some cases had never travelled abroad.

Theoretical framework

This chapter draws on the use of the deconstruction and reconstruction of the visual image to combine it with the cultural reality that has become the Caribbean in the tourist world of trade and travel where the Caribbean is always being consumed, as Pattullo (2005) argues. Nowadays governments are complicit in the engineering of the culture of The Bahamas, so that the country can benefit from the spoils of cultural tourism, that is really about capitalising on an already 'known' product, carnival, and exploiting that, adopting it in the local economy of tourism and adapting to it, so that it drives the tourism product. Where both Benítez-Rojo (1992) and Thompson (2007) argue that these were external forces implicating themselves on the country, they have now become internalised into the postcolonial political consciousness of the new leaders and serve to show that tourism is a new style of colonialism where products are bought and sold, destinations are created and packages deployed to attract more tourists, notwithstanding the damage, both physical and intangible to the culturalscape of the country and its people. The engineering of Carnival in the Bahamian cultural space is only the latest in this process. There is also the physical rescaping that is afoot; a battle has been launched against this by many different groups and individuals, including Walcott in his Nobel acceptance speech. Bethell-Bennett, a visual display exhibited during NE7 at the National Art Gallery of The Bahamas in 2014, demonstrated how the country was being physically altered by these new deracination projects. This may seem disjointed from the cultural economy of tourism and carnival, but it is in fact one of the drivers of this project: governments need money, tourism provides foreign exchange, and foreign direct investment provides even more foreign exchange, so that they all seek to lure the largest most promising new resort that can attract the most tourism. As a part of this, cultural industries or cultural tourism has become the cash cow for many well-meaning paternalistic postcolonial Caribbean governments. Despite efforts to create a serious mechanism for cultural expression and the development of Bahamian culture and its link to tourism, little has been implemented. Bethel and Glaser (2006) produced a cultural policy for The Bahamas in 2006, which has not been implemented. The Ministry of Tourism does not have a joined-up tourism or culture policy that creates an established road map or plan for development. The Ministry of Youth Sport and Culture has not implemented any concrete plan for the development of cultural tourism. So, what continues to exist is ad hoc and random projects to create cultural tourism that do not examine long-term or even medium-term implications of their efforts. Bethel and Bethel's (1991) observations above serve to further this, perhaps, unwitting buy in to the economy of mass-produced tourism that is meant to save the residents of these countries by providing them with jobs.

The remainder of this chapter will therefore explore how the country and its people are sold to a global market as a carnival product, neatly engineered and packed though not without resistance; however, given the lack of importance given to Bahamian history and the lack of awareness of the past inculcated into Bahamian youth or even the understanding of the cultural importance of Junkanoo, the acceptance should be almost complete. In this instance, what is being argued here is that Junkanoo Carnival is engineered to attract tourist dollars to create jobs but ultimately damages the local cultural reality and works in tandem with the physical rescaping implicit and explicit in Thompson's (2007) work to un-write Bahamian culture and to create a synthetic global Caribbean culture where we can all compete for the tourist dollar. This plays into images of alterity and Caribbean lasciviousness that go along with carnival frolicking to sell a destination. As Padilla (2007), Kempadoo (2004), and Brenan (2004), for example, discuss as the realities of transnational desires and sex tourism in the Caribbean.

To bear this out, in Britain, carnival was sold by travel agents as the place to go, the ultimate experience, but it was also delivered with a warning that condoms there were not as well-made as they were in the United Kingdom. The theme was stock up before heading south. This model speaks to what Padilla (2007) refers to as the *Caribbean Please Industry* and Kempadoo (2004) argues is a sexing of the Caribbean. Dunn (2001) further shows that this results in children being held in the worst forms of exploitation given the pervasiveness of the tourism model that expects to exploit or sexploit. Politicians grasp this as their way of making millions of dollars to provide for their often-corrupt rent-seeking governments.

What has become well known, though, is the freedom, the fun, the frolicking the Caribbean represents, especially during festivals, be it Junkanoo, or Carnival; Caribbean 'folk' are happy to celebrate life. Historically, festivals on New Providence even included festivities around Guy Fawkes, a day when fireworks were let off and guys burnt atop bonfires. As the influence of the United States has increased, the identity of The Bahamas has grown less British-colonised-and more African-resistant, these cultural attributes have disappeared, and new cultural ideas and features have emerge.

The people's festival was high jacked by the state and sanitised for easier tourist consumption. Tourists were warned that the parade was not safe, but because it was on Bay Street they could participate as spectators from the bleachers or behind the barriers. Junkanoo, though, has never been supported and celebrated by the Ministry of Tourism as a tourist product despite the efforts of the Junkanoo groups and other practitioners though Tourism uses Junkanoo to represent Bahamian culture internationally. It is ironic, perhaps, that while Junkanoo is celebrated as a huge tangible part of Bahamian culture, little state investment has allowed it to flourish as the sudden investment in Carnival could arguably do. The new focus lies in selling the destination to those in the global north, particularly the United States. Tourism has become king and culture is led by tourism's direction. While the UNWTO warns of the perils of tourism development and scholars such as Pantojas (2012) and Carrigan (2010) underscore the erasure that is almost automatic, we must read along the lines of the UNWTO:

> To mitigate the tension between tourism development and control over cultural identity, constant dialogue is imperative between communities and the heritage and tourism sectors on the 'limits of acceptable change'. A proactive approach to the creation of tourism products should be adopted, in which assets are transformed with the close involvement of local stakeholders, and whereby local space versus tourist space is negotiated with sensitivity.

The Bahamian government seems to have missed the step of mitigating between local and tourist space as well as the impact on the intangible culture of the country. Perhaps UNWTO's position is clarified when the trend towards a deracinated, or decreolised cultural performance of Junkanoo or what Thompson (2007) refers to as tropicalisation as laid out by Bethel and Bethel (1991) above, is followed.

> Intangible cultural heritage must be thoughtfully managed if it is to survive in an increasingly globalised world. True partnerships between communities and the tourism and heritage sectors can only occur if all sides develop a genuine appreciation for each other's aspirations and values. Tourism stakeholders need to acquire an awareness of cultural heritage management practices, while heritage managers must endeavour to comprehend the complex phenomenon of tourism and its modus operandi.

Conclusions

Government has been beleaguered with their efforts to generate cultural transformation and build a more tropical tourism product that would have worked together with the opening of Baha Mar. Their narrow focus on foreign direct investment for resort properties, empowered as it is by legislation and the ministerial prerogative allows huge cultural shift as large swaths of land are gated off and the landscape utterly altered, as Thompson (2007) offers. This rescaping has been an ongoing effort, as Bethel and Bethel (1991) and Saunders (1997) argue, though it was far gentler prior to the 1990s. The Junkanoo Carnival project has been a revelatory sojourn that as this government sells beach access to foreign companies, barring locals from access and thus from access to making a living, it is engineering a festival that reshapes their culture for a late capitalist neoliberal market. The construct of paradise relies on sexualised, exoticised spaces and bodies and Carnival is a product that tends to encapsulate both. Nixon (2015) offers a keen synthesis of tourism's entanglements with the legacy of slavery and colonialism and because state-sanctioned ministries/boards of tourism help reproduce stereotypical, racialised, sexualised, and heteronormative images of the Caribbean.

Nixon (2015) critiques the local policy endeavours to shift the culture which runs in tandem with the physical change of space. For this, we must look to Thompson (2007) who demonstrates the incisive link between tourism, culture, and cultural transformation. Nixon's observations of culture being engineered to meet tourism's needs and thus negatively impacting Caribbean/Bahamian identity are incisive here. As the Minister pointed out above, culture is tourism and tourism is culture; given this, Thompson (2007) shows how this idea physically changes the space which Bahamians inhabit:

> They physically transformed areas of the islands through planting campaigns or cleanliness drives, in efforts to make the islands appear as they did in photographs-orderly, picturesque and tropical.
>
> (Thompson, 2007, p. 10)

Thompson (2007) captures the engineering involved in creating an image of culture that reflects back to the sender of that image an idea good concept develop of what the home space would be like, how it will sound, how they should live in it. 'Once the islands had become tropicalized in the realm of photography, such representational ideals informed the physical appearance of the islands.' Carnival changes the image and identity of the culture and so the identity of the folk. The images deployed of Bahamian culture move from being of inclusive, community-based Junkanoo, as Bethel and Bethel (1991) demonstrated at the beginning of this chapter and Saunders (1997) and Nixon (2011) underscore through various analyses, to the revelling Carnival, a revelling that the Christian Council argues is almost naked, as compared to Junkanoo that is costumed.

References

Benítez-Rojo. A. (1992). *The repeating island: The Caribbean and the postmodern perspective.* Durham, NC: Duke University Press.

Bethel, E. C., & Bethel, N. (1991). *Junkanoo: Festival of the Bahamas.* London, England: MacMillan.

Bethel N., & Glaser D. (2006). National Cultural Policy for the Bahamas Working Draft Ministry of Youth Sports and Culture, 2 February 2006, Bahamas, https://ifacca.org/en/news/2006/02/02/national-cultural-policy-for-the-bahamas/

Brenan, D. (2004). What's love got to do with It?: Transnational desires and sex tourism in the Dominican Republic. Durham, NC: Duke University Press.

Carrigan, A. (2010). *Postcolonial tourism: Literature, culture, and environment.* New York, NY: Routledge.

Dunn, L. (2001). Investigating the worst forms of child labour. No. 8 Jamaica situation of children in prostitution: A rapid assessment. Geneva, ILO. www.ilo.org.

Kempadoo, K. (2004). *Sexing the Caribbean. Gender, race and sexual labour.* New York, NY: Rouledge.

Martin, N. P., & Storr, V. (2009). 'Whose bay street: Competing narratives of Nassau's city centre'. *Island Studies Journal,* vol. 4, pp. 25–42.

Nixon, A. (2011). 'Imaginings in/of paradise: Bahamian literature and the culture of a tourist economy'. *Anthurium: A Caribbean Studies Journal,* vol. 8, pp. 1–21, viewed 1 October 2015. http://scholarlyrepository.miami.edu/cgi/viewcontent.cgi?article=1044&context=anthurium

———. (2015). *Resisting paradise: Tourism, diaspora and Sexuality in Caribbean culture.* Jackson: University of Mississippi Press.

Nunley, J., Bettelheim, J., & Bridges, B. (1988). *Caribbean festival arts; each and every bit of difference.* Seattle: University of Washington Press.

Padilla, M. (2007). *Caribbean pleasure industry: Tourism, sexuality, and AIDS in the Dominican Republic.* Chicago, IL: University of Chicago Press.

Pantojas Garcia, E. (Julio-diciembre 2012). 'Turismo y Desarrollo Económicoen el Caribe: El auge de las "Industrias del Pecado"'. *Investigaciones Turísticas* N° 4, pp. 49–76.

Pattullo, P. (2005). *Last resorts: The cost of tourism in the Caribbean 2nd edition.* Latin London, England: American Bureau.

Powles, L. D. (1996). *The land of the pink pearl* (1888). London/ Nassau: University of Michigan Library/Media Publishing.

Saunders, G. (1997). 'The changing face of Nassau: The impact of tourism on Bahamian society in the 1920s and 1930s'. *New West Indian Guide/Nieuwe West-Indische Gids*, vol. 71 nos.1 & 2, pp. 21–42.

Thompson, K. (2007). *An eye for the tropics: Tourism, photography, and framing the Caribbean picturesque.* Durham, NC: Duke University Press.

UNWTO (2012). Summary: Study on tourism and intangible cultural heritage. Madrid, Spain: www.unwto.org/tourism-and-culture.

Part II
Governance

7 Tourism governance, panarchy and resilience in The Bahamas

Michelle McLeod

Introduction

The purpose of this chapter is to explore the nature of tourism governance using The Bahamas as a case example to clarify the role of governance in supporting the sustainability of an economic activity such as tourism. Tourism governance is based on the principle that the tourism industry can be steered in a manner that promotes its development and growth. Laws, Richins, Agrusa and Scott (2011, p. 1) define governance as "the set of tasks such as decision making, enforcement decisions, communication of rules and measurement of performance that allow these functions of a system to proceed." The idea of governance suggests that the rate of progress of the tourism industry is an attribute of the actors and actions of the stakeholders within the tourism sector. Actors of tourism governance are the public and private sectors and non-governmental or civil society organisations involved in advancing the tourism sector. On the one hand, governance of the tourism sector may also occur based on the achievement of certain objectives such as sustainability (Bramwell and Lane, 2013). On the other hand, clarity is needed as to the realities of tourism governance as a process. A theoretical basis is needed to explore tourism governance and Holling's (2001) concept of panarchy. This may bring some insights, wherein both the hierarchical and networking aspects of a system that contribute to building system resilience can be analysed. Actor Network Theory (ANT) (Latour, 2005) may also provide insights to understand tourism governance in relation to the human and non-human actors involved in advancing the consequences of a tourism industry. Consequences are the outcomes and can either be positive or negative or both positive and negative.

No doubt, governance of tourism activities within countries may both promote and constrain benefits of tourism or the development of the tourism industry (McLeod and Airey, 2007). The nature of governance suggests it starts with the government who sees its primary role as being the body responsible for a country's economic, social and environmental development. A government's governance role is conducted in tandem with several partners who may or may not have the same objectives of the government.

Tourism governance is further complicated by the fact that tourism is an international industry that crosses a country's border. A range of international and regional bodies is involved in the governance of the tourism sector. Tourism governance should occur in a manner that allows for effective development and growth of the tourism sector to ensure its continued success. Detotto, Giannoni, and Goavec (2017) analysed relationships between good governance and the performance of the tourism industry. They found that governance quality has a positive significant impact on tourism revenue. Schembri (2016) assessed the impacts of tourism on Small Island States (SIS) and noted that good governance, in terms of political stability, influences whether visitors visit a tourist destination. In that regard, The Bahamas, a country with a dominant tourism industry, will be explored to determine its tourism governance characteristics and allow for some lessons learnt to be applied to tourism governance in other countries. The Bahamas is a successful tourism destination with over six million visitors annually, the majority of that figure is cruise ship excursionists to the capital of Nassau, New Providence (Ministry of Tourism, 2018a). If one is to understand the importance of tourism governance to provide resilient tourism destinations, then an exploration of The Bahamas, an island archipelago in the Caribbean, provides an ideal context to study system processes in small island environments.

Overview of tourism governance, panarchy and resilience

Governance in tourism relates to the effective management of resources distributed among tourism actors that are largely public, private and non-governmental entities (Valente, Dredge and Lohmann, 2015). Pechlaner and Volgger (2013) conceptualised governance as an intermediary space between government (the state) and management (the firm). Communication and governance are key to the social system as flows and materials are to the natural system (Holdschlag and Ratter, 2013). First, a system of tourism governance is complex from several different levels, not in the least is the fact that tourism is an international industry regulated by international laws and tourism actors operating in the local tourism destination are controlled by foreign entities. With such diversity, the adaptive nature of a tourism destination to external forces requires expanding theoretical lens of understanding a complex adaptive system. Second, the idea that governance has only to do with governmental actions has been challenged (Hall, 2011). Government's role in the development of the tourism sector is important based on the large sums of investment required to build hotel rooms, port and airport facilities, but the inability of government to obtain the necessary capital may result in control of the tourism sector from foreign entities. Third, panarchy theory and ANT facilitate understanding of the multi-realties of governance in an industry such as tourism wherein several diverse actors including public and private sector actors, non-governmental organisations and civil society interact with or without common interests to achieve some benefit from tourism activities.

Farmaki (2015) noted the importance of governance structures in the achievement of sustainable tourism utilising network-based structures that involve tourism stakeholders. The context within which tourism governance occurs is also important as the social, economic and environmental challenges can affect the effectiveness of governance in the context of resilience to climate change (Luthe, Wyss and Schuckert, 2012). Within an archipelago context, tourism governance at the island level does require a particular approach. Local tourism governance can differ and Beaumont and Dredge (2010) found that at a local level tourism governance can be council-led, participant-led and Local Tourism Organisation (LTO)-led. Luthe and Wyss (2016) found that the level at which tourism governance should occur, whether at the regional level or municipal level, depends on whether adaptation is gradual such as climate change (a regional level governance needed) or whether the change is sudden (a municipal level governance needed). The role of government at various levels to promote a regulatory framework that encourages tourism investment is also an important activity of tourism governance (Detotto et al., 2017).

While destination network leadership can set a path to destination development the ability of the network to meet challenges of tourism governance has to be studied from the smallest level. Baggio, Scott and Cooper (2010) suggest that destination governance adopts an adaptive management approach, which utilises knowledge about the destination network characteristics as the tourism destination is explored as a complex adaptive system. Utilising the concept of tourism network governance to advance knowledge about resilience is important. Luthe and Wyss (2016) note that limited research has been conducted on resilience using a network governance perspective. Concerns about long-term tourism decline, and rejuvenation in relation to a destination's resilience (Bec, McLennan and Moyle, 2016) requires consideration of governance issues. The notion of sustainability is inherently related to that of resilience as the latter is the essential ingredient to achieve the former. Authors have approached sustainability from the perspective of a multilevel evolutionary framework that involves social-ecological states, cultural change, cooperation dynamics and multilevel social-ecological interactions (Waring et al., 2015); however, for understanding a resilient consequence the granularity of a network and its processes should be analysed.

An approach that may be taken to understand the workings of tourism governance may be from actor network ontology. An actor network includes both humans and non-humans and network actors' interactions have consequences. Networks exist within the tourism sector to advance several objectives including the management and development of the tourism sector. A network is comprised of nodes or actors and ties or flows. The complex web of relationships that are involved in steering the tourism sector towards its development and growth means that an exploratory approach is warranted utilising a network perspective. Tourism activities have been explored as actor networks (Van der Duim, Ren and Jóhannesson, 2012; see McLeod, 2013). As a system operates, both human, social actors and non-human, physical actors interact and this enactment forms a pattern that results in certain consequences. ANT provides theoretical lens to explore the socio-ecological aspects of island environment systems (McLeod, 2018), and thereby, deconstruction of the human and non-human elements of these systems facilitates understanding of changes within the system. Some authors have utilised Social Network Analysis (SNA) to illustrate ANT to understand five countries' open data ecosystem (McLeod and McNaughton, 2016) and regional resilience to climate change (Luthe et al., 2012).

Analysis of a tourism system of actors warrants application of an overarching theory that exemplifies the evolution of the system, such as panarchy. Allen, Angeler, Garmestani, Gunderson and Holling (2014) defined panarchy as a system characterised by a structural pattern with various processes at different scales. A scale is based on space and time such as a forest that extends to several miles for centuries (Allen et al., 2014). Within the system, the "panarchical" process according to Holling (2001, p. 390) is illustrated by "Each level is allowed to operate at its own pace, protected from above by slower, larger levels but invigorated from below by faster, smaller cycles of innovation. The whole panarchy is therefore both creative and conserving." Within panarchy, hierarchies and adaptive cycles determine the resilience of a system. Based on panarchy, an adaptive renewal cycle has been proposed that involves exploitation, conservation, release and reorganisation (Holdschlag and Ratter, 2013). According to Holling (2001), hierarchy is the structure, natural, human and human-natural systems, and an adaptive cycle operates as a process within the system. Adaptation occurs through time, such as longer periods of accumulation and shorter periods of innovation through which processes of exploitation, reorganisation, conservation and release occur (Hollings, 2001). The concept of an adaptive cycle has been applied to recent research. Slight, Adams and Sherren (2016) noted that certain leverage points can create change as an adaptive process with reference to a rural community including seeds of innovation, cultivation of creativity, colonisation of ideas and laying fallow work together to transform the community.

Building resilience through good governance is important. Whether a system of actors is stable or resilient relates to the management of resources (Holling, 1973). The extent to which civil society should be involved in tourism governance is another consideration. The range of tourism activities, whether by residents or visitors, forms the basis for an evolution of the tourist destination and therefore the social concept and social actors should be considered in the tourism governance framework. The social aspects of vulnerability and resilience, as human agency has a role, cannot be under-estimated. Actions of actors in the process of changing circumstances to mitigate vulnerability and strengthen resilience have to be considered in the creating of good governance of tourism. Calgaro, Lloyd and Dominey-Howes (2014) point to an innovative framework using a systems approach and identify exposure, sensitivity and system adaptiveness as the key elements of the Destination Sustainability Framework (DSF). Exposure is based on the destination's characteristics including the natural, human and built characteristics, sensitivity relates to the pre-existing economic, social, political and environmental conditions, and system adaptiveness relates to responses to the impact and is based on the effectiveness of governance structures, preparedness and capacity (Tompkins and Adger, 2004 in Calgaro et al., 2014). Perch-Nielsen (2010) developed a vulnerability framework for the tourism sector including indicators relating to exposure, sensitivity and adaptive capacity and found that populous countries' high vulnerability is based on low adaptive capacity combined with high exposure, whereas small island states have a range of adaptive capacities and exposures but high sensitivity. Application of governance to a tourism system could change how the destination responds to unpredictable shocks. The Bahamas was explored in order to analyse governance of the tourism sector utilising the systems' approaches of panarchy and ANT.

The Bahamas

An exploratory descriptive research approach was utilised for the close identification of the circumstances of tourism governance in The Bahamas. Timang, Antariksa and Ari (2014) applied an approach of explorative descriptive research as an analytical method and included physical and non-physical characteristics to understand a destination's tourism development strategy, and Lussetyowati (2015) utilised explorative descriptive methods to conduct a study about preservation and conservation through cultural heritage tourism. An explorative descriptive approach explains the characteristics of phenomena, which in this case relates to the tourism governance characteristics of The Bahamas and therefore is appropriate for this chapter. In addition to an exploratory approach, descriptive analysis of secondary data was utilised to outline the situational factors that result in particular types of tourism governance characteristics. Setyaningsih, Nuryanti, Prayitno and Sarwadi (2016) conducted descriptive analysis of observation and interview data to understand creative-based tourism in an urban settlement. Descriptive studies are useful for providing understanding about the characteristics of a situation in a systematic manner that allows for the further development of ideas and to make certain decisions (Sekaran, 2003).

Vulnerability to natural disasters and complex governance structures affect the tourism industry in The Bahamas. Such vulnerability was realised with the recent events of Hurricane Dorian in 2019. Tourism is by far the largest industry in The Bahamas with well over six million visitors per annum; however, the islands within The Bahamas are not all progressing with a consistent growth in tourist numbers. McLeod and Scott (2018) explored the tourism industry in Grand Bahama Island (GBI) and noted the challenges that have resulted in tourist destination decline. GBI has been plagued with a series of catastrophic hurricanes and consistent decline in available hotel rooms. Added to this, the network analysis revealed three Destination Management Organisations (DMO) involved in tourism activities. A lack of cooperation among DMOs in the destination is resulting in stymied tourism development (McLeod and Scott, 2018). A multi-DMO governance structure has challenges for destination coordination particularly in adaptive management when the destination is in crisis. Data about Eleuthera revealed an almost 44.4% decline in the number of hotel rooms from 612 in 1999 to 340 in 2016 (Ministry of Tourism, 2018b). In September 1999 Eleuthera and Abaco were devastated by Hurricane Floyd. GBI had devastating hurricanes in 2004 (Hurricanes Frances and Jeanne) and 2016 (Hurricane Matthew). A trend exists whereby catastrophic hurricanes are preventing some destinations from regaining a footing in the tourism industry.

As tourism is the dominant sector in The Bahamas, the country is challenged to achieve sustainable growth on a continual basis (Hepburn, 2016). One important example of this is the marine resources that form part of the tourism product of The Bahamas. The Bahamas has the first land and sea park in the world designated the Exuma Cays Land and Sea Park in 1958 (Marine Conservation Institute, 2018). Duarte, Doherty and Nakazawa (2017) explored the planning and governance issues of the Exuma Cays Land and Sea Park in relation to a shared governance structure between the Government of The Bahamas and the Bahamas National Trust (BNT) and noted that co-management did not eliminate frictions among stakeholders. Governance involves managing the competing interests among stakeholders and without some consensus the process can be different and outcomes unrealised. A divergence of interests was noted in the paper. In George Town, Exuma, economic performance was very important, while in Nassau marine protection was more important (Duarte et al., 2017). McLeod and Airey (2007) similarly found the tourism interests of stakeholders in Tobago were economically related and those stakeholders in Trinidad were concerned about the environment. In addition, Wise (2014) noted some challenges of managing Marine Protected Areas (MPA), including forming consensus among stakeholders, foreign development, corruption within the permitting process, inadequate participation, shift in political agenda and weak institutional frameworks, are some of the challenges of implementing an MPA (Wise, 2014).

Expansive coastal resources within The Bahamas pose the greatest challenge to its resilience as a tourist destination. In 2013, The Bahamas' MPA spanned over two million acres and the goal is to expand this to 11 million acres by 2020 (Bahamas Reef Environment Educational Foundation, 2014). Areas with an MPA include in the Northwestern Bahamas – Walker's Cay National Park, Crab Cay Marine Reserve, Black Sound Cay National Reserve, Fowl Cays National Park, No Name Cay Marine Research, Pelican

Cays Land and Sea Park, Andros North Marine Park, Andros South Marine Park, Andros Westside National Park, Bonefish Pond National Park, South Berry Islands Marine Reserve; in the Central Bahamas – Exuma Cays Land and Sea Park, Moriah Harbour Cay National Park, The Exuma Marine Reserve, Conception Island National Park; and the Southern Bahamas – Little Inagua National Park, Union Creek Reserve (Bahamas Reef Environment Educational Foundation, 2014, p. 6).

Coastal management of marine resources is a prime concern in The Bahamas. Silvy, Peterson, Heinen-Kay and Langerhans (2017) noted the illegal harvesting of marine resources and suggest solutions for marine resource management are needed to ensure the sustainability of marine life. Marine resources are important for tourism and other livelihood purposes in the islands. As in the case of Andros, informants believed that illegal harvesting of marine resources is associated with a lack of alternative livelihoods, the need for food or monetary gain and a lack of enforcement (Silvy et al., 2017). Converting from the harvesting livelihood to one based on tourism is a temporary solution and other sustainable livelihood alternatives are needed. The governance of these resources through regulations seems to be challenged by the view that "regulations were instituted by educationally and economically privileged people largely from other islands and countries operating under a benevolent, though paternalistic, model of using evidence-based decisions to protect resources for the future" (Silvy et al., 2017, p. 12). Also, a conflict occurs based on the difference in interests between local fishermen and tourism practitioners regarding the protection of marine areas as the former requires these areas as livelihood and the latter as a tourism product (Silvy et al., 2017).

Holdschlag and Ratter (2013) explored environmental stressors, knowledge and social response of three social-ecological subsystems in The Bahamas including interactions within socio-ecological systems that are storm systems, terrestrial and nearshore systems and marine systems. The Bahamas case illustrates cross-scale linkages (Allen et al., 2014) and adaptive cycles (Holling, 2001) of panarchy. Adaptation from a storm system was based on cross-scale interaction with international organisations and feedback loops after hurricane events are crucial. The social complexity meant that individual and community engagement are important as indifference and the lack of individual prevention and preparedness were seen as drawbacks to adaptation (Holdschlag and Ratter, 2013). On the one hand, in terms of governance the storm system in the case study has a cross-scale multi-agent network of actors and this facilitates adaptation. On the other hand, the terrestrial and nearshore systems revealed a governance challenge being the failure of governmental coordination through the Bahamas National Geographic Information Systems (GIS) Centre as the Centre has not built up comprehensive information that can facilitate adaptation (Holdschlag and Ratter, 2013). On the social front, the divergent interests and agendas of local and non-local actors have proven to challenge adaptation within the terrestrial and nearshore systems. Similar challenges with various interests' groups being involved in the management of resources have been identified by other authors (see Duarte et al., 2017, and Silvy et al., 2017). The over-exploitation of fishing resources has resulted in stricter monitoring of fishing grounds as the Department of Marine Resources receive support from the Defence Force to enforce the regulation (Holdschlag and Ratter, 2013).

Adaptive management to build resilience is important as appropriate institutions are identified to achieve effective results. Management in this context involves an actor network of human and non-human actors who steer the resilience processes. The social element of interactions is important. Stojanovic et al. (2016) promote the social concept of social in social-ecological systems in the context of coastal sustainability as interactions between humans and their environments have consequences for its sustainability. Also important is the institutions that will guide adaptive management. The recent formation of a Ministry of Disaster Preparedness, Management and Reconstruction in The Bahamas to manage the rebuilding process on Abaco and GBI, islands devastated by Hurricane Dorian, is one example of adaptive management. The interactions between a core institution and the stakeholders in a dominant sector such as tourism should be mapped and carefully monitored to ensure resilience.

Conclusion

Island destinations are an appropriate context to explore tourism governance, panarchy and resilience theories. Hall (2010) points to the system dynamics of islands and the impacts of these on humans and McLeod (2018) argues for a stream of island tourism research that considers network methodology using islands as an ideal research ground. This chapter explores literature regarding tourism governance, panarchy and resilience and explored the tourism governance characteristics of The Bahamas in brief to exemplify the application of panarchy and ANT as bases that could guide resilience of tourist destinations. The tourism governance characteristics that emerge from this chapter are based on an underlying concept of network governance wherein various actors enact within an ecosystem. Network governance means that tourism actors are working together to achieve among other achievements a successful tourism destination. Enactment of the government actors when a destination is in crisis is particularly important to avert tourist destination decline; however, this enactment can only be facilitated by better understanding of the actor network of the tourist destination. Such a network of actors must be clearly identified and inter-actions understood, given certain natural disaster scenarios that require greater coordination of all the actors involved.

One possible success of good governance is resilience. Resilience has to do with adaptability to change, and governance facilities the preparedness for adaptation to waves of change whether these are slow moving or fast. Preparedness has to become a priority that will focus energies on recovery and adaptation. Human agency played an important role in the governance of various ecosystems in The Bahamas and therefore the social characteristics, as to the preparation and response to certain shocks, of a destination are important to produce resilience. While others have focussed on the community level of resilience (Bec et al., 2016) any study of resilience in the tourism industry must explore the full extent of tourism activities both internal and external to the tourist destination. Through the theoretical lens of panarchy and an actor network, the workings of natural and human phenomena to build tourist destination resilience are constructed.

References

Allen, C. R., Angeler, D. G., Garmestani, A. S., Gunderson, L. H., & Holling, C. S. (2014). Panarchy: Theory and application. *Ecosystems, 17*(4), 578–589.

Baggio, R., Scott, N., & Cooper, C. (2010). Improving tourism destination governance: A complexity science approach. *Tourism Review, 65*(4), 51–60.

Bahamas Reef Environment Educational Foundation (2014). Marine Protected Areas of The Bahamas. https://breef.org/wp-content/uploads/2015/03/Breef-MPAGuideBooklet.pdf

Beaumont, N., & Dredge, D. (2010). Local tourism governance: A comparison of three network approaches. *Journal of Sustainable Tourism, 18*(1), 7–28.

Bec, A., McLennan, C. L., & Moyle, B. D. (2016). Community resilience to long-term tourism decline and rejuvenation: A literature review and conceptual model. *Current Issues in Tourism, 19*(5), 431–457.

Bramwell, B., & Lane, B. (Eds.). (2013). *Tourism governance: Critical perspectives on governance and sustainability.* London: Routledge.

Calgaro, E., Lloyd, K., & Dominey-Howes, D. (2014). From vulnerability to transformation: A framework for assessing the vulnerability and resilience of tourism destinations. *Journal of Sustainable Tourism, 22*(3), 341–360.

Detotto, C., Giannoni, S., & Goavec, C. (2017). *Does good governance attract tourists?* (No. 002). Laboratoire Lieux, IdentitÃ© s, eSpaces et ActivitÃ© s (LISA).

Duarte, F., Doherty, G., & Nakazawa, P. (2017). Redrawing the boundaries: Planning and governance of a marine protected area-the case of the Exuma Cays Land and Sea Park. *Journal of Coastal Conservation, 21*(2), 265–271.

Farmaki, A. (2015). Regional network governance and sustainable tourism. *Tourism Geographies, 17*(3), 385–407.

Hall, M. C. (2010). Island destinations: A natural laboratory for tourism: Introduction. *Asia Pacific Journal of Tourism Research, 15*(3), 245–249.

Hall, C. M. (2011). A typology of governance and its implications for tourism policy analysis. *Journal of Sustainable Tourism, 19*(4–5), 437–457.

Hepburn, E. (2016, July). Investigating the understanding, interest and options for Agri-tourism to promote food security in The Bahamas. In *Proceedings of the 30th West Indies Agricultural Economics Conference.* http://www. caestt. com/home/documents/30thConference/3_Investigating_the_Understanding_Interest_and_Options_for_Agri-tourism_to_Promote_Food_Security_in_the_Bahamas. pdf. Accessed (Vol. 14).

Holdschlag, A., & Ratter, B. M. (2013). Multiscale system dynamics of humans and nature in The Bahamas: Perturbation, knowledge, panarchy and resilience. *Sustainability Science, 8*(3), 407–421.

Holling, C. S. (1973). Resilience and stability of ecological systems. *Annual Review of Ecology and Systematics, 4*(1), 1–23.

Holling, C. S. (2001). Understanding the complexity of economic, ecological, and social systems. *Ecosystems, 4*(5), 390–405.

Holling, C. S., and L. H. Gunderson. 2002. Resilience and adaptive cycles. *in* L. H. Gunderson and C. S. Holling, editors. *Panarchy: understanding transformations in human and natural systems.* Washington, DC: Island Press, pp. 25–62.

Latour, B. (2005). *Reassembling the social: An introduction to actor-network-theory.* Oxford: Oxford University Press.

Laws, E., Richins, H., Agrusa, J., & Scott, N. (Eds.). (2011). *Tourist destination governance: Practice, theory and issues.* Oxfordshire: CABI.

Lussetyowati, T. (2015). Preservation and conservation through cultural heritage tourism. Case study: Musi Riverside Palembang. *Procedia-Social and Behavioural Sciences, 184,* 401–406.

Luthe, T., & Wyss, R. (2016). Resilience to climate change in a cross-scale tourism governance context: A combined quantitative-qualitative network analysis. *Ecology and Society, 21*(1), 1–18.

Luthe, T., Wyss, R., & Schuckert, M. (2012). Network governance and regional resilience to climate change: Empirical evidence from mountain tourism communities in the Swiss Gotthard region. *Regional Environmental Change, 12*(4), 839–854.

Marine Conservation Institute (2018). Bahamas. http://www.mpatlas.org/region/country/BHS/

McLeod, M. (2018). Developing a network analysis methodology for island tourism research. In M. McLeod & R. Croes (Eds.), *Tourism management in warm-water island destinations* (pp. 178–191). Mona: The University of the West Indies.

McLeod, M., & McNaughton, M. (2016). Mapping an emergent Open Data ecosystem. *The Journal of Community Informatics, 12*(2), 26–46.

McLeod, M., & Scott, N. (2018). Destination management: A network perspective. *Tourism Management in Warm-water Island Destinations,* 147. Oxfordshire, England: CABI.

McLeod, M. T. (2013). Actor-network theory and tourism, ordering, materiality and multiplicity. *Tourism Management, 37,* 48–49.

McLeod, M. T., & Airey, D. (2007). The politics of tourism development: A case of dual governance in Tobago. *International Journal of Tourism Policy, 1*(3), 217–231.

Ministry of Tourism (2018a). Air, sea, landed and cruise arrivals 2017. http://www.tourismtoday.com/sites/default/files/air_sea_landed_cruise_arrivals_2017_0.pdf

Ministry of Tourism (2018b). Hotel rooms available in The Bahamas 1967–2016. http://www.tourismtoday.com/sites/default/files/hotel_rooms_available_in_the_bahamas 967-2016.pdf

Pechlaner, H., & Volgger, M. (2013). Towards a comprehensive view of tourism governance: Relationships between the corporate governance of tourism service firms and territorial governance. *International Journal of Globalisation and Small Business, 5*(1–2), 3–19.

Perch-Nielsen, S. L. (2010). The vulnerability of beach tourism to climate change-an index approach. *Climatic Change, 100*(3–4), 579–606.

Schembri, M. H. (2016). *The impacts of tourism on small island states* (Master's thesis, University of Malta).

Setyaningsih, W., Nuryanti, W., Prayitno, B., & Sarwadi, A. (2016). Urban heritage towards creative-based tourism in the urban settlement of Kauman-Surakarta. *Procedia-Social and Behavioral Sciences, 227*, 642–649.

Silvy, E. H., Peterson, M. N., Heinen-Kay, J. L., & Langerhans, R. B. (2017). Illegal harvest of marine resources on Andros Island and the legacy of colonial governance. *The British Journal of Criminology, 58*(2), 332–350.

Slight, P., Adams, M., & Sherren, K. (2016). Policy support for rural economic development based on Holling's ecological concept of panarchy. *International Journal of Sustainable Development & World Ecology, 23*(1), 1–14.

Stojanovic, T., McNae, H., Tett, P., Reis, J., Smith, H. D., & Dillingham, I. (2016). The "social" aspect of social-ecological systems: A critique of analytical frameworks and findings from a multisite study of coastal sustainability. *Ecology and Society, 21*(3), 15.

Timang, V. V. S., Antariksa, A., & Ari, I. R. D. (2014). Tourism development strategy of Buntula'bi Balusu sub-village, North Toraja regency based on tourist perception. *Journal of Indonesian Tourism and Development Studies, 2*(3), 95–102.

Tompkins, E. L., & Adger, W. N. (2004). Does adaptive management of natural resources enhance resilience to climate change? *Ecology and Society, 9*(2), art 10.

Valente, F., Dredge, D., & Lohmann, G. (2015). Leadership and governance in regional tourism. *Journal of Destination Marketing & Management, 4*(2), 127–136.

Van der Duim, R., Ren, C., & Jóhannesson, G. T. (Eds.). (2012). *Actor-network theory and tourism: Ordering, materiality and multiplicity.* London: Routledge.

Waring, T., Kline, M., Brooks, J., Goff, S., Gowdy, J., Janssen, M., … Jacquet, J. (2015). A multilevel evolutionary framework for sustainability analysis. *Ecology and Society, 20*(2), 34.

Wise, S. P. (2014). Learning through experience: Non-implementation and the challenges of protected area conservation in the Bahamas. *Marine Policy, 46*, 111–118.

8 Atlantis

A case study in the experience economy

Zhivargo Laing

The experience economy at-a-glance

Can the evolution of the birthday cake reflect the entire history of economic progress? Joseph Pine II and James H. Gilmore believe so, and proffered as much in their ground-breaking article entitled "Welcome to the Experience Economy," first published in the *Harvard Business Review* in 1998. As they described it in their article, in the earliest stages of economic development, mothers used ingredients (milk, eggs, flour, sugar, etc.) produced on their farms to make birthday cakes for their children for pennies at a time. As the commodity-based economy gave way to the goods-based economy, parents paid a dollar or two to purchase pre-mixed ingredients to make birthday cakes for their kids. As the goods-based economy surrendered to the service economy, parents purchased their cakes from stores for about $5–$10 at a time. In the 1990s, however, a new phenomenon developed such that parents would outsource the entire birthday celebration experience to places like Chuck E. Cheese's or Discovery Zone for about $100 or more with the birthday cake included for free. According to Pine and Gilmore, 1998, the latter represented the emergence of what they termed "The Experience Economy."

The "Experience Economy," according to Pine and Gilmore, is one in which "experience" itself is traded as a value in the economy. In other words, rather than a product or service being the offering provided by a merchant in the economy, the merchant would use a product or service essentially as a prop or stage to provide customers with a value for which they would be prepared to pay in and of itself. Taking the birthday cake at Chuck E. Cheese's as an example, kids would gladly pay for the experience of being at Chuck E. Cheese's to celebrate their birthday, even if the birthday cake was not included. The experience of being at Chuck E. Cheese's with its games, characters, and tickets which could be refunded for toys was worth the dollars their parents paid for it. For Pine and Gilmore (1998), exploiting the distinct value that such experiences offered represented a new evolution in economic development and one that companies needed to understand and exploit.

For Pine and Gilmore (1999), the "Experience Economy" is all about staging. "An experience occurs when a company intentionally uses services as the stage, and goods as props, to engage individual customers in a way that creates a memorable event. Commodities are fungible, goods tangible, services intangible, and experiences *memorable*" (Pine & Gilmore, 1998). The additional value of the experience, Pine and Gilmore contend, should be something for which customers pay a fee. For them, not only is charging a fee for the additional value of an experience appropriate, it is also something that compels the seller to offer even more value when challenged with the notion of charging a fee for that value. For example, shopping malls should charge an entrance fee as does Disney World, but in order to do so, the mall would have to mount such a compelling experience that customers see no difficulty paying the charges.

Boswijk et al. (2011) go even further to suggest a new perspective on the "Experience Economy." For them, the "Experience Economy" is not just about staging, but about taking account of the customer's "personal experience: his or her everyday world and societal context." By moving beyond the organization and its offering to look at the individual and the meaning they might derive from an experience, "the experience moves beyond mere enjoyment to take on 'meaning' for the customer. The experience economy is more than just 'excite me,' 'feed me,' and 'entertain me.' Businesses and organisations can play a meaningful role in helping the individual to find his or her own way" (Boswijk et al. 2011). They see the experience economy as a "co-creation," in which the buyer and seller together produce the unique experience.

The essential characteristic of an experience as reflected in the "Experience Economy" is that it is "memorable" (Pine & Gilmore, 1998). In their table of "Economic Distinctions," they note that the nature of the economic offerings is such that commodities are fungible, goods are tangible, services are deliverable, and experiences are memorable (see Table 8.1).

Table 8.1 Economic distinction (Pine & Gilmore, 1998)

Economic distinctions

	Commodities	Goods	Services	Experiences
Economic offering				
Economy	Agrarian	Industrial	Service	Experience
Economic function	Extract	Make	Deliver	Stage
Nature of offering	Fungible	Tangible	Intangible	Memorable
Key attribute	Natural	Standardized	Customized	Personal
Method of supply	Stored in bulk	Inventoried after production	Delivered on demand	Revealed over a duration
Seller	Trader	Manufacturer	Provider	Stager
Buyer	Market	User	Client	Guest
Factors of demand	Characteristics	Features	Benefits	Sensations

Memorability, as the principle characteristic of an experience that distinguishes it from a product or service, may seem unconvincing. As Poulsson and Kale (2004) argued,

> A lot of consumption experiences in relation to goods and services are indeed memorable (like wearing a finely tailored evening gown for the first time or being treated terribly by the waiter at a gourmet restaurant), but these need not qualify as experiences.

For Poulsson and Kale (2004), a commercial experience is best defined as "an engaging act of co-creation between a provider and a consumer wherein the consumer perceives value in the encounter and in the subsequent memory of that encounter." While this definition attempts to move experience beyond the realm of simply a strong memory, to embrace the notion that the consumer sees the overwhelming value that the provider intended, it remains too abstract to offer a functional appreciation of the concept. "Experience" as a value offering in the economy thus remains unclear in its definition.

Products can produce very strong experiences and quite memorable ones. The purchase of a brand-new Tesla or home can provide a lifetime of memories, receiving exquisite services at a high-end restaurant where a significant other proposes or taking the Glacier Express in Switzerland from Zermatt to St. Moritz are all quite memorable as services. Yet, they might miss Pine and Gilmore's definition of "experiences," because they are not necessarily purchased for the experiences themselves. Nonetheless, it is difficult to argue against the distinct memorability of them as experiences.

There is no question that memorability is essential to the experience offering. However, for decades' people have been paying for memorable experiences in which products and services for sale have not been props and staging in the same. Helicopter flights over scenic terrain, climbing Mount Everest, or riding a roller coaster involve no products or services for sale. The experience is the offering, and might rightly be regarded as a service, an entertainment service provided by the various vendors. For Poulsson and Kale (2004), the experience economy can be regarded as a part of the service sector, with the one distinct difference being that "service is what is done for you" while experience is "done to you." Is this a difference without distinction?

A haircut is a service. It is done for you, but is it correct to say it is not done to you? Truth is that, it is done both for you and to you. The same is true for a train ride, a plane ride, or a helicopter ride. Poulsson and Kale argued that while the

> Goods, services and experiences all have a consumption phase, what differentiates an experience from the other two offerings is that here the consumption phase itself is the main product. Purchase of a good leaves you with a physical object to keep, and a service will leave you with

something done for you or your possessions or on your behalf. With an experience, however, what is of essence is only what happens between the customer and the experience provider in that extended and intensified consumption phase, and the memory of the encounter.

This does provide a more definitive distinction, which still can be augmented by one additional consideration.

What might add to Poulsson and Kale's (2004) description of commercial experience is the notion that in the "Experience Economy," the experience leads. In the product economy, the product leads, meaning whether one gets a lasting memory or not from a product is incidental to the fact that one's lead intent is to purchase the product for some utility and this may or may not be related to a memorable experience. The product itself leads the way. When one purchases a service, whether it provides a lasting memory or not is secondary to the service itself; the service itself leads or motivates the purchase. With an experience, the motivation to purchase is the enjoyment and, directly or indirectly, the memory consequent on that enjoyment itself. Whether there is a product or service delivered in the process of purchasing the experience is only incidental; the consumer is purchasing the experience in whatever mode it is delivered. It could be delivered in a product-mode, as in the purchase of "shark lips" in a Chinese restaurant or a Bluetooth Beats Speaker by Dr. Dre from Amazon. It could be delivered in service mode as in a skydive over Palm Jumeirah in Dubai or an underwater cave dive in Grand Bahama, The Bahamas. In the "Experience Economy," it is always the experience that attracts the customer, not the product or service mode in which it is delivered; and the provider leads with the experience as an offering, knowing that it is what the customer seeks. In the "Experience Economy," the principal exchange between the buyer and the seller is an experience, the consumption of an intangible stimulation or enjoyment involving some or all senses, the lasting impact of which is a memory valued by the customer. Even when companies use experience to attract customers to their products or services, the experience leads and puts them in the "Experience Economy." "Business-to-business marketers increasingly create venues as elaborate as any Disney attraction in which to sell their goods and services" (Pine & Gilmore, 1999).

> Experience marketing is a new and exciting concept. And it is not only of interest to academics. Marketing practitioners have come to realize that understanding how consumers experience brands and, in turn, how to provide appealing brand experiences for them, is critical for differentiating their offerings in a competitive marketplace.
>
> (Schmitt, 2011)

According to Pine and Gilmore (1999), Disney World is the pioneer of the "Experience Economy." In the 1990s, famed South African developer, Sol

Kerzner, followed Disney's lead in the development of one of the most themed resorts in the world, The Atlantis Resort, Paradise Island, in The Bahamas. Both in terms of Pine and Gilmore's (1999) "Four Realms of Experience" and "Designing Memorable Experiences," The Atlantis Resort is a case study in the "Experience Economy." Its success helped to lift the economy of The Bahamas out of a significant lull to enjoy almost a decade of stellar growth and prosperity.

The case of the Atlantis Resort, Paradise Island

In 1994 when Sun International, a consortium led by Sol Kerzner, purchased the defunct Paradise Island Resort and Casino, the Ocean Club, and Paradise Island Beach Resort for $125 million, the Bahamian economy was growing at about 1.34%, an increase over a contraction of 1.55% the year before. GDP per capita in that year was estimated at around $11,813 and unemployment at about 13.3%. Total visitor arrivals were some 3.5 million of which air arrivals amounted to 1.3 million, and total spending was estimated at $1.3 billion, of which stopovers or air arrivals accounted for $1.2 billion. Foreign reserves, important to maintaining the value of the Bahamian dollar, were about $173.4 million.

By 1998, some four years following the development, completion, and opening of Atlantis Phases I and II, The Bahamas' economy was growing at a rate of 6.8%, five percentage points from 1994. GDP per capita increased to $18,467, an increase of some 56.3% over the 1994 figure. Unemployment decreased to 7.8%, a drop of almost 50% below the 1994 level. By 2002, some four years after the opening of Atlantis Phase II, total visitor arrivals had increased to 4.4 million, an increase of about 25.7% above the 1994 figure, while total visitor expenditure had increased to $1.6 billion, which was 23% above the 1994 number. By 1994, foreign reserves had increased to $373.2 million, an increase of 86.8%. That Atlantis was singularly responsible for the bulk of these improvements in the Bahamian economy is not in doubt, as between 1994 and 2002, it was the most significant direct investment in the country, and certainly the most impactful touristic development in the nation. Of the $1.01 billion direct investment in the country from 1998 to 2002, Atlantis accounted for some $650 million, about 64.4%. Of the 25,250 jobs created between 1994 and 2002, Atlantis conservatively accounted for some 10,000 of them directly, or about 40%.

By the end of 2002, Sol Kerzner's investment group had invested about $1.5 billion to transform a rundown resort property, once bearing the name of Trump (the now President of the United States), into a world-class resort, featuring some of the most unique offerings anywhere in the western hemisphere. The Group created a resort featuring: (1) hotel rooms at The Cove, Royal Towers, Coral Towers, Beach Tower, The Reef and suites at Harborside Resort and (2) amenities including Atlantis Marina, Atlantis Adventures, Aquaventure, Dolphin Cay, marine habitat, pools, beaches, spas, golf, casino, fitness centre, shopping, dining, fine dining, casual dining, cafes and quick bites, bars and lounges, outdoor dining, dining plans, entertainment, Aura Night Club, etc. In the process, the resort created more than 3,000 construction jobs during development and some 7,000 permanent jobs following the opening of all three phases. Today, it remains the largest private sector employer in The Bahamas, second overall only to the Government of The Bahamas, and a storied resort among the international travel press.

Pine and Gilmore (1999) contend that experiences can be thought of across two dimensions, one in which "customer participation" is key and the other in which "customer connection" is key. As to participation, a customer's experience can range from passive – where the customer essentially observes the performance and does not affect it. As to connection, the customer helps to create the experience by their active participation. Figure 8.1 is Pine and Gilmore's figure showing "The Four Realms of an Economy."

Atlantis may well be a resort offering accommodations to visitors to The Bahamas, and selling products of all types to its guests, but it essentially uses its rooms and products as props and staging for a mystical experience unique in the hemisphere. Looking at the chart above, in each of the four

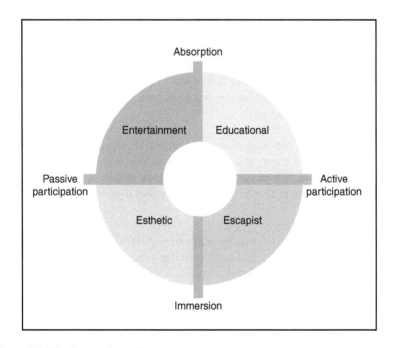

Figure 8.1 The four realms of an economy.

quadrants, Atlantis' experience offering is clear. Atlantis' guest can experience "entertainment" passively with more absorption than of immersion such as when they watch the approximately 50,000 sea creatures swim around in some 11 million gallons of water or attend a concert featuring K-ci and JoJo. An educational experience might be listening to a tour guide provide details of the various marine life at the resort or taking a dive lesson, in which case the experiences involve more active participation, "but students (customers, if you will) are still more outside the event than immersed in the action" (Pine & Gilmore 1999).

If guests want to have "Escapist" experiences they can swim with the dolphins, dance in the Aurora night club or participate in a Junkanoo "Rush-Out" at Marina Village which involves both entertainment and education. For the visitor merely walking around the Royal towers or in "The Dig" for the first time, viewing its elaborate design and mythical features has an "aesthetic" impact tantamount to standing in the remains of The Colosseum in Greece, where they are immersed in the environment but do not impact it much. The totality of Atlantis' offering does produce a kind of "sweet spot," as Pine and Gilmore terms it, where "aesthetic," escapist, entertainment, and education come together, this occurs when a guest is hurtling down a glass water slide that takes them underwater and into a pool of live sharks. The idea that such an offering produces a life-long memory is unmistakable.

Pine and Gilmore (1999) outline five principles that underlay the effective design of a memorable experience. These include: (1) theme, (2) indelible impressions, (3) absence of negative cues, (4) availability of memorabilia, and (5) the engagement of all five senses. Any stay at Atlantis resort will reveal that this formula was followed by the developer. The name of the resort itself, "Atlantis," is a clear clue as to its theme. The resort fashions itself after Plato's mythical tale told some 2,300 years ago about a people who were half-god and half-human who created a utopian civilization. These people were told to be naval experts.

> Their home was made up of concentric islands separated by wide motes and linked by a canal that penetrated to the centre. The lush islands contained gold, silver, and other precious metals and supported an abundance of rare, exotic wildlife. There was a great capital city on the central island.

according to *National Geographic* magazine. Atlantis, the myth continues, suffered a cataclysmic fate and sank into the ocean, no one knows where.
Pine and Gilmore insist that,

> While the theme forms the foundation, the experience must be rendered with indelible impressions. Impressions are the "takeaways" of the experience; they fulfil the theme. To create the desired impressions,

companies must introduce cues that affirm the nature of the experience to the guest. Each cue must support the theme, and none should be inconsistent with it.

From colour scheme, to architecture, to the relics found in "The Dig," to elaborate chandeliers, guests at Atlantis never forget that they are feigning a stay in the mythical city of Atlantis. Visual cues are everywhere, and sounds and smells at the water features enhance the same.

Pine and Gilmore say that negative cues can undo the effects of positive cues, if they contradict the theme. They suggest that nothing does this more than "poor service." When Atlantis first began operating, many of the native Bahamians complained that its work standards reflected some kind of apartheid treatment meted out in South Africa, the native land of Atlantis developer, Sol Kerzner. The complaints became a political issue, but the developer insisted that what was being done was to train staff to deliver the world-class service the resort's high theme demanded. They persevered and the service excellence achieved complimented the resort's theme. Service seldom detracted, in so far as travel reviews revealed, from the positive cues the resort provided guests.

As for availability of memorabilia at Atlantis, there is no shortage of the same. From shirts and mugs bearing images of Atlantis, to actual takeaways from "The Dig," Atlantis provides many opportunities for guests to take a piece of itself with them when they return home, further cementing the memories of their stay.

As required by Pine and Gilmore in the design of an effective experience, Atlantis engages the sense of sight, hearing, touch, smell, and taste. From the sight of winged horses raising out of the fountain in front of the Royal Towers to hypnotic jelly fish in an underground aquarium, the eyes of Atlantis' guests are filled with imagery from the undersea world. From the sounds of goat-skin drums beaten during a Junkanoo rush-out, to the consistent beat of waterfalls and water sprays, the ears of guests get their fill of acoustics. Guests feel the splashing water from spraying fountains, and taste meals of many types under pavilions reminiscent of the City of Atlantis.

In the Experience Economy, argue Pine and Gilmore, more and more companies must learn to charge for the distinct experiences they provide to their customers in order to add this value to the revenue base. In their minds, malls and retailers like movie theatres should charge an entry fee for patronizing the store because the experience inside will be so compelling. Atlantis does not charge an entry fee, per se, at least not to its guests outside of the cost of rooms per night like any resort. However, non-guests do pay one hundred dollars or more to enjoy its amenities, and seem to do so gladly. This much is true, since, room rates across The Bahamas' tourism industry have gone up and Atlantis has led the way to this economic boon, largely due to its unique experience offering.

Policy implications for The Bahamas

Tourism remains the mainstay of the Bahamian economy, contributing some 45% directly to gross domestic product (GDP). As Atlantis found it in 1994, so it is today, with limited growth. While a new mega resort, Baha Mar, holds the hope of boosting the sector's growth, it does not appear to be a game changer as was Atlantis in those days of the 1990s. Baha Mar does not appear to be an experience-based offering, but is much like any upscale resort that could be a good experience for guests. Policy makers in The Bahamas could do well to examine the concept of the experience economy closely and look across the globe at its application. Today, examples of the experience economy are abundant, too many with which to keep up (Pine and Gilmore, 2013).

From these case studies the tourism sector of The Bahamas, as a whole, might be refashioned. It might be that The Bahamas itself could be viewed as an experience for which an entry fee could be charged. It might take on a theme that is authentic to itself, test the same with its target audience(s), and design accordingly. Each island in the chain might represent a cue in the flow of the offering weaving a fabric in the experience unmatched in the world. Beyond tourism, it might promote the concept broadly to the private sector, encouraging more and more companies to upgrade their offerings to embrace the concept in meaningful ways. Micro-states, like The Bahamas, have always had a difficult time carving out a niche in the global marketplace, especially where commodities dominated, and services were regarded at a lesser degree. In the experience economy, they might find more fertile ground, since human experiences can be so vast. Over the years, knowledge in the design of experience-driven enterprises has increased significantly. This knowledge can be called upon by policy makers to help shape a new era of economic growth and development for The Bahamas. In this new era The Bahamas could be for the region, what Atlantis was for the country, a great example of the benefits of the Experience Economy.

Conclusion

> The world has indeed become more intentionally experiential. Yet one point needs to be repeatedly emphasized: this all represents a fundamental shift in the very fabric of the global economy. Focusing on goods and services alone leads down the road of economic austerity. Experiences are a distinct form of economic output, and as such hold the key to promoting economic prosperity.
>
> (Pine & Gilmore, 2013)

Indeed, experience is a new focus of the global economy. It is not that the world has invented anew this concept of experience as an offering, but as Pine and Gilmore (1998) noted, it has "discovered" it as something to offer as a lead value. Atlantis Resort, Paradise Island, began its journey into the experience economy more than 20 years ago, and by skilfully applying the design principles of effective experience, it has enjoyed success as a unique offering in the region, if not in the world of resorts. Its success points the way for policy makers and private sector participants alike to forge ahead in the competitive global tourism industry. For policy makers, they might take up Pine and Gilmore's challenge to consider what the country might need to do if it were charging an entry fee into The Bahamas itself. What themes, cues, memorabilia, and sensory effects might it employ in order to justify such a fee? Each private sector participant must too engage themselves in how they might stage experiences that compel the attention, and more importantly, hard-earned income of customers. Perhaps in doing so, The Bahamian economy might more fully welcome itself into the "Experience Economy."

"Today, around the world, goods and services must give way to experiences as the predominant form of new economic output, the foundation of growth in gross domestic product (GDP) and the source of new job creation." The downturned economies around the planet, spawned by the desperate financial attempts to prop up a world of goods, now make it the perfect time to take a closer look at the still untapped upside to experience-based innovation and economic expansion. This chapter, therefore, looks at the past of the experience economy – how it was discovered and where it came from, with many never-before published details; at the present of the experience economy – our current understanding of it, plus the implications and issues that arise from it; and finally, at the future of the "Experience Economy" – where it must head in the years and decades to come.

References

Boswijk, A., Thijssen, T. and Peelen, E. (2011). A New Perspective on the Experience Economy. [online]. Available at: https://www.researchgate.net/publication/260917972_The_experience_economy_past_present_and_future. [accessed on Dec 3, 2017].

National Geographic. (May 16, 2008) [online]. Available at: https://www.nationalgeographic.com/archaeology-and-history/archaeology/atlantis/. [accessed on Dec 15, 2017].

Pine II, J. and Gilmore, J. H., (1998). *Welcome to the Experience Economy.* Harvard Business Review. July–August 1998 Issue. [online]. Available at: https://www.researchgate.net/publication/260917972_The_experience_economy_pastpresent_and_future [accessed on Dec 17, 2017].

Pine II, J. and Gilmore, J. H. (1999). *The Experience Economy: Work is Theatre & Every Business a Stage.* Brighton, MA: Harvard Business Press.

Pine II, J. and Gilmore, J. H. (2013). The Experience Economy: Past, Present and Future. [online]. Available at: https://www.researchgate.net/publication/260917972_The_experience_economy_pastpresent_and_future [accessed on Dec 17, 2017].

Poulsson, S. and Kale, S., (2004). *The Experience Economy and Commercial Experiences (PDF Download Available)*. [online]. Available at: https://www.researchgate.net/publication/44104494_The_Experience_Economy_and_ Commercial Experiences [accessed on Dec 3, 2017].

Schmitt, B. (2011). Experience Marketing: Concepts, Frameworks and Consumer Insights. [online]. Available at: https://www8.gsb.columbia.edu/sites/globalbrands/files/Experience%20Marketing%20-%20Schmitt%20-%20Foundations%20and%20Trends%202011.pdf. [accessed on Dec 17, 2017].

9 The economics of smiling

A history of the Bahamian courtesy campaign 1955–1970

Edward Minnis

The selling of the paradise myth is a fickle business and friendliness is an intrinsic part of the Bahamian product. The tourist arrives in the islands with expectations of smiling service because friendliness is a central facet of the craving for a mythic paradise, a place free of the impersonality of modern urban life.[1] If, however, paradise turns out to be unfriendly, the guest leaves unsatisfied. Mythic expectations are encouraged and promoted in tourist advertising – in print, on radio and television – luring the foreigner, typically a white American, to vacation in The Bahamas. At the same time, other media are used by the local government to manage the responses of the population once the tourist arrives. The tourist returns home, hopefully satisfied, and the cycle begins again.

Given the primary place of tourism in the Bahamian economy it is understandable why successive governments have guarded the industry fiercely and have employed varying strategies to secure its clientele. These strategies have, over time, translated slow and inefficient service into the rustic charm of "island time." But when the slow and inefficient degenerates into the mean and belligerent, simple rebranding is not enough. It is then that the government turns to the courtesy campaign. These programmes, conducted at regular intervals, are designed to remind the population that tourists *are* the economy and should be treated accordingly. In the process, the campaigns gloss over significant social problems and inequalities implicit in, or brought about by, tourism, with heavy doses of conditioning that can essentially be boiled down to the maxim: "the customer is always right." Over the years the Bahamian has learned that smiling service is essential to their economic well-being and that discourtesy is the equivalent of treason.

Historiography

Since *The Fergusons of Farm Road* radio show, the object of this study, is a product of the ongoing Bahamian courtesy campaign, it is appropriate that we first attempt to understand the originating phenomenon. In the small pool of literature that is the field of Bahamian history, the courtesy campaign has been largely ignored. This neglect is surprising given its importance to the maintenance of the modern Bahamian tourism apparatus.

These campaigns earn only brief mentions in even the best histories of the islands, that is, if they receive any mention at all. For example, the second part of Michael Craton and Gail Saunders' *Islanders in the Stream*, the first attempt to write a comprehensive national history of the modern Bahamas to date, devotes one half of one sentence to the phenomenon in almost five hundred pages of text.[2] Craton gives a fuller three-sentence coverage of the campaigns in his 2002 biography of Pindling, but in that brief space he not only manages to conflate two distinct campaigns but also gives the erroneous impression that Pindling was still minister of tourism in 1970, when in actuality he had already passed the tourism baton twice.[3] Courtesy campaigns in the Caribbean have received similar scant attention. Polly Pattullo provides only a snapshot of these campaigns, or "tourism awareness programs" as she calls them, in the form of a three-page subheading in *Last Resorts,* her classic study of Caribbean tourism.[4]

The only substantive treatment of courtesy campaigns in general, and the Bahamian version in particular comes courtesy of Ian Strachan in his 2002 book, *Plantation and Paradise: Tourism and Culture in the Anglophone Caribbean*, in which he analyses aspects of the Bahamian "Pride and Joy" courtesy campaign of 1984 and the memorable enactment of courtesy in 1990 by Sir Lynden Pindling who "worked" various tourist-related jobs, for example, becoming a bell boy for a few hours, to show Bahamians how things were supposed to be done.[5] While he is both informative and analytical, and correctly situates the campaigns as a part of "the long tradition of [paradisiac] mystification," Strachan does not attempt to trace the origins of the Bahamian courtesy campaign nor does he fully explicate its place as a significant and recurring method of social control of the modern Bahamian state.[6]

The smattering of coverage in the literature has also perpetuated a persistent myth about Bahamian bad service and thus the need for corrective courtesy campaigns: namely that they are the direct outcome of majority rule and were thus ushered in by the Progressive Liberal Party (PLP) with its electoral victory of 1967. While this argument seems reasonable enough on the surface, it becomes ludicrous and demeaning to black Bahamians under closer scrutiny. This chapter then represents the first comprehensive discussion of the Bahamian courtesy campaign that this author is aware of. It defines the phenomenon as a significant form of social control that has been a recurring feature of the local landscape since at least the dawn of mass tourism in the 1950s. Gordon K. Lewis memorably described the Bahamian ruling classes in 1968, as "paranoid tourist-worshippers" – the courtesy campaign is testament to the continuing perfection of that faith.

Courtesy as national emergency

In 1961, six years after the Bahamas Hotel Association's (BHA) original award scheme, the courtesy campaign returned to The Bahamas. This was three years after the general strike of 1958 and after the 1960 by-elections

in which the Progressive Liberal Party (PLP) had secured several important victories that helped them increase their presence in the House to ten
Members of the House of Assembly (MHA). The PLP's influence had even
reached the point where it felt that it had an excellent chance of winning
the general elections due the following year. Through the political pressure
of the PLP and other fledgling black parties, the United Bahamian Party
(UBP) had become somewhat more responsive to popular demands, or at
least more responsive than before. On policy issues, however, the opposition
could hardly be differentiated from the government; both supported continued tourism development and foreign investment. It could be said that the
difference between the parties lay in their perspective for wealth-distribution
derived *from* tourism, that is, where the money would ultimately go. The
variation in their concepts was predictably defined along racial lines. The
PLP angled for a bigger slice of the pie for the common black while the UBP,
formed in 1958 with hardly a black MHA to be found, advanced the white
status quo.[7]

Meanwhile, tourism had continued its rapid growth and arrivals had shot
up 224% to 341,977 by 1960. Contrary to the 1955 argument, desegregating
Nassau's hotels did not kill the tourist industry. In fact the opposite was
true, as the Development Board was actually spending money advertising
"in key [U.S.] Negro publications to assure The Bahamas of a substantial
share of that important tourist market."[8] Times had definitely changed.
However, tourism figures had taken a sharp dip in Florida as well as other
resort islands in the region due to a mild economic recession, and it was
feared that the same would soon happen in The Bahamas.[9] For its part,
Florida had found it necessary to initiate a courtesy campaign to improve
business, a move that was apparently a "great success." Continuing its role
as government mouth-piece, a *Nassau Guardian* editorial suggested that a
similar programme was "badly needed" in The Bahamas since it was also
suffering from a colony-wide deterioration in civility.[10]

It was not long before the UBP answered the *Guardian's* call. On May 31,
1961, it sent an urgent appeal to the Governor as if it were a matter of national security – for in their minds it probably was.

> Whereas, this House is concerned about the deterioration in the degree
> of courtesy accorded visitors to the colony; ...
>
> Be it therefore resolved, that His Excellency the Governor ... is hereby
> requested to take such steps as may appear necessary ... to ensure that
> the necessity of the utmost courtesy to visitors is fully impressed on all
> persons within the colony who come into contact with visitors. [11]

If the "Courtesy Conscious" drive in 1955 provided a carrot for Bahamian
workers, the proposed campaign employed the stick. Gone were the subtle
hints, rewards and the general tone of encouragement. The message was far
clearer – tourism was the lifeline of the colony and discourtesy would kill it.

The story was similar to that of 1955, but the animosity towards "those who deal[t] with tourists" was amplified. The Guardian editorial lamented that

> there are too many of us who, as individuals are not pulling our weight. We have stressed over and over again that "service is not servility." Yet the commonest complaint heard from visitors is that they have been subjected to surly, uncooperative and inefficient service in hotels, restaurants and other public places. [12]

While Sands had referred to those not "pulling their weight" in generalized tones in 1955, the *Guardian* was much more specific. This time the phrase referred almost exclusively to the black Bahamian worker. That the writer would find it necessary to stress "over and over" that "service is not servility" makes this point clear, as few white Bahamians, less than 20% of the population, would be concerned about issues of servility, especially since so few of them actually worked in the service sector.

The Development Board had contacted tourists in their home environment after their Bahamian holiday and had conducted surveys. Apparently these

> studies showed that 45 per cent of the tourists – which would be more than 140,000...- found some reason to complain and that more than half of these complaints concern a lack of courtesy shown by service personnel with whom they came in contact.[13]

This was reason for concern. For the Development Board the ideal tourist was one who spread good word-of-mouth and acted as "unofficial salesman."[14] Sands heard the complaints loud and clear and created a courtesy committee in June, comprised of leaders of main Nassau tourism organizations to oversee the campaign.[15]

The coming courtesy campaign would be multi-faceted with full exposure on various media and in the press. Radio ZNS was seen as an essential component in the effort. Sands said that

> Radio spot commercials not only reach a large percentage of those whose work brings them into direct contact with tourists, but those commercials emphasizing courtesy will deliver the message to hundreds of others of all classes. I have said before that courtesy is contagious, and this may be a very good means of spreading a very worthwhile infection. [16]

Anthropologist Nicolette Bethel concurs with Sands' assessment, contending that The Bahamas is primarily an oral society and that because of this "radio, and not the press, is the bearer of information, the provider of any kind of central, organised unity in the nation."[17] Therefore the use of radio, an oral medium, was the ideal conduit for the "infection," and with monopoly control over the colony's air waves, the UBP used that power to their advantage to remind Bahamians that they were "naturally a pleasant and courteous people."

In his speech, Sands called courtesy "the key part of the real Bahamian way of life." It should be remembered that only a few years earlier the "Bahamian way of life" meant holding onto social segregation. The dynamic had changed, but the phrase still referred to the ways that the colony could be marketed to foreigners. Courtesy had replaced segregation as another key ingredient next to sun, sand and sea in the Development Board's sales pitch. And following the old maxim, "charity begins at home" to its logical end, Sands also concluded that the solution to the problem of service must emanate from the black Bahamian home.

> Courtesy should be a lesson learned early. Human relations are all important. For this reason the Department of Education could assist by undertaking a courtesy campaign in the schools, emphasizing its importance in everyday living as well as its vital significance in keeping our tourist industry successful.[18]

If the black family was failing to produce workers who were courteous, the state should step in and provide the appropriate training.

Public reaction

A feature of *The Nassau Guardian* of Monday, July 3, 1961 called "The People Speak" gives us a good window on the opinions of ordinary Bahamians on the courtesy campaign. While those interviewed acknowledged that there was a problem with courtesy, they generally preferred the 1955 campaign. While one respondent said that the current campaign was "one of the best things they could ever think of doing," four of the six interviewees wanted a return to cash prizes as rewards for courtesy. If they were going to be nice to tourists, this small sample of black workers wanted to be paid for it, as one respondent coyly said "after all, courtesy always pays." Sands himself was amenable to the idea of monetary reward, but he left this to the discretion of individual storeowners and the BHA.[19]

This small sample of public opinion also touched on an issue previously ignored in courtesy propaganda – the unreasonable demands of some tourists. Bryce Maycock, a tour conductor, said that "Admittedly we cannot satisfy all the tourists, because some of them are just impossible and expect too much."[20] Courtesy was generally a one-way street and the "impossible" guest did not make many appearances in government exhortations to courtesy. There were also Bahamians who simply felt that their leaders were being hypocrites about the entire exercise. Take, for example, the sarcastic comments of Suzanne Wanklyn of Prospect Ridge who wrote, in a letter published May 31, 1961, that "in the last sessions of the House several members [of the House of Assembly] most certainly forgot their manners at every sitting."[21]

The timing of the courtesy campaign deserves mention. Was it a pre-emptive strike against dips in tourist arrivals or was it a more sinister attempt to beat back black desire for majority rule? A definitive answer is difficult to give but it is noteworthy that the PLP defeat at the polls in the 1962 general elections came as a surprise to many. Colin Hughes argues that "some of the explanation [for the PLP defeat] no doubt lies with the growing prosperity, closely linked to the rising number of tourists" while Saunders and Craton attribute the defeat to wide-spread "fear of the consequences of black majority rule."[22] Both might agree to describe the results as a victory for Bahamian conservatism; expansion of tourism had put the economy in "bonanza" mode and it seems that many did not want to agitate the water by siding with unproven stewards. One is tempted to suggest that the message of the courtesy campaign was taken to heart or at least reinforced this conservatism.

The above examples should make it abundantly clear, though, that bad service was not invented with the narrow PLP victory on January 10, 1967, but rather, that it has a long history that stretches back at least to the beginnings of mass tourism in the 1950s and that the question of service in the tourism industry was freighted with more than the simple mechanics of hospitality – it was an issue of social control and reward. Contrary to UBP claims, they had not only employed the courtesy campaign during their time in power, but had pioneered the techniques that the PLP was then using in the "Look Up, Move Up" campaign to manipulate worker attitudes.

Friendliness through understanding

With the alarm bells ringing in unison and the country in a suitable panic, a courtesy campaign was announced as a programme of "mutual understanding" on Monday, March 2, 1970. As if reading directly from the Checchi Report, Clement Maynard said "the Bahamian must be made aware in very specific terms of what tourism means to his personal pocketbook and the future welfare of his family and the nation." He diverged from the script as he continued, saying,

> the visitor must be made aware of the customs of our country, understand that they may differ from those of his own country, and that his readiness to adapt – rather than resist – will be repaid with a spontaneous desire to please on our part.[23]

The concept was ambitious, Maynard was proposing a programme that would condition both sides of the equation to the potential benefit of the government. How much "understanding" would be coaxed out of the visitors, however, remained to be seen.

The programme was called "Friendliness Through Understanding" (FTU) and was officially launched by Prime Minister Pindling on Wednesday March 25, 1970, and like the programme in 1961, it was multi-tiered and intensive, targeting every single Bahamian demographic through multiple media, making maximum use of ZNS radio.[24] Similar to the 1968 elections, the courtesy campaign was tied into the "holy season" of Easter.[25] Pindling gave a presentation to church leaders prior to launching the campaign on ZNS, so that the ministers could incorporate the theme into their Easter sermons. Tying the campaign to Christianity was perhaps an attempt to exploit the feelings of sacrifice that the Easter season can evoke, or as simply a means to give the programme the legitimizing blessing of the church as it already had a workable degree of social leverage over Bahamians.[26]

Components of understanding

Once the FTU programme began in earnest, even the most casual radio listener would have heard several messages a day. There were one-minute radio spot ads by world-famous Bahamian actor Sidney Poitier. The content of these spot ads can be ascertained from Etienne Dupuch's complaints about them:

> Several times a day the voice of Sidney Poitier comes over Z.N.S. urging our people to be friendly to tourists.
>
> Black hands, white hands, brown hands and yellow hands must all be clasped in good fellowship if we are to have a good country, Mr. Poitier declares.[27]

Poitier's voice was paired with additional radio spots, featuring a similar message, performed by well-known local writer Susan Wallace.[28]

Beginning April 8, at 6:30pm there were daily broadcasts entitled "One in A Million" that presented excerpts of actual tourist exit interviews – both good and bad – giving their candid reactions to the islands. It was described as "the programme that lets you know what people are saying about you and your country." The press release continued,

> The five-minute spots end with a thought-provoking question addressed to all listeners: "What have I done for our country today?" The reply from each person should be: "All I could do and just a little bit more!"[29]

The title neatly manipulated the ratio of tourists to Bahamians for maximum effect and by linking tourist joy or dissatisfaction to individual performance the ads personalized tourism in a somewhat different way than the Checchi Report had admonished.

School-age children were conscripted into the campaign from above and below. Minister Maynard spoke on the theme of the "Teacher's role in a

Tourist Economy" to the faculty and students of The Bahamas Teachers College on May 1. His audience would eventually graduate to become high school and primary-level teachers. Perhaps getting a bit carried away with his message, he described tourism as an opportunity for spiritual growth. He told them that "a consciousness of the importance of service and a willingness to serve are essential to the spiritual growth of any people."[30]

The children themselves received their own propaganda. Students from ages 8 to 18 were able to participate in a "Friendliness through Understanding" essay contest. The "preferred essay topics" are as follows: Courtesy in The Bahamas; Is friendliness important to Bahamians? and Are Bahamians still a friendly people?[31] The last question is the most intriguing, for it asks the essayist to presume that Bahamians were, at some point in the past, naturally friendly. Given that majority rule had come only three years before, how were the children to imagine generations of racially oppressed and often impoverished Bahamians as "friendly"? The ability of this seemingly innocuous question to gloss over and mystify centuries of problematic history is impressive and to do so this soon after that very history was the central issue in the colony is nothing short of breath-taking.

The national FTU programme inspired others to create similar initiatives. The King's Inn and Golf Club in Freeport decided that it could encourage friendliness through competition. Employees in contact with tourists earned "Sunshine Points" through the recommendations of tourists on "Guest Questionnaires" or by sending "Happy Letters" back to the hotel on their return home. "Back of the house" employees not in direct contact with tourists were not left out as they could earn their points by staff recommendations. The points would be accumulated over the course of the year and the grand prize winner would receive a trip for two to England.[32] Similar focus on financial reward spawned a "Mystery Shopper" programme conducted in Nassau that gave prizes to the "friendliest retail sales person of the week."[33]

As the title of the campaign, "Friendliness through Understanding," implied, there were attempts to help tourists better understand the ways of the native. Leaflets were distributed to visitors upon arrival in The Bahamas explaining to them "the difference between the customs and traditions of The Bahamas and those of the United States."[34] Some of the timely advice given in the pamphlet included the following:

> We drive on the left, our currency is the equivalent of yours (even though it doesn't carry a picture of George Washington) We are a proud people, we don't move with the frenzy of a New Yorker or a Londoner – so relax and enjoy the slower pace for which you came. Please enjoy it to the full and return home revitalized. [35]

A few gentle pointers were all that the tourist needed to get, while Bahamians were bombarded with the ministry's hard-line message night and day. It was Bahamians who needed to understand that tourism was vital to the country; they who needed to understand that each tourist represented income and their country's future. "Smile," the campaign seemed to say, "your life depends on it."[36] This was ultimately the only "understanding" that the programme was designed to promote.

The Fergusons of Farm Road

The most imaginative portion of the "Friendliness Through Understanding" programme was no doubt its "Education-Entertainment" component. The Interpublic Group had crafted a radio serial drama, based on the enduring British Broadcasting Corporation show, *The Archers,* to promote the principles of FTU entitled *All about the Albury's.* Initially recorded with foreign actors, Maynard felt that the programmes' American accents would not get through to Bahamians – perhaps using the opportunity to exercise authority in an area where *he* was the undisputed expert. The ministry tried to recycle the Interpublic scripts using Bahamian vocal talent, but the actors found the scripts to be unappealing. Maynard then turned to the young lawyer and playwright Jeanne Thompson.[37]

Jeanne was the second child of Ellison and Sybil Thompson, a middle-class couple who eventually had five children. Ellison, born on the Out Island of Eleuthera, had made a successful career for himself as a civil servant, and had held a wide variety of posts. He began his varied career in 1930 as a public school teacher, then served as an assistant commissioner in the far south Out Island of Acklins and then as a commissioner in Mayaguana. He returned to Nassau in 1942, working in the public treasury and the Attorney General's chambers. In 1967, he was made First Assistant Secretary in the post office and public works departments and two years later Deputy Permanent Secretary. On February 10, 1970, while the FTU programme was likely under active development, he was appointed permanent secretary for the ministry of tourism under Clement Maynard, having been moved at Maynard's behest from his previous post in the ministry of works.[38]

The two eldest daughters, Dawn and Jeanne, had moved to Jamaica in 1955 to attend the Wolmers girls' boarding school for sixth form, which was the final two years of secondary schooling when students, usually between 16 and 18 years of age, prepared for their A-level examinations. It was at this boarding school that they first met Sonia McPherson.[39] The trio became fast friends and even after graduating they kept in contact. Their paths crossed again in London in the early 1960s while they all pursued post-secondary degrees – Jeanne pursued a law degree at Middle Temple at the Inns of Court in London after a year at University College; Dawn obtained a postgraduate certificate in education (PGCE) at Durham University; and Sonia studied French, journalism and politics at L'ecole Superieure de Journalisme and l'Institut de Sciences Politiques in Paris and Birkbeck College, London University.

Jeanne returned to The Bahamas with law degree in hand and joined her uncle's practice becoming only the second female lawyer in The Bahamas when she was called to the bar in 1965. She was very active in the local arts scene and was a leading Bahamian playwright, director, actress and prominent member of the local theatre group, "the Bahamas Drama Circle." Her plays up to that point were satiric affairs that skewered recent Bahamian politics, two of which were the evocatively titled and self-explanatory *Peoplexodus* in 1967 and *Le Noir Supreme* in 1969.[40] As a self-proclaimed feminist, she battled what she described as "a considerable degree of prejudice against women lawyers, both inside and outside the legal profession and among the general public."[41]

Sometime after returning to Jamaica in the mid-1960s, Sonia joined the Jamaica Information Service Radio Unit, headed by Elaine Perkins who would become renowned as the Jamaican radio serial pioneer. Perkins first serial was the pro-development soap opera *Life in Hopeful Village* conceived by then Minister of Development Edward Seaga to promote the five-year development plan. Perkins eventually left *Hopeful Village* and the government service to pursue the development of her own commercial soap opera, *Dulcimina: Her Life in Town,* which became immensely popular. Perkins departure left Sonia in charge as the show's main writer, a post she held for nearly two years. In 1967, she married Don Mills, a Jamaican civil servant and veteran of the Jamaican Central Planning Unit.

The following year Don was recruited by the Bahamian Ministry of Development to serve as its permanent secretary and thus began the task of transferring his family to The Bahamas. There was apparently a delay in processing his request through the official channels, and Sonia relates that they were surprised to be told, informally, by Prime Minister Hugh Shearer, that the main reason for the delay was the concern that the minister of development, Edward Seaga, had about finding a replacement for Sonia to keep *Hopeful Village* alive.[42] The transfer eventually came through and the Mills family finally came to The Bahamas. Sonia was employed with the ministry of tourism, and served in a number of capacities, where she was eventually placed in charge of promotional brochures and informational literature for tourists.

The arrival of the Mills family in The Bahamas also served to reunite Jeanne and Sonia. Thus when Jeanne was offered the opportunity to write a Bahamian radio serial by the minister of tourism, she immediately called her good friend. Although Thompson had written a number of plays, she had no prior experience with the radio serial format or the soap opera aesthetic, and she was reluctant to take on the project. Mills had no such trepidation and encouraged Thompson to take the job. Although Mills' involvement was not officially sanctioned, the pair agreed to work together on the serial.[43]

Feeling that the ministry seemed to appreciate alliteration, they changed "Albury," a common white Bahamian name, to its opposite, the black folk name of Ferguson. They then combined this with a reference to the

Over-the-Hill area, where Thompson had grown up and created *The Fergusons of Farm Road*.[44] The pair recruited actors from Thompson's immediate family, the Nassau theatre community, working-class Bahamian straw vendors and even a few work acquaintances. The programme they produced remains to this day a singular instance of Bahamian creative collaboration and, as far as this writer is aware, was also the first national narrative ever provided to the Bahamian people in an extended popular format. The genesis of the *Fergusons* also has a distinct Pan-Caribbean flavour as it traces its lineage directly to the early Jamaican pro-development serials.

The inaugural broadcast of *The Fergusons of Farm Road* aired on ZNS at 7:30pm, Wednesday May 13, 1970 and was repeated the following day at 12:30pm. Under the headline "Courtesy Show on ZNS," a press release in the *Guardian* announced *The Fergusons* as an "all-Bahamian soap opera."

> All the parts are played by Bahamians and through the characters they portray, the theme is set to emphasize the importance of courtesy and a constructive outlook not only towards the resort's visitors but between Bahamians and their fellow country men and women.[45]

Under the original terms agreed on between the parties, the *Fergusons* were only to exist for 13 episodes and then it was to fade away with the rest of the FTU courtesy campaign. The show immediately attracted the attention of Bahamians who had never before heard a fictionalized version of their daily lives, and within weeks they began to congregate around their radios to hear the latest 15 minute instalment.[46] Had the colony finally found a medium that conveyed the importance of courtesy to their mainstream industry without invoking colonial attitude of subservience and obsequiousness? Stay tuned.

Notes

1 Strachan, *Paradise and Plantation*, 116.
2 Craton and Saunders, *Islanders Vol. Two*, 357, 8.
3 Craton, *Pindling*, 162.
4 Pattullo, *Last Resorts*, 70–73.
5 Strachan, *Paradise and Plantation*, 116–124.
6 Ibid., 116.
7 Hughes, *Race and Politics*, 80, 1, 6.
8 Anonymous, "Coming Season Seen Most Competitive in Travel History: Board Here Sets Tourist Campaign, " *The Weekend Guardian*, August 5–6, 1961.
9 Anonymous, "Sands Addresses Chamber on Courtesy Campaign, " *The Nassau Guardian*, Tuesday, June 13, 1961.
10 Editor, "Time for Courtesy, " *The Nassau Guardian*, Friday, May 12, 1961. Editor, "Courtesy Campaign, " *The Nassau Guardian*, Monday, June 12, 1961.
11 Anonymous, "House to Air Flagging Courtesy to Visitors, " *The Nassau Guardian*, Wednesday, May 31, 1961.
12 Editor, "Time for Courtesy."

13 Shell Nulty, "Service Groups Supporting Colony-Wide Venture: Be Courteous!, " Monday, June 12, 1961.

14 Anonymous, "Sands Addresses Chamber on Courtesy Campaign."

15 Nulty, "Service Groups Supporting Colony-Wide Venture: Be Courteous!."

16 Anonymous, "Sands Addresses Chamber on Courtesy Campaign."

17 Nicolette Bethel, "Navigations: National Identity and the Archipelago, " *Yinna* 1 (2000).

18 Anonymous, "Sands Addresses Chamber on Courtesy Campaign."

19 Ibid.

20 Anonymous, "The People Speak: On Courtesy Campaign, " *The Nassau Guardian and Bahamas Observer*, Monday, July 3, 1961, 10.

21 Suzanne Wanklyn, "Bravo! Well Spoken Mr. Symonette, " *The Nassau Guardian*, Friday, June 2, 1961.

22 Hughes, *Race and Politics*, 92. Craton and Saunders, *Islanders Vol. Two*, 314.

23 Anonymous, "'Mutual Understanding' Programme Slated, "*The Nassau Guardian and Bahamas Observer*, Tuesday, March 3 1970.

24 Connie Jo Justice, "'Friendship through Understanding' Campaign Launched, " *The Nassau Guardian and Bahamas Observer*, Thursday, March 26 1970. Now we can finally examine the error in Craton's statement found on page 162 of *Pindling: The Life and Times of Lynden Oscar Pindling First Prime Minister of the Bahamas, 1930–2000*, that "in March, 1970, [Pindling] initiated and starred in a well-publicized 'Friendliness' Campaign." Pindling only 'initiated' the campaign in the sense that he launched it with a speech – he likely had as little to do with its development and execution as did Maynard, who, if we read between the lines of his autobiography, was probably no more than a mouth-piece for Chib at the time. On page 161, Craton says that Pindling was the minister of tourism in 1970; this is simply wrong. If, however, he wishes to use 'Pindling' as metonym for the entire PLP government, then of course, he is ultimately correct, but only in the most misleading of ways. When Craton writes that Pindling 'starred' in the campaign, he is likely thinking about his movie role in the 'Look Up, Move On' campaign of 1968, and is likely conflating the two separate campaigns.

25 Hughes, *Race and Politics*, 138.

26 Bahamas Ministry of Tourism, *1970 Annual Report: Tourism in the Commonwealth of the Bahama Islands*, 1970 (Nassau, Bahamas) 17.

27 Etienne Dupuch, "Charity Begins at Home, " *The Tribune*, Saturday, May 16, 1970.

28 Tourism, *Annual Report 1970*. 17.

29 Anonymous, "Daily Broadcasts to Aid Tourism, " *The Nassau Guardian and Bahamas Observer*, Wednesday, April 8, 1970.

30 Anonymous, "'Education Should Begin at Home' Says Minister, " *The Nassau Guardian and Bahamas Observer*, Thursday, May 7, 1970.

31 Anonymous, "Essay Contest to Push 'Friendship Campaign', " *The Nassau Guardian and Bahamas Observer*, Saturday, May 30, 1970.

32 Anonymous, "Freeport Club to Promote 'Smile' Campaign Yearly, " *Nassau Guardian and Bahamas Observer*, Thursday, May 7, 1970.

33 Tourism, *Annual Report 1970*.

34 Bill Cole, "Visitor Figures Discreditors Lashed by Tourism Minister, " *The Nassau Guardian and Bahamas Observer*, Tuesday, March 3, 1970.

35 Anonymous, "Mutual Understanding."

36 See Strachan, *Paradise and Plantation*, 131.

37 Claire Belgrave, *Theatre in the Bahamas: From Ol' Story to Rep Theatre* (Nassau: Guanima Press, 2007), 104. The writer's name is pronounced Jean-nie. Thompson is also this writer's aunt.

38 Anonymous, "Deputy Is Appointed Permanent Secretary, " *The Nassau Guardian and Bahamas Observer*, Tuesday, February 10, 1970.
39 Don Mills, *Journeys & Missions: At Home and Away* (Kingston: Arawak Publications, 2009), 107.
40 Belgrave, *Theatre in the Bahamas: From Ol' Story to Rep Theatre*, 148.
41 Lambert, "Jeanne Thompson – Girl Lawyer."
42 *Hopeful Village* survived until 1975. See Cambridge, "Mass Media Entertainment", 346.
43 Belgrave, *Theatre in the Bahamas: From Ol' Story to Rep Theatre*, 104.
44 Jeanne Thompson, interview by author, Nassau, Bahamas, January 21, 2009. The series title was apparently not an automatic choice – an early draft of the first episode has the family living on Peter Street.
45 Anonymous, "Courtesy Show on Z.N.S., " *The Nassau Guardian and Bahamas Observer*, Wednesday, May 13, 1970.
46 Belgrave, *Theatre in the Bahamas: From Ol' Story to Rep Theatre*, 148, 9.

Part III
Sustainable development

10 Assessing sustainability in small island developing states

A comparative analysis of sustainability assessment tools and their applicability to small island developing states

Stacey Wells-Moultrie

Introduction

In September 2015, the United Nations member countries adopted the Sustainable Development Goals (SDGs). Along with these agreed goals are recommendations on indicators to measure their achievement. This research seeks to answer one primary and two secondary research questions:

- Primary question – Are existing sustainability assessment tools applicable to SIDS, based on their unique characteristics?
- Secondary questions:
  - If they are not, should a SIDS-specific tool be developed?
  - What would be the features of such a tool?

This research provides a comparative policy analysis of the use of sustainability indicator systems and their suitability for SIDS.

The comparative analysis involved a series of steps that are outlined in Figure 10.1 and detailed in Sections Results of analysis, Discussions and Conclusions.

Sustainability

With finite space and resources, sustainability is vital for small island developing states (SIDS). The first step for SIDS in achieving sustainability is to define it for their national context. Once it is defined, clear policy directives for achieving sustainability then need to be developed. The directives should outline the goals the country wants to achieve to develop sustainably.

Sustainability is a term that was coined during the 1987 World Commission on Environment and Development (WCED). It is often used interchangeably with the term "sustainable development" and is defined as "development that meets the needs of current generations without compromising the ability of future generations to meet their needs and aspirations" (WCED, 1987).

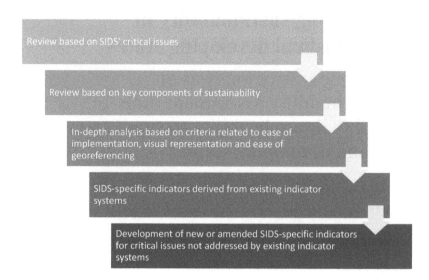

Figure 10.1 Steps in the comparative analysis of indicators.

Davidson (2011, p. 352) challenges this definition and refers to the 1987 WCED Report (also referred to as the Brundtland Report) as "largely empty rhetoric":

> ...sustainable development has been conflated with the idea of "sustained economic growth", implying that the world economy, which is currently based on human consumption, should and can grow indefinitely, as long as resources can be replaced faster than they are used... Sustainable development has become, in essence, a version of environmental protection that does not pose a threat to the current economic structures of modern industrial societies, including the loci of power and wealth, such as leaders in politics and commerce.
>
> (Davidson, 2011, p. 352)

Davidson (2011, p. 359) makes the important point that "economic growth does not necessarily provide a critical measure of individual and community well-being [or whether practices are sustainable or unsustainable]."

The Brundtland Report's definition of sustainability fails to acknowledge that resources are finite, not limitless, though many would wish them to be. Pursuit of sustainability has to include finding ways to limit our use of these finite resources. This chapter proposes that the Brundtland definition of sustainability is too narrow and proposes an alternate definition:

> Sustainability requires limits to growth but allows substitutability of capitals only with the support of appropriate green design or

technologies. It also seeks to preserve the environment, achieve social justice, equity and freedoms as described by Sen (1999) while allowing for the development of a viable economy.

This definition is adapted from Davidson's work to compare political economy typologies' interpretation of sustainability and fits more with her social democratic typology along the continuum of weak versus strong sustainability[1] (Davidson, 2011).

An indicator system of sustainability would then track changes in policies, processes and behaviours towards limiting use. Davidson (2011, p. 353) purports that very strong sustainability would mean there is no substitutability of capitals. The definition of sustainability for the purposes of this chapter would require limits to growth but allow substitutability of capitals only with the support of appropriate green design or technologies. As an example, any new building construction would require at least partial use of green design or technologies, such as solar panels or energy-efficient building materials. It would also seek to preserve the environment, and achieve social justice and equity while allowing for the development of a viable economy (Davidson, 2011, p. 355).

Sustainability indicators

Since WCED, there have been many efforts, global and local, to determine what the components of sustainability are, how countries and communities can achieve sustainability and how to measure progress towards sustainability. Singh et al (2009) alone have identified 70 such indicators. The Sustainable Development Goals (SDGs) process has identified more than 300 indicators. There are also numerous examples of integrated sustainability models including A Multidirectional Optimum Ecotope-Based Algorithm (AMOEBA) and the Ecological Footprint.

Assessing sustainability through the use of indicators should "provide decision-makers with an evaluation of global to local integrated nature-society systems in short- and long-term perspectives in order to assist them to determine which actions should or should not be taken in an attempt to make society sustainable" (Kates et al, 2001, p. 191).

Dahl (2012, p. 16) purports that "The most coherent indicator sets are those...that have been mapped to a national strategy or concept of sustainability. This ensures that each indicator is policy relevant." He gives Switzerland as an example of a country that has achieved this through its national office for sustainable development.

Small island developing states

Small island developing states (SIDS) are a unique group of countries, many of which are working to achieve sustainability as they develop. Their unique characteristics include (adapted from Blancard and Hoarau, 2013; Briguglio, 1995):

1　Geographic – small size, remoteness, isolation, exposure to major natural hazards;
2　Environmental – fragile ecosystems, limited water resources, high vulnerability to sea level rise, storm surges and ocean acidification;
3　Historic – external dependence, close political links to former colonial powers, such as the United Kingdom;
4　Social – low intensity and volatility of human capital, weak institutional structures, labour market instability, insecurity;
5　Economic – small economies of scale, limited local markets, dependence on a narrow range of exports, lack of diversification activities, cost of access to external resources, high communication and transportation costs, prevalence of natural monopolies, oligopolistic structures, dependence on foreign sources of finance and limited development options.

These island nations are found in areas such as the Caribbean Sea, Pacific Ocean and off the coast of Africa. The Economic Commission for Latin America and the Caribbean (ECLAC) (2010, p. 65) notes the constraints Caribbean SIDS face in implementing international and national sustainable development strategies – inadequate capacity (human, financial and technical), lack of information for decision-making, lack of legal authority and institutional capacity for implementation and enforcement, and challenges communicating sustainable development to the populace.

In planning for development, planners and decision-makers in SIDS need indicators or some type of assessment tool to determine whether they are achieving their sustainability goals. Once the indicators or the assessment tool are developed, SIDS also face challenges with their continued monitoring. Hirano (2008, p. 8) notes that "SIDS commonly cite the need for assistance and training in data collection, analysis and management, ... Lack of data, [and] the low quality of existing data ...are all barriers to the overall goal of achieving sustainable development."

Methodology

The study design can be described as cross-sectional and retrospective prospective. The methodology used is applied research and more specifically, a comparative policy analysis of the use of indicators for measuring sustainability in the context of SIDS. The information gathered through this research can be utilized for policy formulation, planning, community involvement in decision-making, and enhancing understanding of phenomena (e.g. climate change) – all aspects of sustainability.

Sustainability is an important goal for SIDS with their limited resources – natural, human and financial. These countries need some means of measuring their progress towards sustainability to ensure they are moving in the right direction and making informed decisions. This research seeks to assist SIDS in identifying indicators and potentially an assessment tool to measure their progress.

The strengths of the study design are that it could be done relatively quickly and in a cost-effective way. It enabled review of tools developed in the past and will generate recommendations for a future tool. As applied research, it will form the basis for development of a tool that can be used to benefit SIDS; the tool will be created and tested in future efforts involving the action research methodology.

The main limitation of the research methodology utilized would be the inability to review every existing indicator and tool or to identify and interview every expert in the field, either because of time constraints or their unavailability. Therefore, the indicators or models assessed, and the experts interviewed are a representative sample of the entire field. It is possible that important information has been missed that could provide specific insights.

The data collection methodology consisted of a literature review and interviews that were structured and unstructured. The structured component of the interview consisted of an interview schedule detailing specific questions that were asked of experts. The unstructured component consisted of a research guide that outlined issues that were raised during the interview. The interviews focussed on those persons who could potentially participate in the tool implementation to determine successes and deficiencies.

The sampling design for the expert interviews was expert and snowball sampling. Experts were identified through the literature review of secondary sources of data. These experts were contacted and those who agreed were interviewed. Experts were also asked to recommend other experts or institutions that should be contacted about the research topics as a means of snowball sampling.

Primary data sources were the existing assessment tools themselves and the responses from the expert interviews. Secondary data sources were journals, textbooks and websites of organizations, such as the United Nations Statistical Commission (UNSC).

There are countless indicators existing or proposed to monitor sustainability and sustainable development. It was not feasible to analyse every indicator, so with each of the systems reviewed using a series of questions, a sample of those indicators that were deemed most relevant to SIDS were selected for further analysis.

In determining relevance or appropriateness of existing indicators to SIDS, several criteria were used:

- Did the indicators address issues critical to SIDS?
- Did the indicator monitor key components of sustainability as defined in this chapter?
- Could the data collected be visually represented and could each indicator be georeferenced?

Table 10.1 Criteria in determining relevance of sustainability indicators

Addressed issues critical to SIDS	Monitored key components of sustainability	Criteria for further analysis
Vulnerability to sea level rise	Limiting economic growth	Ease of implementation
Building resilience to climate change (adaptation)	Measures of a viable economy	Visual representation
Individual and community well-being	Substitutability of capitals	Ease of georeferencing
Geographic	Change in dynamic systems	
Environmental – limited water resources, marine resources	Environmental preservation or conservation	
Historic – external dependence	Designation of tipping points	
Social – low human capital, weak institutional structures	Social justice	
Economic – existing mechanisms	Equity	

Table 10.1 provides a summary of the criteria applied in determining relevance of indicators to SIDS as the analysis was further refined.

Whether indicators addressed issues critical to SIDS was determined by asking the following questions as summarized in column 1 of Table 10.1:

1   Geographic – Was it relevant to SIDS geographic characteristics versus being more appropriate for large continental land masses?
2   Environmental – Was the indicator monitoring an issue of significance to SIDS, such as limited water resources or climate change?
3   Historic – Would it enable an examination of SIDS' external dependence and be able to monitor change in the relationships with organizations, such as former colonial powers or donor agencies?
4   Social – Did it look at issues relevant to SIDS and could it still be monitored considering these issues, such as low human capital and weak institutional structures?
5   Economic – Were there already mechanisms to monitor the indicator, thus negating the costs associated with having to create new mechanisms?

Relevance of indicators was also determined based on whether they monitored the key components of sustainability as defined by this chapter and summarized in column 2 of Table 10.1. These key components were:

1   Planetary sustainability at global and national levels
2   Change in dynamic systems
3   Environmental preservation or conservation
4   Designation of tipping points

5 Capacity to analyse alternative scenarios
6 Values or ethical principles
7 Social justice – human rights, political freedoms, social opportunities, transparency guarantees, safety nets
8 Equity
9 Substitutability of capitals only with appropriate green design and technologies
10 Measures of a viable economy
11 Limiting economic growth

Limiting the analysis to indicators that addressed these issues was also seen to determine whether an assessment tool of 10–15 indicators could be feasible.

Sustainability indicators are a means to track whether sustainability policy goals are being achieved. For SIDS, these indicators must meet certain criteria which are summarized in column 3 of Table 10.1 and detailed below:

Ease of implementation – SIDS' limited resources include limited human resources. The most numerous human resources are found in schools and colleges in the form of students. Indicators should not be so complicated that only PhD-level students or professionals can understand and implement them. Indicators need to be at a level where students, starting from tenth or eleventh grade through final year bachelor's degree, can monitor them. Ideally, schools and colleges, not government agencies (which are short-staffed and over-worked), should take the lead in monitoring sustainability indicators as a part of their contribution to national development. Colleges or universities would coordinate data collection by students at the various levels and work cooperatively with national statistical offices to design the data collection process, analyse the data and input into the assessment tool.

Visual representation – If there was a visual component to indicator tool or system, it could aid in decision-makers' and citizens' understanding of the indicators and the role they play in helping the country to achieve sustainability.

Ease of georeferencing – As technology progresses, utilizing indicators that can be georeferenced will become the norm. SIDS will need to be able to do this in their national statistical offices.

These last three criteria were used for further analysis of the 37 indicators and the results of this analysis are presented in Section Results of analysis.

Results of analysis

Using the criteria for determining relevance of sustainability indicators as described in Section Methodology, the 304 indicators proposed by the Bureau of the UNSC and the 229 indicators proposed by the Inter-agency and Expert Group – Sustainable Development Goal (IAEG-SDG) were reduced to 152 indicators deemed as SIDS-appropriate. Because this number would be considered burdensome for SIDS to monitor on an annual basis, the list was further reduced to 37 indicators. These 37 indicators form the basis of further review using the criteria of ease of implementation, visual representation and ease of georeferencing. Where no SIDS-appropriate indicator was provided by either UNSC Bureau or IAEG-SDG report for sustainability components deemed critical, alternative indicators or amended indicators are proposed in Section Discussion.

Each of the 37 indicators were selected because they were deemed SIDS-appropriate and aligned in some way with the sustainability definition for this chapter. The indicators were further assessed based on the following criteria:

- Ease of implementation – Scores were assigned based on the level of education necessary to enable sound data collection. High school (H) level was given a score of 3, bachelor's degree (B) level was given a score of 2 and Graduate (G) level was given a score of 1. Those variables that were easiest to implement are what SIDS should seek to monitor;
- Visual representation – Being able to visually represent the indicator is important to communicating findings to decision-makers and the general public. "Yes" provided a score of 1 and "No" received a score of 0;
- Ease of georeferencing – Selecting many indicators that cannot be easily georeferenced for a national system could prove problematic in the future. "Yes" provided a score of 1 and "No" received a score of 0.

An indicator could receive a maximum score of 5 and a minimum score of 1. The scoring system is summarized in Table 10.2.

A summary of the results of the scoring is provided in Table 10.3. High scores are highlighted in *italics* and low scores in **bold**. It is important to note that this scoring system is simplified and may result in loss of valuable insight. For example, ease of implementation could be based on any number of criteria, including cost-effectiveness, timeframe for data collection, and necessary equipment, and not only be limited to the level of education of data collectors. Multi-criteria analysis would provide a more robust and objective scoring system and should be a goal for future research.

Table 10.2 Scoring system for indicator analysis

Ease of implementation	*Visual representation*	*Ease of georeferencing*
High school – 3	Yes -1	Yes -1
Bachelor – 2	No -0	No -0
Graduate – 1		
Maximum score – 5		
Minimum score – 1		

It is also important to note that the scoring may also be influenced by the researcher's bias as a citizen of a Caribbean SIDS and familiarity with other Caribbean island nations. The issues prioritized in the analysis may be most applicable to Caribbean SIDS, but not necessarily SIDS globally, such as women involved in government. This potential bias can only be eliminated through future research with case studies in other SIDS regions.

One indicator received a low score of 2: Progressivity of tax and social expenditures, e.g. Proportion of tax contributions from bottom 40%, Proportion of social spending going to bottom 40%. This was because it required graduate degree-level data collectors and it cannot be easily georeferenced. It was only one of the two indicators deemed necessary to have graduate degree-level data collectors. The majority of the indicators could be monitored using bachelor's degree level collectors.

Seven indicators received the maximum score of 5 as indicated in *italics* in Table 10.3. The maximum score was received because these indicators required high-school-level data collectors, could be visually represented and could be easily georeferenced. These indicators would be best suited for SIDS with their limited highly skilled human resources and limited financial resources. High school students could be trained in data collection methodology initially and data analysis eventually. Their work could be overseen by more experienced data collectors and statisticians to ensure data quality and adherence to data standards.

Discussion

Of the 37 indicators assessed, seven were deemed best suited for SIDS and could be incorporated into a new SIDS-specific assessment tool. Monitoring these seven indicators should enable SIDS to track their progress towards sustainability. Each country will need to adopt a definition for sustainability and formulate a national policy or plan for achieving sustainability. Indicators must be linked to the goals and targets within a national policy or plan for their results to have meaning. SIDS may decide to adopt the SDG and targets as they are to serve as their national sustainability policy or plan, or they can opt to develop an instrument that is unique.

The seven indicators that are suggested for use by SIDS can support decision-making. For example, percentage of financial support that is allocated to the construction and retrofitting of sustainable, resilient and resource-efficient buildings is an indicator of SDG 11. It is specifically related to SDG Target 11.c on support to least developed countries through various means including financial and technical assistance to construct sustainable and resilient buildings utilizing local materials. This indicator alone relates to several issues critical to SIDS – vulnerability to sea level rise, improving resilience to climate change, change in the relationship with former colonial powers or donor agencies, use of appropriate green design and technologies, and development of a viable economy. For SIDS to achieve sustainability,

Table 10.3 Analysis of indicators

No.	SDG target	Indicator	Ease of implementation	Can be represented visually	Can be easily georeferenced	SIDS suitability score
4	2.1	Prevalence of Undernourishment (PoU)	B	Yes	No	3
5	2.4	*Percentage of agricultural area under sustainable agricultural practices*	*H*	*Yes*	*Yes*	*5*
6	3.4	Mortality of cardiovascular disease, cancer, diabetes, or chronic respiratory disease	B	Yes	No	3
11	5.5	*Proportion of seats held by women in national parliaments and local governments*	*H*	*Yes*	*Yes (by state, constituency or district)*	*5*
12	6.1	Percentage of population using safely managed drinking water services	B	Yes	Yes	4
14	6.3	*Percentage of bodies of water with good ambient water quality*	*H*	*Yes*	*Yes*	*5*
16	7.a	Improvement in the net carbon intensity of the energy sector (GHG/ TFC in CO_2 equivalents)	B	Yes	No	3
18	9.3	Percentage of small-scale industries with a loan or line of credit	B[a]	Yes	Yes	4
19	**10.4**	**Progressivity of tax and social expenditures, e.g. Proportion of tax contributions from bottom 40%, Proportion of social spending going to bottom 40%**	**G**	**Yes**	**No**	**2**
20	10.6	Percentage of members and voting rights of developing countries in international organization	H	Yes	No	4
22	11.c	*Percentage of financial support that is allocated to the construction and retrofitting of sustainable, resilient and resource-efficient buildings*	*H*	*Yes*	*Yes*	*5*
23	12.5	National recycling rate, tons of material recycled	B	Yes	No	3
25	14.3	*Average marine acidity (pH) measured at agreed suite of representative sampling stations*	*H*	*Yes*	*Yes*	*5*

No.	SDG target	Indicator	Ease of implementation	Can be represented visually	Can be easily georeferenced	SIDS suitability score
26	15.1	Forest area as a percentage of total land area	B	Yes	Yes	4
28	15.5	*Red List Index*	*H*	*Yes*	*Yes[b]*	*5*
30	15.a	Official development assistance and public expenditure on conservation and sustainable use of biodiversity and ecosystems	B	Yes	No	3
31	16.1	*Number of victims of intentional homicide per 100,000 population, by age group and sex*	*H*	*Yes*	*Yes[c]*	*5*
32	16.5	Percentage of persons who had at least one contact with a public official, who paid a bribe to a public official, or were asked for a bribe by these public officials, in the previous 12 months, disaggregated by age group, sex, region and population group	B	Yes	No	3

a There is no reason that a high school student could not collect this data except that business owners would probably be reluctant to provide data to a person under the age of 18 years.
b It can be georeferenced by the country, but it would be more difficult to do by species natural range within the country, particularly if little data exists on the species and its distribution.
c Where victims were killed can be georeferenced and where they lived before being killed.

improving their resilience to climate change and natural disasters should be a priority. Communicating this priority to donors[2] should inform the funding and technical assistance provided to SIDS for addressing this issue. Setting the baseline for financial support for this type of construction and then tracking it over the years can inform decision-makers of several things or raise questions that need to be addressed:

1   Whether donors are providing the funding for a priority as identified by SIDS or whether their funding is driven by something else;
2   If it is something else, is it aligned with sustainability goals for SIDS? If it is not aligned, is it making achievement of sustainability more difficult?
3   If it is making achievement of sustainability more difficult, can donors be convinced to address SIDS' priorities?
4   If donors cannot be convinced, should the relationship be severed and other donors sought?

Just tracking this single indicator can also lead to questions about other related issues, such as:

1   If funding is increasing and construction proceeding, does this directly translate into resilience to natural disasters, such as hurricanes? If it is, resilient buildings should sustain minimal damage as compared to buildings traditionally constructed.
2   If more resilient buildings are being constructed, what are the cost savings to governments when substantial repairs after hurricane damage are no longer necessary and how are those savings being utilized for other sustainability issues, such as social justice?

This single indicator can lead those in power to make informed decisions about foreign policy, international negotiations, foreign and local investments, economic development, and training priorities. This one example also highlights the connectivity or complementarity of indicators and how this can strengthen the system. It is tracking indicators in this way that can help The Bahamas to plan for natural disasters, such as Hurricane Dorian. Dorian hit the islands of Abaco and Grand Bahama in September 2019, causing damages to homes and infrastructure estimated at $3.4 billion.[3] To recover from catastrophic impacts such as this, creating communities that are resilient must be a priority and adopting a national indicator system for sustainability can assist decision-makers in ensuring that it is prioritized in development activities.

An additional 13 indicators are also recommended as components of the tool because some issues critical for SIDS were not adequately covered by indicators proposed through the United Nations SDG process:

1   Education – Development of primary- and secondary-level curriculum including civics or CAS (creativity, activity, service) courses/activities that are mandatory
2   Viable economy – Proportion of SMEs with access to loan, credit or overdraft facilities
3   Viable economy – Percentage of tourism market share that is locally owned
4   Employment – Percentage and number of persons engaged in forced labour, per sex and age group (disaggregated by the worst forms of child labour)
5   Resilient infrastructure – Percentage of critical infrastructure able to withstand 50-year storm or The Intergovernmental Panel on Climate Change (IPCC) sea-level rise projections through 2100
6   Adaptation – Total official international support adaptation programmes/projects focussed on creating sustainable and resilient infrastructure

7 Inequality – Total resource flows for development disaggregated by recipient and donor countries, type of flow and target national plans and programmes

8 Production patterns – Third-party audits of companies to include evaluation of sustainable practices and publication of results

9 Conservation of marine resources – Percentage of coastline and marine territory with formulated or implemented integrated coastal management or maritime spatial plans based on an ecosystem approach, that builds resilient human communities and ecosystems, and provides for equitable benefit sharing and decent work

10 Preventing biodiversity loss – Benefits (in US dollars) derived from national legislative and administrative frameworks, including permits, for utilization of genetic resources according to guidelines of the Nagoya Protocol

11 Preventing biodiversity loss – Programs for Invasive Alien Species (IAS) control based on national legislation, including prevention, detection, control and monitoring, established and regularly assessed

12 Global partnership for sustainability – Number of policy changes in investment regimes incorporating sustainability objectives

13 Global partnership for sustainability – Developing countries' and least developed countries' share of global exports derived from sustainable management of natural resources.

Of the 20 indicators recommended for inclusion as a part of the SIDS-specific tool, seven are at the global level or associated with global impacts – average marine acidity, Red List Index, international adaptation programmes, total resource flows for development, programmes for IAS control, number of policy changes in investment regimes, and developing countries and LDCs share of global exports. The remaining indicators are at the national or local level.

Limiting the tool to 10 or 15 indicators could be done, but it would provide a limited perspective of all the many facets of sustainability. With the initial indicator recommendations, the number of indicators is already at 20 and there are still indicators needed for designation of tipping points and values. It may also be argued that these 20 do not sufficiently address social justice issues and the tool would need to incorporate some of the less-suited SDG indicators or propose alternatives.

A new SIDS-specific tool would need to include system dynamics models, resilience indicators, designation of tipping points, and the capacity to analyse alternative scenarios with indicators at both the planetary and individual levels (Dahl, 2012, p. 17). Trying to balance a manageable number of indicators and still capture all the complexities of sustainability would be the challenge. Because of this challenge, all of the existing indicator systems reviewed are largely based on data that is already being collected to eliminate the challenge of having to collect data related to new indicators. Using existing data sets has its own challenges, such as poor-quality data and gaps remaining for key sustainability issues, such as equitable distribution of wealth.

To address this challenge, the tool could be designed based on the 5M principles proposed by Evrendilek (2014) – measuring, monitoring, mapping, modelling and managing (see Figure 10.2) – and developed in a phased approach over time rather than all at once.

The five components feed into each other in an iterative process with continued data collection improving the system as it evolves. A tool based on these principles incorporates concepts of visual representation and georeferencing which were highlighted as important criteria for a SIDS sustainability assessment tool. Modelling could also provide a means for forecasting change in system dynamics or developing trade-off scenarios. Policies and management actions based on this evolving tool could be adaptive, i.e. as information inputs improve, policies and management decision could be changed accordingly.

The goal for SIDS could be to build the system in a phased approach, focussing initially on measuring and monitoring as inputs to managing and then progressing to mapping and modelling as capacity improves within the country. SIDS could be supported in the development of this tool by multilateral agencies. Targeted Official Development Assistance (ODA) could fast-track tool development.

The Consortium of SIDS Universities is a potential vehicle for implementation of a SIDS-specific sustainability assessment tool with data collection and analysis being led by the universities in respective countries. The Small

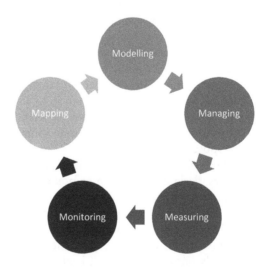

Figure 10.2 The 5M components of SIDS Sustainability Assessment Tool.

Island Developing States Network (SIDSNET) described as "a vital knowledge management portal for SIDS" could potentially serve as the platform for data collected and analysed (ECLAC, 2010). Partnering with universities or research centres to support countries through dedicated training for environmental monitoring is recommended by Working Group on Audit of Extractive Industries (WGEI) (UNEP, 2014, p. 11). The Global Partnership for Sustainable Data may be the possible basis/platform for developing a SIDS-specific tool.

Nita (2008, p. 11) makes the important point that

> if cash handouts or answers and solutions are given to people who have not developed the capacity to generate and sustain wealth and build their own solutions, this does not bring about the achievement of sustainable economic development. Instead the seeds are sown of a dependent relationship.

Developing a SIDS-specific assessment tool is not sufficient in achieving sustainability. It must be accompanied by efforts to build systems that can support application of the tool through robust data collection, trained data collectors, skilled data analysts and platforms where data can be shared and integrated. This is reinforced by the Council of Foreign and Community Relations (COFCOR), which called for "the systemic approach to strengthening the statistical systems in SIDS" at its Sixteenth Meeting held in Trinidad and Tobago in May 2013 (United Nations Environment Programme Regional Office of Latin America and the Caribbean [UNEP ROLAC], 2013).

While the SDGs now exist, they are more focussed on sustainable development, not sustainability. For SIDS, it is the latter that needs to be pursued. To aid them in their pursuit, indicators of sustainability as a part of an assessment tool specific to their needs is required.

Conclusions

It is a recommendation of this chapter that a SIDS-specific tool be developed in a phased approach, focussing initially on measuring and monitoring as inputs to managing and then progressing to mapping and modelling as capacity improves within each country. SIDS could be supported in the development of this tool by multilateral agencies and targeted ODA could fast-track tool development. The recommendation to involve more stakeholders in the process, particularly students, is a means by which national capacity can be built.

Recommendations for further research include estimating cost-effectiveness of monitoring the 20 indicators proposed as a part of the SIDS-specific tool in this chapter, estimating the cost of developing the tool, identification of additional indicators that measure sustainability and those components that are required to develop an assessment tool that SIDS can utilize in spite of their constraints and challenges rather than creating more for these island nations.

Future research activities would be designed as action research. The intent would be to conduct the research followed by eventual development of a SIDS-specific sustainability assessment tool to help decision-makers to choose actions that will increase their country's attainment of sustainability goals. The research would begin with a case study of The Bahamas and then progress to analysing other SIDS to eventually build a global picture of these countries.

As action research, the initial case study in The Bahamas would be a collaborative process engaging with key stakeholders including the Office of the Prime Minister, Department of Statistics, University of The Bahamas, and teachers and students from at least one high school at either the level of Grade 10 or 11 as well as experts from other fields as needed to develop components of the tool. These experts could include GIS specialists, software developers, and graphic designers.

A SIDS-specific assessment tool coupled with development of a national policy or plan based on a clear definition are key to small island nations achieving sustainability which is vital to the well-being of each country and its citizens. The successful development of the tool in a single SIDS country could be replicated in other SIDS as well as larger countries, particularly LDCs that share many of the same challenges faced by SIDS.

Notes

1 Davidson's continuum was as follows: Neoliberal – Liberal – Social Democratic – Radical. Neoliberal philosophy would espouse weak sustainability with approaches such as total substitution of natural capital for any other type of capital, trade liberalization and privatization of public enterprises being promoted. At the other end of the continuum, the radical philosophy would espouse strong sustainability where no substitution for natural capital is allowed.
2 Donors may include former colonial powers, multilateral agencies, regional banks or foundations; methods of funding may include grants, loans or concession-based lending.
3 IDB News Release 15 November 2019. https://www.iadb.org/en/damages-and-other-impacts-bahamas-hurricane-dorian-estimated-34-billion-report

References

Blancard, S., & Hoarau, J. (2013). A new sustainable human development indicator for Small Island Developing States: A reappraisal from data envelopment analysis. *Economic Modelling*, 30, 623–635.

Briguglio, L. (1995). Small island developing states and their economic vulnerabilities. *Development*, 23, 1615–1632.

Dahl, A. (2012). Achievements and gaps in indicators for sustainability. *Ecological Indicators*, 17, 14–19.

Davidson, K. (2011). Reporting systems for sustainability: What are they measuring? *Social Indicators Research*, 100, 351–365.

ECLAC (2010). *Caribbean regional report for the five-year review of the Mauritius strategy for the further implementation of the Barbados programme of action for the sustainable development of small island developing states (MSI+5)*.

Evrendilek, F. (2014). The 5M principles of sustainability dynamics: Ecosystem-level measuring, monitoring, modelling and managing of natural capital. *Journal of Ecosystem and Ecography*, 4(2). doi: 10.4172/2157-7625.1000e121

Hirano, S. (2008). The development of national sustainable development strategies in small island developing states. In Strachan, J. and Vigilance, C. (eds.) *Sustainable development in small island developing states: Issues and challenges*. Economic Paper 80. London: Commonwealth Secretariat.

Kates, R.W. et al. (2001). Sustainability science. *Science*, 292, 641–642.

Nita, A. (2008). Risk, consultation and participation in the creation of a national sustainable development strategy in Papua New Guinea. In Strachan, J. and Vigilance, C. (eds.) *Sustainable development in small island developing states: Issues and challenges*. Economic Paper 80. London: Commonwealth Secretariat.

Sen, A. (1999). *Development as freedom*. New York: Alfred A. Knopf, Inc.

Singh, K., Murty, H.R., Gupta, S.K., & Dikshit, A.K. (2009). An overview of sustainability assessment methodologies. *Ecological Indicators*, 9, 189–212.

Sustainable Development Solutions Network (SDSN). (2015). *Indicators and a monitoring framework for sustainable development goals – Launching a data revolution for the SDGs*. Retrieved from http://unsdsn.org/wp-content/uploads/2015/05/150612-FINAL-SDSN-Indicator-Report1.pdf

UNEP. (2014). *Proposal of the working group on environmental indicators to the forum ministers of the environment of latin America and the Caribbean*. Mexico: Nineteenth Meeting of the Forum of Ministers of Environment of Latin America and Caribbean (Ref UNEP/LAC-IGWG.XIX/4. Rev.2).

UNEP ROLAC. (2013). Concept note: Strengthening the collection, management and use of environmental data and information to support decision making on environment and sustainable development in Caribbean SIDS. In *Strengthening regional networks and national capacities for environmental information in Latin America and the Caribbean – Focus on Caribbean SIDS*. Barnwell, G. (2013). 1–11. Panama City, Panama.

The World Commission on Environment and Development (WCED). (1987). *Our common future: Report of the world commission on environment and development*. Retrieved from http://www.un-documents.net/wced-ocf.htm

11   Toward a blue economy

Ragged Island: a case for sustainable development for the islands of The Bahamas

Bridgette Rolle

Even before the story of The Bahamas was formally written, our forefathers had stories to tell about how "the islands" as they would call them, became colonized. Many people, myself included, if challenged, can link our ancestry to several groups of people. My 90-year-old mother for example tells the story of how she remembers her grandmother as a woman with "long straight jet-black hair that reached almost down to the floor, and women who spoke very little English". This could mean then that this woman could very easily have been of Indian decent or as historians would call them, Amerindian. Several articles have highlighted Bahamians heritage and speak directly to the fact that people who travelled to some of the islands of The Bahamas came as far away as Africa, Spain, France and Britain (Albury, 1975; Craton & Saunders, 1999; Curry, 2017).

Because of the archaeological makeup of The Bahamas, most of the island settlers made their living from the sea after salvaging their bounties from wrecks (skilful diversions of ships) where they were parleyed into what was then vibrant economies (bahamas.com).

> The Bahamas also prospered and became a base for Confederate blockade-running, bringing in cotton to be shipped to the mills of England and running out arms and munitions (Tinker, 2018). None of these provided any lasting prosperity to the islands, nor did attempts to grow different kinds of crops for export.

One such industry that seemed to have had a degree of sustainability was the salt industry which proved to be quite lucrative for many of the Bahamian islands (Erickson, 1987; Saunders, N/D). Although little is known about the Great Ragged Island, other than it was given the name of Duncan Town after its founder who developed the island's salt industry. Ragged Island is believed to have been a pirate safe house at one point, with its rocks and caves offering great hideaways. Blackbeard's Bay and Blackbeard's Well suggest that the pirate may have established his headquarters near the well because of its unique location (bahamas.com).

Pre Hurricane Irma in 2017 (one of the many hurricanes in recent times to have dealt a crippling blow to small island economies in The Bahamas (Neely, 2019), Ragged Island was known for its quiet and serene characteristics, a complete opposite of its name (ragged), and have long been home to fewer than one hundred people. The island generally attracted the avid fishermen, with its unmatched flats that are ideal for bone fishing. It was not uncommon to catch copious amounts of grouper, snapper, barracuda, tuna and king fish during just one day on the water (myguidebahamas.com). Ragged Island had a variety of beaches that were mostly unexplored. Several historical landmarks, authentic Bahamian handicraft and quaint towns scattered throughout the island would have been what tourist happened on while visiting (myguidebahamas.com). Post Hurricane Irma life as we knew it was completely changed forever on this island. Already one of the tiniest island's population-wise, the infrastructure was destroyed and many of the islands had to for safety reasons vacate the island and move to either New Providence or one of the other islands in The Bahamas (Maura, 2017; Neely, 2019). For sure, those who remained witnessed first had the evaporation of a once lucrative and prosperous economy. Those who remained however, were considered the hardy bunch who vowed to stay and rebuild their beloved island (Russell, 2017; Lockhart, 2018). Conversations of and about the blue economy and other innovation mechanisms to refuel these small islands that were devastated became the talk of the day in government circles (Caribbean Journal, 2017; Maura, 2017; Russell, 2017).

Emergence of the blue economy

The emergence of the "blue economy" concept arose from the 2012 United Nations Conference on Sustainable Development, or Rio+20, and offered a new pathway by which small states could develop and achieve some of their sustainable goals and objectives (sustainabledevelopment.un.org). While these goals embraced many of the features of a "green economy", including environmental sustainability, this new approach to looking at the economy delves into how the ocean and marine life could sustain an economy.

The United Nations (2017) defines the blue economy as a long-term strategy aimed at supporting sustainable and equitable economic growth through oceans-related sectors and activities. In addressing the UN Conference on Trade and Development (UNCTAD) in 2014, Kituyi (2014), Secretary-General, lamented the fact that the blue economy was much like the green economy in that it shared similar outcomes which seek the improvement of human well-being and social equity, while significantly reducing environmental risks and ecological scarcities. This new approach aims to scale up traditional uses of the ocean, using the latest technologies and steered by new, enabling public policies (World Wide Fund for Nature [WWF] 2015).

The United Nations General Assembly of December 22, 2015, adopted a resolution 70/226 to support the implementation of Sustainable Development

Goal 14: Conserve and sustainably use the oceans, seas and marine resources for sustainable development to support the implementation of Sustainable Development Goal 14.

The world's oceans, seas and coastal areas are the largest ecosystems on the planet and a precious part of the natural heritage. They are considered an important part of the livelihood and food security of billions of people globally, and to the economic prosperity of most countries (World Wide Fund for Nature [WWF] 2015). Many of these countries are being threatened today by burgeoning populations, overdevelopment and misguided and uncoordinated human activities. Developed and developing countries are however quickly becoming aware of the need to implement coherent, evidence-based policies to manage their economic development of environment and the ocean. The importance of the ocean to economic development cannot be understated as the need to maintain a balance between improvements of standards of living and the health of ecosystems is imperative.

The origin of the concept of Blue Economy is often traced to the book titled *The Blue Economy: 10 Years, 100 Innovations, 100 Million Jobs*, written by Gunter Pauli, first published in 2010. Pauli's business model examines a transforming society looking specifically at the notion of scarcity to abundance, with the help of locally available resources, which have been adopted using innovative measures to address environmental and related problems. The concept of blue economy is now being widely used to refer to human activities based on oceans although it carries many meanings and interpretations, which have done nothing but create doubt in the minds of the interested public on the subject. It also appears that some interest groups have tried to emphasize the ecological perspectives, while others have considered it merely as a parasol or catchment term for all economic activities in the maritime sector, carried out using ocean resources, without any reference to sustainability aspects (Senaratne, June 2017).

Senaratne wrote in a June 17, 2017 copy of the NATION that

> Oceans cover two thirds of the earth's surface and over three billion people are estimated to depend on marine and coastal systems for their livelihoods, directly and indirectly. Important maritime activities, such as fishing, sea transportation, tourism, offshore mining, and energy generation, play a significant role in the national economies of many countries.

Much of these sentiments are shared for archipelagic island nations like The Bahamas that still rely in large parts on the proceeds of the ocean for seafood, recreation and transportation. Senaratne also noted that

> Marine ecosystems fulfil environmental functions that are essential for the survival of humans and other living beings. The oceans absorb a major share of carbon dioxide emissions that humans produce, play an

important role in the stability of global climate systems, and accommodate and protect a major part of global biodiversity, making the world habitable for all of us.

There are several measures that signals support for the blue economy and should help to broaden its definition. These include, but are not limited to, ecosystem services that are provided, regulated, supported and seek to enrich the cultural uses of coastal and marine ecosystems worldwide (UNEP, 2015). An examination of the report also found that ecosystem services were intricately associated with the sustainability and the opulence of key industries within the Blue Economy.

Prospects for blue economy in The Bahamas

Felicity Ingraham, in the October 23, 2017 issue of the Tribune reported that Minister of Agriculture and Marine Resources Renward Wells is keenly watching current economic trends and the emergence of the "blue economy", which he believes has the ability to decrease the national deficit and increase revenue to The Bahamas. The country, he says, "with its vast natural aquatic resources, is poised to benefit from the focus the world is currently placing on the ocean, as new ways are explored to sustain the earth's population". Ingraham (2017) further reported that Minister Wells had spent the past months analysing the country's current budget allocations for import and export trends, and was considering the necessary legislation to make "meaningful changes in agriculture and marine resources". She noted that he had "high hopes the initiatives which will pay off, including the introduction of two major greenhouses, more incentives for local producers and a focus on the blue economy".

The Agriculture and Marine Resources minister also stated in the Tribune (2017) that "We are also looking at how to maximize the economic impact an ocean can have on a people; The Bahamas is over 100,000 square miles. I believe the wealth of this country lies mainly in the ocean". He further noted that The Bahamas could look at aquaculture, which is growing fish on the land, through a process of open ocean fishing.

> East of Cat Island, Eleuthera and Abaco, out in the Atlantic for 200 miles, is our exclusive economic zone. It is the territory of The Bahamas under international law and we have exclusive right to fish it, mine it and use its resources, noted Wells.
>
> (Ingraham, 2017)

Enabling conditions

Prime Minister Dr Hubert Minnis declared on Monday that the destruction wrought by Hurricane Irma on tiny Ragged Island in The Bahamas has rendered it uninhabitable and urged the remaining 18 residents to evacuate as early as Tuesday.

Minnis, members of his Cabinet, members of the opposition, officials of the National Emergency Management Agency (NEMA) and the media visited Ragged Island, Acklins and Crooked Island on Monday.

When members of the prime minister's group moved throughout the island, they were shocked. Many exclaimed that it was the worst disaster they had ever seen. No home was left untouched by the Category 5 hurricane. Many of the homes had no roof, windows or doors. Other homes were destroyed, with only rubble remaining on the foundation. Most, if not all, of the power lines were down. The roof of the clinic, school and administrator's office were gone. (Travis Cartwright-Carroll, Nassau Guardian Senior Reporter, September 13, 2017).

The Caribbean Journal reported, September 16, 2017

While much of The Bahamas escaped the wrath of Hurricane Irma, the southern island of Ragged Island bore the brunt of the damage, with most homes destroyed or damaged, power lines down and public buildings damaged or destroyed.

Now, Bahamas Prime Minister Dr Hubert Minnis is vowing to transform Ragged Island into the first "fully green island" in the region.

"Out of the devastation and the destruction, a new Ragged Island will emerge including stronger building codes, improved zoning, and strategies to mitigate against Climate Change and rising sea levels," Minnis said. "I assure the wonderful people of Ragged Island that their island will be rebuilt. We will work with private institutions, international agencies and foreign partners to create a more sustainable island-community at Ragged Island."

"Most homes are destroyed or severely damaged. Power lines are down. Utilities are non-functioning. Public buildings, including the government-operated school, the clinic and other public facilities are severely damaged or destroyed. The numbers of dead animals pose a serious health risk," Minnis said.

The island will have to be rebuilt through a combination of public and private efforts, he said, with a number of Ragged Islanders already having offered their assistance for recovery and rebuilding.

Given the current situation in Ragged Island, the researcher suggests that the Prime Minister and the Minister for Agriculture and Marine Resources continue the dialogue about the redevelopment of this small island (Figure 11.1). This can be done initially by identifying enabling mechanisms that would be critical to the transition to a Blue Economy. Some of the major mechanism could include, but would not be limited to:

Figure 11.1 Photograph showing hurricane damage on Ragged Island. Photograph courtesy of Ian Bethell-Bennett.

- Finance: Determining existence finances for family island development and leveraging that with new sources of funding, like those already identified. According to Minister of Public Works, Desmond Bannister in an article written by Smith (2017)

  > We also are ensuring that there is amazing input and assistance to those people and so you're going to see some of the biggest companies in the world get involved in the Ragged Island project and when you see Ragged Island again in a short while, it is going to be an example that we can follow for the rest of the world what we are doing down there.

- Minister Bannister further added:

  > For example the Carbon War Room is involved. Tesla is involved. A number of things are involved that require international input and I can tell you that the people who are leading this are very, very concerned about Ragged Island, but they're also concerned that if Ragged Island is hit by another hurricane we are not going to see that kind of devastation (again).
  >
  > (Russell, 2017)

- Trade and Investments: Bring to bear the necessary policies for the establishment of a Blue Economy that would be consistent with the overall National Development Plan for The Bahamas, the Rio + 20 Sustainable Development Goals and Caribbean Community (CARICOM).

- Steering Committee: Establish a steering committee that would comprise the relevant members of the government and government agencies like the Department of Fisheries, the Marine division of the Port Department, the Ministry of Tourism, etc.; non-governmental organizations such as the Bahamas National Trust and the Bahamas Nature Conservancy; public, private partners (PPP) such as the LJM Maritime Academy and the University of The Bahamas; technical advisers; local residence and neighbouring residence(from Exuma Island) and those persons that may have a vested interested in the redevelopment of a "New" Ragged Island featuring a Blue Economy.

These participatory meetings should occur at least twice monthly in the first instance to diagnose and assess the situation on the ground. At this time, smaller technical groups could be established that will be directly responsible for various aspects of the redevelopment, some of which are:

- Determine what definitions should be used when referring to The Bahamas as a "Blue Economy" and not a "Green Economy" particularly as it relates to marine activities and its uses.
- Providing technical advice on issues relative to rezoning of the waterfronts, dredging of the harbour, new water mains (which has already started), new building codes, and other basic infrastructure such as electricity, telephone and cable.
- The management of Ragged Island as this will now be a "Model" that could be replicated on other smaller islands of The Bahamas.

Further to these initial meetings, broader stakeholder consultations should take place to keep current residents and potential residents up to date on plan changes and to explain in detail the tenets of what a Blue Economy would look like, versus that of the proposed Green Economy that the Prime Minister of The Bahamas has promised. This would be an opportunity for the government to garner local and international experts in the field to submit proposals of how the redevelopment would look and the impact it would have for residents and The Bahamas as a Diaspora. These proposals could then be shared through town meetings held on Ragged Island, where the greatest impact would be felt and timely feedback could be sourced. This view was expressed in a study of residents in Abaco, Bimini and Exuma, they wanted to be a part of development plans for their islands because they lived there (Minnis & Blackwell, 2018). At this point, the local media would be invited to document and share the messages to a wider audience.

The way forward and lessons learned

"I heard the comments by Mr. Cooper", Mr. Bannister said ahead of the morning session of Cabinet yesterday, referring to remarks Mr. Cooper made about the Prime Minister making false promises about Ragged Island rebuilding (Russell, 2017).

> They were very unfortunate. The government has a number of private sector partners who are working with us to ensure that Ragged Island is rebuilt properly. I think all of you went to Ragged Island and you saw how the buildings were initially put up. We have to ensure that we build according to code now.
>
> (Russell, 2017)

Adrian LaRoda, president of The Bahamas Commercial Fishers Alliance, suggested that because of Ragged Island's location within the Great Bahama Bank it is ideal for what he calls a Satellite Fisheries Outpost/SFO that could sustain the economy of not only this island, but also that of The Bahamas. He further noted that this kind of development could be ideal for the Commercial Seafood Engineers/Fishermen because they could then establish and maintain seafood storage and processing plants to export seafood, using Ragged Island as a base. Additionally, this "fishing hub", once created, could in fact:

- Support longer fishing days at sea
- Provide fuel storage and distribution
- Facilitate safer product storage
- Encourage product processing and distribution
- The development of Export Service and Customs Brokerage mechanisms
- Digitally driven Roll-on & Roll-off Shipping Services
- A fully functioning Medical facility
- A Military Outpost which can support and protect local Seafood Engineers/Fishermen as well as their fishing vessels
- A Satellite Fisheries Outpost which when fully operational, can support up to two hundred (200) full-time jobs with a minimum Gross Domestic Product (GDP) of more than 7.3M per year.

Conclusion

In conclusion, since the Hurricane (Irma) of 2017, Ragged Island saw its very existence turned upside down. The island was so devastated that the Prime Minister declared it uninhabitable, calling on remaining resident to vacate for health and safety concerns (Maura, 2017). However, Ragged Island residents have demonstrated that they are resilient as attested to many remaining on the island to ride out several hurricanes over the years. Ragged Island has the potential of becoming a major player in the Bahamian economy. The government of The Bahamas since Hurricane Irma has opted to make Ragged Island a green island in order to mitigate against hurricanes or other natural disasters and make the island more sustainable

(Caribbean Journal, 2017). Ragged Island can serve as the model for future island developments in the archipelago. Further, in addition to maintaining a green economy, it is vital for the government to encourage and maintain a blue economy as well. Fishing is one of the economic mainstays of the island residents (myguidebahamas.com). By developing enabling mechanisms as outlined above, for the establishment of a vibrant "Blue Economy", utilizing local expertise and its proximity in the Great Bahama Banks (one of the country's richest fishing grounds), Ragged Island can and will be restored and be sustainable in the future.

References

Albury, P. (1975). *The story of The Bahamas.* London, ENG: MacMillan Caribbean.

Caribbean Journal Staff. (16 September, 2017). Bahamas vows to build a "new" Ragged Island. www.caribbeanjournal/2017/09/16/bahamas-vows-build-new-ragged-island.

Cartwright-Carroll, T. (2017). Opposition leader supports mandatory evacuation. *The Nassau Guardian.* Retrieved 15 August, 2018. www.thenassauguardian.com.

Craton, M., & Saunders, G.(1999). *A history of the Bahamian people: From aboriginal times to the end of slavery.* Vol. 1. Athens: University of Georgia Press.

Curry, C. (2017). *Freedom and resistance. A social history of black loyalists in The Bahamas.* Gainesville: University Press of Florida.

Erickson, M. O. (1987). *Great Inagua.* Garrison, NY: Cariole Press.

Ingraham, F. (2017). Embracing the benefit of the 'blue economy' insight@ tribunemedia.net pg. 9.

Islands of The Bahamas. (N/D). Our history. Remembering our past. Retrieved 17 February, 2020. https://www.bahamas.com/our-history

Islands of The Bahamas. (N/D). Ragged Island. Retrieved 17 February, 2020. www.bahamas.com/islands/ragged-island.

Kituyi, M. (20 January, 2014). Blue economy summit. United Nations Conference on Trade and Development. Retrieved 5 May, 2018. https://unctad.org/en/pages/newsdetails.aspx?OriginalVersionID=597

Lockhart, S. (29 May, 2018). Local organisation donates more than $18,000 to Ragged Island families. Retrieved 17 February, 2020. www.freeportnews.com/news/local-organisation-donates-18000-ragged-island-families

Maura, M. (13 September, 2017). PM: Early evacuation helped save a generation of Ragged Islanders. Retrieved 17 February, 2020. www.bahamas.gov.bs.

Minnis, J., & Blackwell, M. (2018). Living on islands: Tourism and quality of life on three islands Abaco, Bimini and Exuma. A case study. Unpublished paper.

Neely, W. (2019). *The greatest and deadliest hurricanes to impact The Bahamas.* Bloomington, IN: iUniverse.

Pauli, G. (2010). *The blue economy: 100 years, 100 innovations, 100 million jobs.* Internet Archive. Taos, New Mexico: Paradigm Pubns.

Russell, K. (13 December, 2017). Rebuilding Ragged Island to cost tens of millions. *The Tribune.* Retrieved 2 September, 2018. www.tribune242.com.

Saunders, G. (N/D). Exuma salt. https://www.exumamap.com/exuma-salt.htm

Senaratne, A. (2017). 'Nations". www.ips.lk/wp-content-uploads/2017/03/Nations_17June_Oceans-and-Sri-Lanka's-future.pdf.

Smith, S. (13 December, 2017). "Tens of millions" to rebuild Ragged Island. *The Nassau Guardian.* Retrieved 2 September, 2018. www.thenassuguardian.com.

Tinker, K. (2018). *Perspectives on Nassau and blockade running 1860–1865.* Bloomington, IN: Xlibris.

The Caribbean Journal. (September 16, 2017). Bahamas "back to business" after Irma. Retrieved 2 September, 2018. https://www.caribjournal.com/2017/09/13/bahamas-back-business-irma/

United Nations. (2012). The blue economy concept paper. Retrieved 17 February, 2020. www.sustainabledevelopment.un.org.

United Nations. (2015). The potential of the blue economy: Increasing long-term benefits of the sustainable use of marine resources for small island developing states and coastal least developed countries. Retrieved 3 September, 2018 https://sustainabledevelopment.un.org/content/documents/15434Blue_EconomyJun1.pdf

United Nations. (2017). Exploring the potential of the blue economy. Retrieved 3 September, 2018. www.un.org.

United Nations Environmental Program. (2015). The blue economy: Sharing success stories to inspire change. Retrieved 2 August, 2018. https://wedocs.unep.org/bitstream/handle/20.500.11822/9844/-Blue_economy_sharing_success_stories_to_inspire_change-2015blue_economy_sharing_success_stories.pdf.pdf?sequence=3&isAllowed=y

World-Wide Fund for Nature. (2015). All hands-on deck: Setting the course towards a sustainable blue economy. WWF Baltic Ecoregion Programme. https://wwwwwfse.cdn.triggerfish.cloud/uploads/2019/01/wwf-all-hands-on-deck-rapport-2015-15-6802.pdf

12 Climate change, tourism and sustainable development in The Bahamas

Adelle Thomas and Lisa Benjamin

Introduction

Small island developing states (SIDS) face several capacity constraints, including small economies that are highly dependent upon specific industries such as tourism. These states are also extremely vulnerable to the negative impacts of climate change. Rising sea levels, increases in atmospheric and oceanic temperatures, coastal erosion, changes in levels of precipitation and increased intensity of extreme events are all projected climate change hazards that will affect SIDS (Nurse et al., 2014). The loss of coral reefs and ocean acidification are already impacting the tourism and fishing industries in these states, and negatively affecting the livelihoods of many residents. Coastal erosion and sea level rise are leading to loss of territory, and extreme events are exposing the high vulnerability of coastally based industries such as tourism (Thomas, 2012). These negative trends are anticipated to intensify in the future as the global average temperature continues to increase. Climate change threatens the continued viability of tourism industries and resultantly the economic viability and development trajectories of SIDS.

The Bahamas, an archipelagic state that is both highly vulnerable to climate change as well as heavily dependent on tourism, is therefore likely to face several development challenges associated with these issues. In this chapter, the relationship between climate change and tourism is further detailed, focussing on implications for the industry in The Bahamas. Existing Bahamian policies on climate change are examined, including the National Policy on the Adaptation to Climate Change and the draft National Development Plan, to determine whether policies and plans to further integrate climate change into development planning should be undertaken.

Climate change and tourism: implications for the industry in The Bahamas

Tourism began to be developed in The Bahamas in the late 1800s and intensification of the industry began in the 1950s as a vehicle for economic development (Pattullo, 2005). Currently, tourism contributes more than half of national gross domestic product (GDP) and employment, placing the country as one of the most dependent on tourism for economic stability (WTTC, 2017). The Bahamian tourism industry is largely reliant on sun, sand and sea to attract millions of visitors to the country per year (Thomas, 2012). However, as the impacts of climate change begin to intensify, these valuable environmental characteristics that are at the heart of the industry may be significantly affected. As part of the Caribbean, The Bahamas is in one of the most vulnerable regions in the world to climate change (Nurse et al., 2014). The islands of The Bahamas are of extremely flat elevation with the majority of tourism-related infrastructure, including accommodation, airports and seaports, being near the coastline (Thomas, 2012). This exposes critical aspects of the industry to the impacts of climate change, sea level rise and effects of tropical storms. Indeed, in comparison to other islands in the region, The Bahamas is by far the most vulnerable to the effects of sea level rise (Rahmstorf, 2010). Sea level rise will result in inundation of land as well as altering the wide, sandy beaches that the tourism industry has capitalized upon. Additionally, high percentages of residents are also located near to the coast, making the workers that the industry relies upon also vulnerable to climate change hazards.

One of the key components of a tourism destination is the climate. The tourism climate index is a measure of key climatic variables that are important to tourism, including temperature, humidity, precipitation, sunshine and wind (Mieczkowski, 1985). The index ranges from -20 to 100, with higher scores indicating more attractive climates for tourists. Studies using this index that have included The Bahamas have found that the current high season for tourism in the nation, from December to April, scores over 80 in the index, meaning that the climate is attractive to tourists (Moore et al., 2009). Within the Caribbean, The Bahamas is ranked either first or second in climate attractiveness among all countries for these months. However, between June and September, the index score drops significantly to approximately 40 and the country falls to the last and second last place in the region for climate attractiveness. These months also correspond to the low season for tourism in The Bahamas. Thus, the index accurately recreates the seasonality of Bahamian tourism. When assessing the index and including projections of climate change, the results are alarming. When taking into account the impacts of climate change on important tourism climatic variables, the index score for The Bahamas drops by more than 20 points. The high season scores approximately 60 in the index, a significant drop but still in the range of acceptability. However, scores for the low season are extremely unattractive for tourism, meaning that the country may likely see a significant decline in tourism during these months. Additionally, while the index scores for The Bahamas decrease due to climate change, scores for the key markets that tourists originate from, including North America and Europe, increase (Moore et al., 2009). This means that foreign tourists will have more attractive climate conditions in their home countries than in tropical regions such as The Bahamas. This is expected to result in significant changes to the global flow of tourists, culminating in increased domestic tourism in North America and Europe and decreased international tourism to increasingly hotter tropical regions.

Another significant impact of climate change for tourism is increased oceanic temperatures. Higher temperatures of the ocean result in bleaching of coral. Coral reefs are currently a major attraction for tourists to The Bahamas interested in scuba diving and snorkelling. Within the Caribbean, there have already been several significant coral bleaching events. In The Bahamas in particular, there have been reports of mass bleaching of coral reefs, resulting in loss of the vibrant colours and colourful fish that attract divers (Baker et al., 2008). Just as global atmospheric temperatures continue to rise, so too will oceanic temperatures, resulting in continued mass bleaching of corals, slowing or eliminating future coral growth patterns, detrimentally affecting biodiversity of marine organisms and having resultant impacts on this important sector of tourism.

The extreme hurricanes in 2017 have highlighted the severe implications of tropical storms for the Caribbean region. As an archipelagic nation, The Bahamas is on average affected by a hurricane in some way every three years and suffers direct contact every 12 years (Neely, 2006). Hurricanes such as Frances and Jeanne in 2004 caused significant devastation to numerous tourism establishments in Grand Bahama, resulting in permanent closure of key tourism businesses and a constriction of the economy for the island (Thomas et al., 2015). Hurricane Matthew in 2016 had similar effects for Grand Bahama and called into question the continued viability of depending on large, foreign-owned tourism establishments for economic stability. Hurricanes also affect travel with tourists being advised to leave destinations early and either reschedule or cancel planned trips.

The record-breaking Hurricane Dorian in 2019 tragically highlighted the threat that climate change poses for The Bahamas. The hurricane devastated the islands of Grand Bahama and Abaco, resulting in over 60 deaths, impacts on approximately 30,000 people and losses and damages of over US$3.4 billion (ECLAC, 2019). Tourism was particularly affected, with damages of approximately US$530 million and losses of US$325 million. While the storm directly affected the two most northern islands of the archipelago, tourism in the rest of the nation was also negatively impacted with reduced numbers of visitors. The Government of The Bahamas made significant efforts to publicize to the world that most islands were open for tourism, and visiting the nation would greatly assist the country in recovering from the storm (Peltz, 2019). Hurricane Dorian underscored the extreme risk that hurricanes pose to tourism in The Bahamas and that these storms affect tourism across the nation and not just the particular islands that may be directly impacted.

In an era of climate change, hurricanes are expected to increase in intensity (Nurse et al., 2014). Increased intensity of hurricanes means higher wind speeds, which result in an exponential increase in damages. Increased sea levels combined with more intense hurricanes will also result in higher storm surges and an increase in associated damages. Thus, the tourism industry will likely see increased impacts from hurricanes in future years.

Climate change and development: adaptation and development policies and regulations in The Bahamas

The impacts of climate change are taking a toll on the development trajectories on Caribbean SIDS, including The Bahamas. The annual average losses due to adverse impacts of climate change as a percentage of GDP are much higher in SIDS compared to global averages. The cost of inaction on climate change in the Caribbean region is estimated to amount to over US$22 billion by 2050, accounting for approximately 10% of the entire region's economy (UN-OHRLLS, 2015).

High coastal exposure of populations in these states is anticipated to further exacerbate average annual losses due to tropical cyclone activity. The Bahamas, Montserrat and Dominica are anticipated to have the highest relative risk in the region from storm surge (UN-OHRLLS, 2015). The Caribbean region suffers from more natural disasters per square metre than the rest of the world (Ruprah et al., 2014). The costs of these extreme events are also higher than global averages, and therefore more difficult for smaller economies to absorb. The damages caused by Hurricane Joaquin in The Bahamas in 2015 were estimated to be in the hundreds of millions, and combined with the damage from Hurricane Matthew in 2016, aggregated potential losses are estimated to reach almost US$800 million or approximately 40% of the nation's annual budget, and 9% of GDP (Virgil, 2017). While The Bahamas was largely spared excessive damage in the 2017 Atlantic hurricane season, the country is assisting regional neighbours to cope with climate-induced displacement, and loss and damages in the Caribbean from both Hurricanes Irma and Maria will be severe. Given the high debt-to-GDP ratios of SIDS, including The Bahamas, these events are putting excessive strain on already overstretched public budgets.

These extreme events are causing increased impacts on public safety, livelihoods, public health and infrastructure (Sabin Centre, 2014). The Caribbean region, including The Bahamas, is therefore experiencing increased incidents of loss and damage due to climate change, and these events are having social as well as economic impacts (Thomas and Benjamin, 2017a). At the same time, SIDS are highly vulnerable due to their small size, remoteness and narrow resource bases. Combined with ongoing biodiversity loss and climate change impacts, these events are putting additional strain on the economies and public budgets of these states (UN-OHRLLS, 2015). SIDS are having to borrow in order to address loss of earning resulting from disasters, as well as for investment in disaster relief and reconstruction (UN-OHRLLS, 2015). As Lyster (2015) notes, climate change is leading to uncompensated damages in developing countries, macroeconomic strains such as depleted tax bases, declining reserves and credit ratings, and the diversion of capital from other social programmes towards post-disaster efforts. Infrastructural improvements and adaptation activities to accommodate higher sea levels are expensive, and SIDS are struggling to raise finance for adaptation and investment in public infrastructure development (UN-OHRLLS, 2015). Therefore, the impacts of climate change are preventing future investment in climate change adaptation efforts as well as other developmental priorities such as poverty reduction, health and education (Benjamin and Haynes, 2018). Policies and mechanisms to address loss and damage, including climate-induced migration and displacement, are both necessary but largely absent in SIDS (Thomas and Benjamin, 2017a, 2017b).

There have been a number of regional policy initiatives targeting sustainable development in SIDS. These include the Barbados Programme of Action for the Sustainable Development of SIDS in 1994 (BPoA), the Mauritius Strategy for the Further Implementation for the Programme of Action for the Sustainable Development of SIDS in 2005 (MSI), as well as the SIDS Accelerated Modalities of Action (SAMOA Pathway) in 2015. These declarations all recognize that progress on sustainable development within SIDS has been hampered by the adverse impacts of climate change. The Caribbean Community Climate Change Centre (CCCCC) is the regional body responsible for coordinating the region's response to climate change, and has initiated a number of projects on mainstreaming climate change into national policy agendas and actions.

At a domestic level, The Bahamas developed a National Policy for the Adaptation to Climate Change (NPACC) in 2005. The policy recognizes the special vulnerability of the country due to its extended coastlines, low-lying islands with largely coastal settlements, location in the Atlantic hurricane belt, and archipelagic make up (BEST, 2005). The NPACC also recognizes the limited human and economic resources available to the country to combat climate change (BEST, 2005). In addition, the policy recognizes that the country's small size and heavy reliance on tourism, including coastal development, makes it highly susceptible to fluctuations in the tourism market. The policy contains several directives, including the integration of climate change adaptation into national policies, plans, projects and national budgetary processes, as well as adequate physical and socio-economic planning which caters for the impacts of climate change. The NPACC has a section specifically dedicated to tourism and contemplates potential damage to the tourism industry from climate change, including destruction of coastal properties and natural resources attractive to tourists such as coral reefs and beaches, higher temperatures and less benign weather. Policy directives aimed to mitigate these impacts include research as the basis of sound decision-making, environmental impact assessments and appropriate physical planning guidelines, including coastal setbacks and dune protection for tourism developments, which integrate climate change considerations.

Most of these policy directives included in the NPACC have not been implemented, as recognized by the draft National Development Plan (NDP) (NDP, 2016). The NDP also recognizes the significant environmental challenges facing the country, including lack of public infrastructure planning, lack of geographic information systems (GIS) and hazard planning, and a lack of preparedness for climate change. Goal 11 of the NDP includes integrating disaster risk reduction into planning, sustainable management of natural resources and positioning the country as a leader in climate change adaptation research. The NDP envisions modern public infrastructure built to withstand climate change, accompanied by a long-term capital investment plan and asset inventory, as well as the establishment of a Climate Change Task Force and an Integrated National Land Use Plan, which incorporates better land use planning and disaster risk reduction.

While national policies on climate change adaptation and incorporation of climate change into the draft NDP are positive steps, the NPACC is outdated and lacks reference to loss and damage or climate-induced displacement and migration which are important issues related to climate change. Additionally, the draft NDP has yet to be implemented. While the country has a Planning and Subdivision Act 2010, it is largely unenforced (Benjamin and Thomas, 2019). As a result, the country lacks comprehensive planning on climate change adaptation, despite being subject to current and future adverse impacts on climate change, including in the tourism sector. However, lack of policies and mechanisms on adverse climate change impacts, including loss and damage and climate-induced displacement and migration, is not unusual in the region (Thomas and Benjamin, 2017a, 2017b).

Given the heavy reliance of The Bahamas on tourism, it is not surprising that successive governments are reluctant to focus on adaptation and implement strategies such as enforcing restrictions on coastal development which would reduce vulnerability to climate change (Benjamin and Thomas, 2019). Coastal development is one of the primary income generators for the country, and therefore, this dichotomy has engendered conflicting approaches to the management of coastal resources. Despite the negative impacts and excessive costs of climate change, the development of consistent and effective coastal regulation and governance has been identified as problematic both within the region, and in The Bahamas in particular (Benjamin and Thomas, 2019, 2017b). Poor development choices are exacerbating vulnerability of coastal areas in the region to climate change (Mycoo and Donovan, 2017). Poor land use practices, outdated land registration systems, weak enforcement of climate change adaptation policies, combined with "profound deficits in governance and infrastructure" are all resulting in incomplete regulation (Mycoo and Donovan, 2017). These deficits are partly due to spatial constraints, but also due to development pressures accountable largely to the tourism industry. This dichotomy has led to a dissonance in the political economy of states such as The Bahamas, which is facing extreme impacts from climate change, and yet is highly dependent upon coastal development (Benjamin and Thomas, 2019, 2017a). Improved policy interventions on climate change, as envisioned by the draft NDP, are therefore necessary to try to smooth over these hurdles to sustainable development.

Conclusion

This chapter provided an overview of the impacts of climate change for Caribbean SIDS with a focus on The Bahamas, how these impacts may affect the tourism industry in the future and the adequacy of current climate change adaptation and development plans. Climate hazards, sea level rise, rising atmospheric and oceanic temperatures and increased intensity of hurricanes threaten the continued success of the tourism industry for The Bahamas. Critical infrastructure, marine ecosystems and the attractive climate that are all important for the industry are at risk of incurring significant loss and damage. Existing impacts of climate change, including the high costs of responding to extreme events such as hurricanes, place a financial burden on SIDS such as The Bahamas and divert funds that could be allocated to sustainable development.

National policies, the NPACC and NDP, include discussion of climate change impacts and the need to properly adapt to upcoming challenges. However, the lack of implementation of these policies as well as the absence of key issues related to climate change highlight the deficiency of comprehensive planning to address current and future impacts of climate change. This lack of planning places the country at high risk, particularly the tourism industry on which the country is financially dependent. Improved policy interventions on climate change, a focus on sustainable development and a long-term approach to tourism planning are necessary to prevent significant climate change impacts for The Bahamas.

References

Baker, A., Glynn, P. and Riegl, B. (2008). Climate change and coral reef bleaching: An ecological assessment of long-term impacts, recovery trends and future outlook. *Estuarine, Coastal and Shelf Science* 80(4): 435–471.

Benjamin, L. and Haynes, R. (2018). Climate change and human rights in the Commonwealth Caribbean: Case studies of The Bahamas and Trinidad & Tobago. In S. Jodoin, S. Duyck and A. Johl, eds. *Routledge handbook of human rights and climate governance*. Routledge.

Benjamin, L. and Thomas, A. (2019). Political economy of coastal development in the Caribbean: The case study of The Bahamas. In P. Harris, ed. *Climate change and ocean governance*. Cambridge, England: Cambridge University Press.

BEST. (2005). National policy for the adaptation to climate change. Available at: http://www.best.gov.bs/Documents/ClimateChangePolicy.pdf.

ECLAC. (2019) Assessment of the effects and impacts of Hurricane Dorian in the Bahamas. Executive summary. Available at: https://www.iadb.org/en/damages-and-other-impacts-bahamas-hurricane-dorian-estimated-34-billion-report.

Lyster, R. (2015). A fossil fuel-funded climate disaster response fund under the warsaw international mechanism for loss and damage associated with climate change impacts. *Transnational Environmental Law* 6(1): 125–151.

Mieczkowski, Z. (1985). The tourism climatic index: A method of evaluating world climates for tourism. *Canadian Geographer* 29: 220–233.

Moore, W., Lewis-Bynoe, D. and Howard, S. (2009). Climate change and tourism features in the Caribbean. MPRA Paper No. 2140. Munich Personal RePEC Archive.

Mycoo, M. and Donovan, M.G. (2017). *A blue urban agenda: Adapting to climate change in the coastal cities of Caribbean and Pacific small island developing states.* New York and Washington, DC: IDB Monograph. doi: 10.18235/0000690.

NDP. (2016). Draft national development plan. Available at: http://www.vision2040 bahamas.org.

Nurse, L.A., McLean, R.F., Agard, J., Briguglio, L.P., Duvat-Magnan, V., Pelesikoti, N., Tompkins, E. and Webb, A. (2014). Small islands. In V.R. Barros, C.B. Field, D.J. Dokken, M.D. Mastrandrea, K.J. Mach, T.E. Bilir, M. Chatterjee, K.L. Ebi, Y.O. Estrada, R.C. Genova, B. Girma, E.S. Kissel, A.N. Levy, S. MacCracken, P.R. Mastrandrea, and L.L. White, eds. *Climate change 2014: Impacts, adaptation, and vulnerability. Part B: Regional aspects. Contribution of working group II to the fifth assessment report of the intergovernmental panel on climate change.* Cambridge, UK and New York, NY: Cambridge University Press, pp. 1613–1654.

Pattullo, P. (2005). *Last resorts: The cost of tourism in the Caribbean.* New York, NY: NYU Press.

Peltz, J. (2019). In Dorian's wake, Bahamas appeals for climate action at UN. Available at: https://apnews.com/443f91abfe004209a42739fc2342915e

Rahmstorf, S. (2010). A new view on sea level rise. *Nature Reports Climate Change* 1: 44–45.

Ruprah, I., Melgarejo, K. and Sierra, R. (2014). *Is there a Caribbean Sclerosis? Stagnating Economic Growth in the Caribbean.* Washington, DC: Inter-American Development Bank Monograph; 178.

Sabin Centre for Climate Change Law. (2014). Climate change and forced displacement: Calling for an international dialogue on the legal rights of persons displaced by climate change and corresponding obligations of national governments. Available at: http://wordpress.ei.columbia.edu/climate-change-law/files/2016/10/climate_change_and_forced_displacement.pdf.

Thomas, A. (2012). *An integrated view: Multiple stressors and small tourism enterprises in The Bahamas.* New Brunswick, NJ: Rutgers University; 236.

Thomas, A. and Benjamin, L. (2017a). Management of loss and damage in small island developing states: Implications for a 1.5C or warmer world. *Regional Environmental Change*, 1–10. doi: 10.1007/s10113-017-1184-7.

Thomas, A. and Benjamin, L. (2017b). Policies and mechanisms to address climate-induced migration and displacement in Pacific and Caribbean small island developing states. *International Journal of Climate Change Strategies and Management.* doi: 10.1108/IJCCSM-03-2017-0055.

Thomas, A., Benjamin, L. and McNamarah, C. (2015). A situational analysis of the Bahamian environment. State of the Nation Report. Vision 2040 of The Bahamas. http://www.vision2040bahamas.org/media/uploads/Draft__National_Development_Plan_01.12.2016_for_public_release.pdf

UN-OHRLLS. (2015). Small Island developing states in Numbers. Climate Change Edition 2015. Available at: https://unohrlls.org/custom-content/uploads/2015/12/SIDS-IN-NUMBERS-CLIMATE-CHANGE-EDITION_2015.pdf.

Virgil, K. (2017). Homes still unrepaired after hurricanes in 2016 and 2015. The Tribune, 30 May 2017. Available at: http://www.tribune242.com/news/2017/may/30/homes-still-unrepaired-after-hurricanes-in-2016.

WTTC. (2017). WTTC data gateway. World Travel & Tourism Council. Available at: https://www.wttc.org/datagateway.

13 Marijuana Agro-Tourism Habitat

Sophia Rolle

Research objectives

The major objectives of this study were to show how a Marijuana Agro-Tourism Habitat, dubbed MATH, can serve as a viable sustainable tourism option.

Another intention of this research was to determine the Meta-knowledge of Millennials regarding the UN sustainable development goals (SDGs) and their global impacts on The Bahamas. Many small island developing states (SIDS), including The Bahamas, were mandated by the UN to engage the 17 SDGs and the 169 indicators utilizing a myriad of creative initiatives. Consequently, the development of a MATH on one of the islands in The Bahamas is felt to be an easy fit for the overarching SDG concepts.

The research was also intended to demonstrate that the growth and production of marijuana on a remote island in The Bahamas could readily be achieved by utilizing the existing, very successful and highly functional tourism/ecotourism marketing and distribution channels. These channels employ a multi-destination approach to sell tourism products which range from mass tourism to adventure tourism, to cultural and heritage tourism and in recent years, to sustainable tourism.

Methodology

A convenient non-probability sampling technique was employed in this research. Participants were selected based on convenient accessibility and proximity to the researcher in New Providence, Bahamas, and as previously stated, the research sought millennials' views on the production or growth of marijuana as a market-driven activity linked to tourism and marketed as Agro-Tourism.

A quantitative survey instrument was used to collect data for this study and approximately 120 millennials were surveyed. The purpose of the study was first to find out millennials knowledge of the concepts of sustainability and the SDGs; second to determine millennials thinking about the SDGs as an economic growth and development in The Bahamas; third to introduce the concept of marijuana growth as an economic vehicle for SIDS such as The Bahamas; and finally to determine millennials attitudes towards marijuana growth on one of the remote Out Islands in The Bahamas as an economic vehicle and a means of diversifying the tourism industry.

Individuals between the ages of twenty-five and thirty-five (25 and 35) were the target subjects of the study. The survey questionnaire consisted of five broad sections. They included definitions of frequently used concepts such as SIDS and Agro-Tourism; a demographic section, a section on attitudes towards marijuana as a sustainable development tool and a section on marijuana as a sustainable industry in The Bahamas were represented on the survey instrument.

The instrument was distributed over a two weeks' span. Approximately one hundred (100) persons responded to the survey. The instrument consisted of 24 questions. A consent form was affixed to the front of the instrument, and this explained the reason for the research study and solicited the individual's willingness to participate in the research.

Major findings

Results from the survey revealed that of 120 millennials surveyed, 88 of them or 56.17% were females and 29.21% males. Some 46.06% of all respondents were between the age of 25 and 27. The fewest of the responses came from millennials between the age of 28 and 31, who represented 16.81%. 22.46% of the respondents were between the age of 31 and 35 years. Figure 13.1 reveals that 74% of all respondents knew about the concept of sustainability.

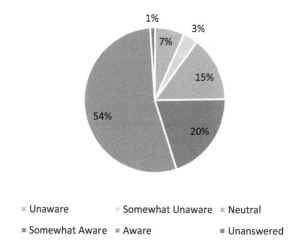

Figure 13.1 Meaning of sustainability by millennials.

The researcher was very careful not to seek answers about legalizing marijuana for the traditional uses of recreation and medicine. Therefore, some 50% of the survey questions sought answers about marijuana as a sustainability tool, creation of an agro tourism habitat on a remote island in The Bahamas or on the possible economic benefits to be derived from the development of this sustainable form of tourism development.

Respondents were asked if they were aware of the SDGs. Figure 13.2 revealed that when combined, some 48% of all respondents were somewhat or completely aware of the SDGs.

An encouraging number of respondents (Figure 13.3), 25.84%, were at least aware of the terminology SIDS (Small Island Developing States) and 42.69% were aware of the terminology Agro-Tourism. A pleasant surprise, especially seeking answers from this demographic, was their awareness of the fact that The Bahamas was considered SIDS. That awareness has implications for how they would potentially receive the suggestions of the creation of a MATH on one of the out islands. It also has implications for their awareness of the potential financial benefits to be derived for the country from such a development.

A striking 44% of millennials (Figure 13.4) indicated that they were at least aware The Bahamas was considered SIDS.

Agro-Tourism as a means of diversifying the tourism industry in The Bahamas was one of the key questions asked of the participants in the survey. We first had to determine if this demographic at least knew of the terminology Agro-Tourism.

Figure 13.5 shows us clearly that 38% of all respondents were aware, 27% were somewhat aware and some 15% were not aware of the concept.

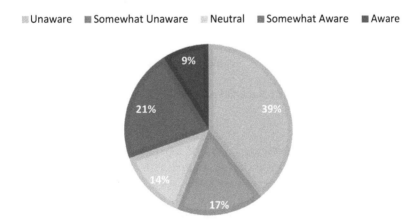

Figure 13.2 Awareness of the United Nations Sustainable Development Goals.

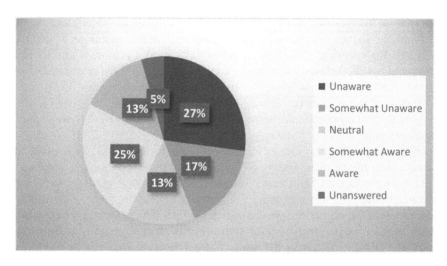

Figure 13.3 Awareness of concept of SIDS.

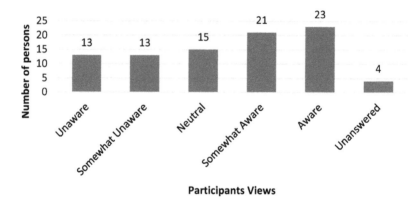

Figure 13.4 Awareness of The Bahamas as a SIDS.

When asked about the legalization of marijuana for the sole purpose of diversifying the tourism industry, Figure 13.6 shows us that 31.46% of the respondents strongly agreed with this suggestion, 25.84% agreed and 17.97% remained neutral on the answer. Only 12.35% strongly disagreed with the notion that growth of marijuana can in fact diversify the Bahamian economy.

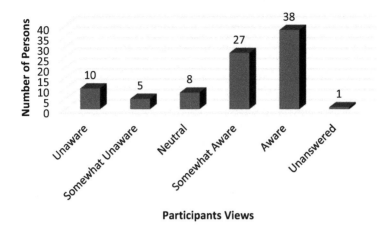

Figure 13.5 Meaning of Agro-Tourism.

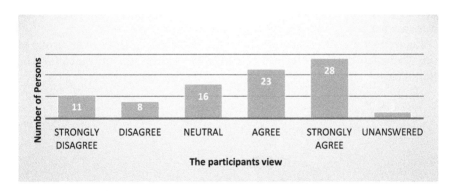

Figure 13.6 Support to producing marijuana.

Neighbouring countries in the Caribbean as well as the United States of America and even as far as Canada have all realized significant monetary gains from either the legalization of marijuana or the production of same. According to the Dangerous Drugs Act of Jamaica (2015), possession of marijuana under two ounces has been decriminalized for personal use. With this step, then came other opportunities for Jamaica to make a profit from this new industry, exporting the first marijuana oil extract product to Canada in 2018 and setting the path for more Caribbean countries to follow in exporting the soft drug for a profit. Could The Bahamas, much like Jamaica, also capitalize on this new industry?

According to the University of Florida IFAS Extension website, the Agro-Tourism industry in the United States generated $704 million in 2012. The legalized marijuana industry in America in the state of California alone has generated $2.75 million dollars to date according to the Forbes online report of 2018.

One of the questions posed in this study was if The Bahamas began to grow marijuana for production purposes, would it be sustainable and specifically, can it enhance the overall GDP of the country. Figure 13.7 indicates that some 40% of the respondents agreed and 20% strongly agreed that the production of this plant would enhance the GDP. While many remained neutral (29%) only 11% either disagreed or strongly disagreed with this notion.

To support this question, we wanted to find out if the marijuana plant in and of itself should be considered an agricultural crop and as such, given the same attention as other agricultural crops in the country. It really was not surprising that this demographic of Bahamians was resolute in their answers to this question. Figure 13.8 shows us just what they thought of this suggestion. The diagram shows us that some 48% of all respondents either agreed or strongly agreed with the suggestion of the country growing marijuana as an agricultural crop. 23% remained neutral, while 18% of them were diametrically opposed to its growth in the country.

Figure 13.9 show us that when surveyed, millennials, as the focus group of this study, felt that the creation of a MATH was a sustainable idea for The Bahamas.

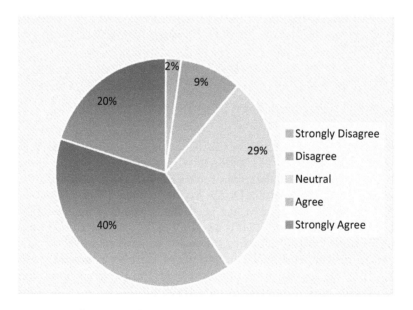

Figure 13.7 Marijuana growing as a toll for increased GDP.

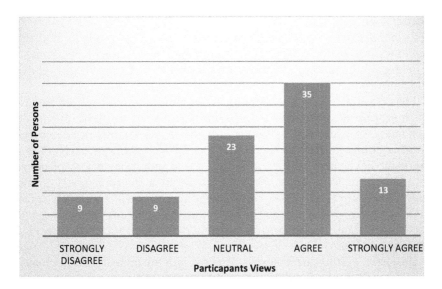

Figure 13.8 Growing marijuana as an agricultural crop.

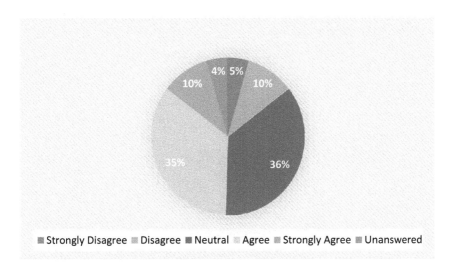

Figure 13.9 A sustainable Marijuana Agro-Tourism Habitat.

In gaging the barometer of how respondents felt about Bahamian owner-ship and foreign investment in the industry, 47.19% of all participants in the survey felt that such an industry should be all Bahamian-owned. Some 87% of all respondents indicated that in the first instance, Bahamians should be the principal investors. This supports the idea of individual entrepreneurs participating in the industry but working together co-operatively for the greater good.

Respondents were also asked about the selection of products that they would want to see being packaged from the growth of marijuana. Some 25 different products were identified. Products such as hemp oil, tea, edibles and hair products were the top products identified.

The creation of jobs must be one of the major factors to be considered when proposing such a development on one of the Family Islands in The Bahamas. As is seen throughout the literature and demonstrated in neighbouring countries, the production or sale of marijuana or derivatives of the plant have the potential to create whole industries which of course translates into jobs. To support the model of a micro industry and as shown in Figure 13.10, 42% of respondents agreed and 25% strongly agreed that such a move would be in the best interest of persons engaged to work on such an island. Less than 10% of participants felt that it would have no economic value.

University settings have always been the hub for innovation and creativity. Research on the feasibility of a MATH should be engaged at the local universities particularly if there are national implications. It is refreshing then to note that of all the millennials surveyed, 48% indicated that they would attend the University of The Bahamas or the Bahamas Agriculture and Marine Sciences Institute if programmes on marijuana cultivation were available at these institutions.

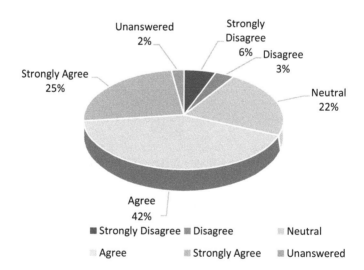

Figure 13.10 Boosting economy of island due to Marijuana Agro-Tourism Habitat.

Discussion and practical implications

Agro-Tourism Habitats

Considering the difficulties with establishing an industry of this magnitude, we can now begin to compare the current data to similar Agro-Tourism Habitats to discern the feasibility of a marijuana habitat on a remote island in The Bahamas. Agro-Tourism is not a new concept to the Caribbean. What is Agro-Tourism? According to Kunasekaran, Ramachandran, Yacob and Shib (2011), Agro-Tourism is a type of rural tourism that allows the tourist to visit a farm and experience a farmer's daily life. Focusing on an Agro-Tourism product where marijuana is concerned can provide a larger work force for this new export industry in The Bahamas. Agro-Tourism will also allow the island and the farmers to enjoy greater economic benefits and retain the next generation of the farming community in these rural areas (Kunasekaran et al, 2011).

Besides developing the MATH to create a diverse tourism industry for The Bahamas, such a habitat on one of the islands would create a robust micro industrial corporation that can quite possibly complement the existing, even though struggling, tourism-based economy that is present on many of the smaller islands. Entrepreneurial opportunities can easily be established using a co-operative methodology that is holistic in its approach to industry development, creates a working model where several small businesspersons can participate, and most importantly, add significantly to the overall gross domestic product for The Bahamas. This model will realize very little leakage, because most of the money generated will stay in the local economy with the Bahamians working there.

The Caribbean Tourism Organization's (2010) tourism bulletin aimed at educating children across the Caribbean called "Making Waves" speaks about engaging youth in agro-tourism career opportunities with examples that span across the region. In the bulletin the different types of tourism touched upon are farm-based tourism, health and wellness tourism, community tourism, culinary tourism, agro-heritage tourism and agro-trade tourism. It describes native fruits and farms, and the activities that you can expect to engage in when you arrive in these places. These activities range from taking care of farm animals, harvesting crops, planting, cooking delicious meals and most importantly engaging in an educational experience about that communities' culture and heritage surrounding the chosen crops or animals in these habitats.

Comparing the CTO's model to a Marijuana habitat in The Bahamas, some of the activities we can expect to recreate would be planting, harvesting and engaging with locals in the act of doing similar kinds of duties. Missing factors will be the linking of this crop to Bahamian heritage or culture and a lack of historical significance to the people who produce this crop.

Environmental

Quite a few implications can be derived from the development of a Marijuana Agro-Tourism Habitat on a Family Island in The Bahamas. From a sustainable development perspective, one must consider the environmental impact. Two main areas of concern are water and energy consumption. In review of the Energy Use in the Colorado Cannabis Industry 2018 annual report, electricity and water consumption were analysed. Of the 1,115 thousand megawatts of electricity produced in the state of Colorado in 2016, only 54,418 thousand megawatts or roughly 2% of the overall amount of this electricity generated was used to process the dried flower product, a derivative of the marijuana plant. Concomitantly, water consumption was even smaller. The marijuana industry only used some 523 AF (Acre-Feet) of water in its growing process. This represented less than half of a percent in the overall 5.3 million AF used by Coloradans in 2016. This is a noteworthy submission because it clearly demonstrates that despite popular belief, the marijuana industry is sustainable and in fact is seen as industry leaders in water efficiency when compared to other agricultural crops.

According to the Water Resources Assessment of The Bahamas (2004), "Water availability is so low that it is considered scarce according to the United Nations criteria". The Water Resource Assessment of The Bahamas (2004) further indicated that the amount of daily available water is 9.63 million gallons; however, the daily demand was 10.62 million gallons. It is reasonable to expect that these demand and supply figures have increased over the years. Given these realities however, one might automatically assume that introducing a marijuana production farm on any island would drain the already limited resources. However, the suggestions are on developing a sustainable water system that draws on the natural production of water and perhaps the use of a Reverse Osmosis Water Treatment Plant that is powered by wind or solar energy. Keep in mind also that the focus will be on a hydroponic growing system that is contained and managed by experienced agriculturalists. Industry experts are also now saying that one of the best ways in the future to reduce overall energy consumption in growing agricultural crops that can potentially require high electricity consumption is to engage in regenerative farming techniques and hyper-efficient, multi-tiered greenhouses. Regenerative agriculture is an approach to agriculture that focuses on improving and revitalizing the soil health during the growing process. Utilization of a combination of these new industry benchmarks and some tried and tested farming methodologies best suited for island farming can potentially yield the results local farmers would be aiming for.

Social impact

Another aspect of sustainability also deals with the social climate of the country. A big part of social understanding is also delegitimizing the public's view that illegal sales are more profitable in the short term. According to the CARICOM's analysis,

> Facing high returns for investment in drug trade, the opportunity costs of legal entrepreneurship, with more limited, long run profits are disadvantaged. As a consequence, in many poor areas of the region, children and young people who have the dream of escaping poverty do not see education and entrepreneurship as a major avenue in their upward mobility career, (those elements being the main catalysts for endogenous development of Caribbean societies), but as a mere loss of a time that would be more profitably spent in drug business in the short run.
>
> (Antoine, 2018)

However, through a MATH initiative, the link between education and entrepreneurship can be established. The other social concerns articulated by CARICOM relating to illegal marijuana use, loss of parents due to incarceration and so on are not intended to be a part of the MATH model.

Economic impact

Several factors are considered when examining economic implications of such a facility in The Bahamas. Though there are differing views for the most part, the literature is conclusive when stating that if done correctly, a legitimized marijuana market can uproot the black market and produce a safer environment for the host community as well as the purchaser. In the CARICOM analysis (2018), there is a marked difference in the model graphs showcasing the market for marijuana sold illegally as well as decriminalized marijuana where the supply is still illegal, but the possession is not an arresting offence. The market seemed to improve where possession was decriminalized versus something the buyer could potentially go to jail for. The analysis further postulates that the cost of illegal marijuana depends on varying factors that increase the price exponentially. A few of the listed causes were the risk of incarceration to those willing to work the supply chain in an environment where the merchandise is illegal, the inherent danger in dealing with a criminal element, as well as the inherent risk the dealer is taking to sell this product to you.

Conclusion

It's easy to juxtapose or compare marijuana production with overuse, overdosing and illegal activities. It is also easy to dismiss the notion that creating a marijuana industry in The Bahamas can inherently go against the "Christian" belief system of the country. It is further easy to suggest that creation of such an industry in The Bahamas may well enhance or influence for some what is an already robust drug trade and illicit activities brought about by the country's gateway status for the transhipment of drugs into the United States. All these concerns are legitimate and have some degree of merit depending on who is asked. However, if The Bahamas is to remain competitive economically, and make some major inroads in diversifying its economy, then at minimum, the conversation must begin with respect to how that will be achieved.

It was important to hear from the next generation of policy makers in country. The Millennials are that group. They represent different views of the way forward and are more exposed to what is presently the apparent norm in other parts of the world. It was not surprising the results that were generated from the questionnaire on the development of a Marijuana Agro-Tourism Habitat on a Family/Out Island in The Bahamas. An overwhelming positive response was given to creating what some term a mix of a traditional tourism with that of a revolutionary production marijuana farm. This will present for The Bahamas, an opportunity to not only diversify the tourism industry and introduce an out-of-the-box experience for visitors to the selected island, but also become one of the first of its kind habitat found anywhere else in the Caribbean. Undoubtedly, a MATH has the potential of contributing significantly to the overall GDP as well as creating several new entrepreneurs in the country.

References

Antoine, R. M. (n.d.). Waiting to Exhale – Safeguarding Our Future through Responsible Socio-legal Policy on Marijuana. Retrieved on 09, March 2018. https://caricom.org/documents/16434/marijuana_report_final_3_aug_18.pdf.

Government of Jamaica. (2015, March 20). Amendment to the Dangerous Drugs Act. Retrieved on 10, May 2018 https://www.japarliament.gov.jm/attachments/339_The%20Dangerous%20Drug%20bill%202015.pdf

Govt to Consider CARICOM Findings on Medical Marijuana. (n.d.). Retrieved on 14, June 2018 http://www.tribune242.com/news/2018/jun/15/govt-to-consider-caricom-findings-on-medical/ for Dr. Duane Sands.

Kunasekaran, P., Ramachandran, S., Yacob, M. & Shuib, A. (2011). Development of Farmers' Perception Scale on Agro Tourism in Cameron Highlands, Malaysia. World Applied Sciences Journal. 12. 10–18.

U. (n.d.). Water Resources Assessment of The Bahamas (2004). Retrieved on 19, July 2018. https://www.sam.usace.army.mil/Portals/46/docs/military/engineering/docs/WRA/Bahamas/BAHAMAS1WRA.pdf

Part IV

Development, governance, sustainability

A look at hurricanes

14 Sustaining tourism after a hurricane

Neil Sealey

In so far as tourism is by its nature already integrated into much of the economic and social fabric of The Bahamas, dealing with the impact of a hurricane disaster such as caused by the recent Dorian (2019), much of what applies to tourism will in fact be partly covered by existing protocols. This includes early evacuation and securing the premises, bearing in mind that The Bahamas has experienced many hurricanes in the past. Nevertheless, although this might seem a simple answer, the reality is that under such stressful circumstances much can be overlooked or ignored, particularly if the hurricane is stronger than expected or varies in its projected path. In the case of Dorian, the impact of a category five hurricane on a major settlement was unprecedented (CEDEMA, 2019).

Tourism workers are of course personally affected, and there is also the potential for employees to abandon work to ensure their property and family will be safe. Although these days there is excellent forecasting and advance warning of a potential hurricane strike, the fact remains that confirmation of exactly which communities and tourist facilities will be hit may not be apparent until one or two days before landfall. For this reason, there should be clear guidelines as to what should be done to safeguard the tourists and the facilities they use. For tourism to be sustainable, tourists should be confident that their safety is ensured, and future tourists will need to be able to verify which services are available. After Dorian the foreign media gave the impression that the whole country had been devastated and it took several months for patrons to resume their visits (BBC News, 2019; France 24, 2019). It should be borne in mind that many potential tourists are not familiar with the geography of the wider Caribbean region, or the multiple islands and destinations within the Bahamian archipelago. Unambiguous and prompt communication, especially to the foreign press and TV, is essential to maintain the industry. New Providence, with the capital city of Nassau, is the prime tourist destination and was unaffected by the damage to Abaco and Grand Bahama, yet this was not widely perceived. On Long Island, over 200 miles south of the affected islands, it has been reported that vacation rentals suffered much lower bookings for at least six months after Dorian (Kemp, 2020).

On islands that are directly impacted by a hurricane, such as Abaco and Grand Bahama by Dorian, there is a crucial need for services to be restored as quickly as possible. Perhaps most important is communications, clearly because advice and knowledge are paramount at such a difficult time. While cell phones may be secure from property damage by being contained on the person, they soon need recharging, and inevitably the power will be off, often for protracted periods. Four months after Dorian hit Abaco, power was still off in Treasure Cay, a major settlement for second homeowners and tourists alike (Rolle, 2019b). In Nassau after Hurricane Matthew (2016) the power was off for at least two weeks in many neighbourhoods, but the telephone landlines were working (Galanis, 2016). As landlines, with some forethought, can be made disaster proof, it would be prudent to have secure lines in shelters, clinics, public buildings and any other structures built according to the national building code. It was notable in Abaco that although the media focused on devastated shanty towns, strongly built buildings survived and became the centre for post-hurricane operations. Nevertheless, it is important to restore power as quickly as possible, and in heavy tourist areas an emergency power distribution system would be a great asset. Even though power might not be restored island-wide due to security issues with downed power lines, an emergency system would ensure that surviving buildings had power and could be a focus for stranded tourists and eventual evacuation. In this situation a solar powered system would be ideal, as has already been constructed on Ragged Island to withstand category 5 hurricane winds (Smith, 2020). A solar array with a battery backup (1.26 megawatts backup was installed on Ragged Island) would store the surplus energy and provide night-time electricity (ZNS Bahamas, 2019)). It is an anomaly that for days after a hurricane strikes and there is no power, or fuel for standby generators, the sun is blazing down creating thirst and unwanted heat when it could be captured where it is most needed. A solar system, unlike a largely unused and expensive standby generator, which only operates during a power cut, solar can of course be used daily to supplement the electricity the tourist facility uses during normal times.

Once communications are available, tourists can move in or out. Although domestic concerns are important, tourists are visitors and will lack the local knowledge that residents have. Not only is it essential that tourists receive help, but they must also know that they will be cared for before the event (Cartwright-Carroll, 2016). Before the hurricane season, and especially before a hurricane strikes, tourists should be assigned staff or aide who will stick by them until they are rescued or returned home. In many cases, tourists will not be in a critical situation, assuming emergency services move in quickly, but tourists must not be neglected as they will certainly be concerned about their immediate situation and how to return home. Preparation is the key to a successful recovery or forced departure, and if the tourist is kept informed there are unlikely to be bad feelings. Apart from compromising return visits, a few bad words about their experience in The Bahamas could undo thousands of dollars of advertising very quickly.

Security is a major concern for all, but especially the tourist. Unfortunately, the impact of a hurricane creates a less monitored environment as the police and other security personnel are involved in first responder activity (Knowles, 2019b). This is compounded by infrastructural damage which aids the criminal but hampers law enforcement. This is a concern that needs to be addressed by the governing bodies. In Abaco a curfew was introduced for this reason, but there were many reports of looting and other criminal activities (Maycock, 2019). The possible impact on tourism diminishes once the tourists have left, another reason why evacuation before and after the hurricane is so important. In Abaco a significant number of foreigners, many do not present during the hurricane, had second homes there (Dixon, ND). Clearly, it was important for their properties to be secure from looting and vandalism, but in the aftermath, this proved very difficult. Given its property investment and labour requirements, some forethought needs to be given to the after-effects of a hurricane on security if a valuable winter tourist industry is to be sustained.

The practical aspects of recovery from a hurricane must come first, but very quickly the social aspects of a tourist's life will take over. Food and drink are not options, and while some provision for feeding will usually be available, shortage of water quickly becomes an issue. Most hurricane rescue operations involve the supply of water (Ritchie, 2019). Without electricity, pumped water systems will not be able to function. In addition, as was clear in Grand Bahama after Dorian, storm surges flood far inland and pollute the freshwater lenses with saltwater (The Tribune, 2019). A back-up supply of fresh water for tourists should make allowance for washing and showers as well as drinking. Ice is not a luxury for tourists who may not be used to the summer heat, and there will be no air conditioning. Freezers that can hold supplies frozen for several days without power are available and need to be considered where tourists are likely to be stranded (Figure 14.1).

Having been supplied with creature comforts but lacking evacuation, tourists may need a more psychological intervention. Again, this is not something that can be offered ad hoc after a hurricane but must be planned. Entertainment is a great diversion and is after all what the tourist expects. The tourist will just want his vacation to continue, however sympathetic he is to local problems. Major resorts may have no trouble with this as they have extensive resources, but smaller hotels that are common in the Family Islands could easily be faced with a dilemma of a shortage of staff, structural damage and lack of power. Without some planning and preparation, this situation can become quite adverse for the tourist. While Family Island communities are resourceful, without some prior organisation a musician might well stay at home, or a comedian feel it unnecessary to entertain visitors. Ideally such persons could be persuaded to visit tourist centres and offer their services without being asked, assuming communications are down.

Figure 14.1 Dead Caribbean pines near Freeport after Hurricane Wilma, caused by saltwater intrusion. Photograph, courtesy of Neil Sealey and Media Enterprises.

One Abaco hotel on Green Turtle Cay was so damaged by Dorian and it was shut for a year and reportedly lost $30,000 a month in room revenue; in addition, its marina was destroyed (Kemp, 2019b). On Abaco the Sandpiper Inn at Schooner Bay was able to re-open in early December, the first hotel on that island to do so (Ritchie, 2019). Hotels in Marsh Harbour and Treasure Cay will not recover until well into 2020 when the infrastructures are restored. Regrettably re-opening hotels can be a protracted business, causing a loss of room availability for tourists and consequent unemployment locally (Ritchie, 2019). Although hotel closures may be temporary, most staff will nevertheless be laid off while the hotel is closed, further compounding the value of tourism for the community (Maycock, 2019). In Freeport after damage caused by Hurricanes Frances and Jeanne in 2004, the Royal Oasis Hotel and Casino closed permanently, and left about 1,200 persons unemployed (Maycock, 2019). A decade later the Grand Lucayan Resort's three hotels were seriously damaged, and the owners declined to repair two of them, leading to a massive crisis in that community. The adjacent Port Lucaya Marketplace (shopping and restaurant plaza) was partly abandoned, and after Dorian it was completely closed for many weeks (McKenzie, 2019). To salvage the situation, the government brokered the sale of the Grand Lucayan Resort and opened it in advance at the nation's expense (Rolle, 2018; The Tribune, 2018). In the light of this situation, it is apparent that the government needs some sort of commitment from hotels to repair, rebuild or otherwise restore their properties (Ritchie, 2019). Many tourist properties are vulnerable to flooding and coastal erosion due to their proximity to a beach. Ideally, they should be far enough away from the shoreline, and well above sea level, in order to provide protection during a hurricane, and to inspire confidence in tourists who are well-informed these days through various social media and news outlets. The well-known Pink Sands Hotel on Harbour Island is well back from the beach and has survived for many years to sustain tourism in this popular island. As The Bahamas is such a large archipelago, a location may not be exposed to a hurricane for many years, so it is not surprising that developments exist that are exposed and vulnerable to even minor hurricanes. As an example of an older and vulnerable resort there is Small Hope Bay Resort, near Love Beach on Andros, which is already suffering from beach erosion (Sealey, 2005). In another location, offshore cabins on stilts have been proposed for the Exuma Cays. In the Bimini Islands a major cruise ship destination has been created on an artificial island which will certainly be vulnerable to even low-category storms (McCartney, 2019). It is assumed the cruise company has prepared a comprehensive evacuation plan for its employees (Diaz, 2019), and the resources to restore the facility after a hurricane strike. For situations like this, it is necessary, once a likely hit is forecast, that all occupants can be evacuated to a safe location (Figure 14.2).

This requires planning, and ideally a test run, to ensure that the tourists will be safe. It is unrealistic to locate all tourist facilities inland and well above mean sea level, although major resorts and large hotels should be well protected, such as the Atlantis and Baha Mar resorts on New Providence. It is notable that of the two oldest Family Island tourist developments that

Figure 14.2 Treasure Cay in Abaco is on low land between the sea and a creek. Photograph, courtesy of Neil Sealey, Media Enterprises.

have succeeded over the years, Stella Maris on Long Island is located away from the shore and on a ridge, while Treasure Cay on Abaco was seriously impacted by Dorian (Semple, 2019) due to its low elevation, many canals and marinas, and extensive building along the main beach. Despite this, it survived some 50 years without serious mishap, so notwithstanding its present status it is difficult to consider it 'unsustainable'. Nevertheless, it was always exposed, and the beach was being eroded before the storm damage, so there is a strong case for careful planning to allow for the occasional hurricane. Abaco is also somewhat more vulnerable to hurricane damage. Apart from direct hits, it is exposed to strong winds and waves from hurricanes passing on a northwards' track offshore in the Atlantic Ocean, such as with Hurricane Hugo in 1989.

Another aspect of hurricane damage, particularly evident after Dorian, is the clean-up and restoration process. For months after Hurricane Andrew *(1992)* struck Miami, its streets and highways were lined with debris, stores were closed, and the whole city remained in emergency mode (Beck, 1992). In The Bahamas after Dorian, the clean-up process was expedited on both islands (Abaco and Grand Bahama), and Freeport (Grand Bahama) quickly regained its tourist appeal (Myers, 2019). Some consideration must always be given to getting the tourist environment back on track, as anyone who has had to stay in a hotel next to a construction site will appreciate that destroyed buildings and temporary facilities are not conducive to sustaining tourism.

There are over 20 plus active airports in The Bahamas, six of which are ports of entry able to accommodate international flights (Ministry of Tourism and Aviation, 2011), and therefore subject to US Transport Security Agency (TSA) requirements (Caribbean Journal, 2013). These are the most convenient way for tourists to enter and leave. New construction should ensure that runways are not compromised, which was the fate of Marsh Harbour International Airport after Dorian (Kemp, 2019; Morgan, 2019b). To compensate a runway near Treasure Cay, approximately 30 miles from Marsh Harbour, had to be used for emergency supplies. At Freeport International Airport the terminal buildings were flooded and destroyed, and the runway was under water for several days (Robards, 2019). Tourism on these islands, even if other facilities are functioning, is not sustainable if the airports are not fully restored. While inter-island flights may be quickly restored, it is a different matter for international flights, where the airports are subject to TSA inspection for US flights. As many as 70% of Abaco tourists (or second homeowners) are from nearby South Florida and fly to that island. Both Marsh Harbour International Airport and Freeport International Airport were closed to US flights for over four months, and tourists had to fly to Nassau and then take a local flight to get these islands (Sachs, 2019). Freeport's privately owned airport's terminal buildings had been previously damaged by hurricanes, and a new terminal able to withstand a major hurricane strike and flooding was projected (Ambrose & Sabatino, 2013).

Part of the issue that tourism faces today is that both the tourists and the environment have changed. Tourists now have access to a variety of social media and internet sites that provide information. Tourist agencies need to be aware of what their clients know and expect, particularly regarding their evacuation, and physical security if they are unable to leave before the hurricane strikes. In the past the tourist relied on magazines, brochures, and travel agencies, because once in a hotel, they were largely isolated from the rest of the world. Today the situation is quite different, for, as well as being fed regular news updates, the tourist can him/herself inform the rest of the world about what is going on. A bad experience is easily sent to friends and family, and news outlets are always keen to broadcast adverse reports as soon as they arrive at a disaster zone, which they can do very quickly. Even though many Abaco properties survived, news photographs were almost exclusively of flattened unauthorised shanty towns, notably The Mudd a shanty town in Marsh Harbour, mostly occupied by Haitian migrants, who were sometimes interviewed as if they were locals. This inevitably gave the false impression of the state of tourism in the country, most of which was still functioning totally normally, both for cruise and longer-term visitors (Brown, 2019) (Figure 14.3).

Apart from the modern tourist, the advent of climate change has also impacted the country (Rolle, 2019). Older properties were less concerned about locating on or near the coast, even though major hurricanes always formed in the region in the past. The difference today is that sea level has risen a small amount, and the percentage of major storms, category three and above, has increased (Latherby et al., 2019), although the total number of storms seems to be consistent with past years. The combined result is that a hurricane strike can create a significant storm surge, and heavy flooding is now the norm. Even a category one storm like Sandy in 2012 created major

Figure 14.3 Flooding after Hurricane Sandy in Nassau. Photograph, courtesy of Neil Sealey, Media Enterprises.

flooding along the north coast of New Providence (Sealey, 2017), partly because it lingered over the island for several days. This was also a factor with Dorian as it passed over the northern Bahamas, and the storm surge from the north penetrated far inland on Grand Bahama, causing salt pollution of the water lenses that supplied Freeport and Lucaya (The Tribune, 2019). This has happened before, after Hurricanes Frances and Jeanne in 2004, and Wilma in 2005 (Charles, 2005; Bahamianology, 2019). It must now be assumed that such low-lying areas will be exposed to flooding almost every summer hurricane season.

Ultimately, to ensure that tourism is sustainable and that tourists will perceive that The Bahamas remains a viable destination, plans are needed well in advance of each hurricane season. Ideally every new tourist facility should be designed to withstand winds and flooding and have plans for the security of their visitors. Overall the relevant government agencies, including the Ministry of Tourism, National Emergency Management Agency (NEMA), and the newly formed Ministry of Disaster Preparedness, Recovery and Reconstruction and Disaster Reconstruction Authority, both created in 2019 in response to the Dorian disaster (Jones, 2019), should be a party to these annual plans.

References

Ambrose, A., & Sabatino, M. (2013). Strong winds and rising currents: A design proposal for Grand Bahama international airport. In Subtropical cities 2013. Braving a new world design: Design interventions for changing climates. ACSA Fall conference proceedings. Editors: A. Abbate, A., Lynn, F., and Kennedy, R. Retrieved from, www.asca-ach.org.

Bahamianology. (6 September 2019). Parts of Freeport and Abaco under six feet of water after double Hurricane Francis and Jeanne both hit in September 2005. *Bahamianology*. Retrieved from, www.bahamianology.com.

BBC News. (2 September 2019). Hurricane Dorian: Bahamas battered by 'monster' storm. Retrieved from, www.bbc.co.uk.

Beck, T. (24 August 1992). Hurricane Andrew rips across South Florida. *UPI*. Retrieved from, www.upi.com.

Brown, O. (9 October 2019). Bahamas still open for business after Dorian officials say. *The Washington Informer*. Retrieved from, www.washingtoninformer.com.

Caribbean Journal. (26 July 2013). Bahamas, United States sign memorandum of understanding on TSA pre-clearance. *Caribbean Journal*. Retrieved from, www.caribbeanjournal.com.

Cartwright-Carroll, T. (4 October 2016). MOT monitoring thousands of tourists ahead of hurricane Matthew. Retrieved from, www.bahamas.com.

CEDEMA. (12 September 2019). Major hurricane Dorian: Situation report No.12. Caribbean Disaster Emergency Management Agency- CEDEMA; St. Michaels, Barbados. Retrieved from, www.cedema.org.

Charles, J. (28 October 2005). Bahamas badly beaten by Wilma. *The Bahamas Network*. Retrieved from, www.bahamasb2b.com.

Diaz, J. (30 August 2019). Hurricane Dorian forces cruise lines to change itineraries. *Sun-Sentinel*. Retrieved from, www.sun-sentinel.com.

Dixon, H. (ND). Paradise lost: Hurricane survivors rebuild their lives against a backdrop of death. *The Telegraph*. Retrieved from, www.telegraph.co.uk.

France 24. (9 September 2019). One week after Hurricane Dorian, Bahamas residents struggle amid the ruins. *France24*. Retrieved from, www.france24.com.

Galanis, P. (17 October 2016). Matthew and the indomitable Bahamian spirit. *The Nassau Guardian*. Retrieved from, www.thenassauguardian.com.

Jones Jr., R. (22 September 2019). Iram Lewis appointed minister of state for new disaster preparedness ministry. *Eyewitness News*. Retrieved from, www.ewnews.com.

Kemp, Y. (6 December 2019a). December 16 target set for Abaco airport re-opening. *The Tribune*. Retrieved from, www.tribune242.com.

Kemp, Y. (6 December 2019b). Dorian: Abaco hotel losing $30K monthly. *The Tribune*. Retrieved from, www.tribune242.com.

Kemp, Y. (3 January 2020). Long Island vacation rentals hit by Dorian. *The Tribune*. Retrieved from, www.tribune242.com.

Knowles, R. (3 December 2019a). 50% unemployment on Grand Bahama. *The Nassau Guardian*. Retrieved from, www.thenassauguardian.com.

Knowles, R. (10 December 2019b). Dorian caused murder spike. *The Nassau Guardian*. Retrieved from, www.thenassauguardian.com.

Latherby, L., Rojanasakul, M., & Roston, E. (1 September 2019). Hurricane seasons are getting more severe. *Bloomberg*. Retrieved from, www.bloomberg.com.

Maycock, D. (8 January 2019). Ten murders on Grand Bahamas as crime falls by 10%. *The Tribune*. Retrieved from, www.tribune242.com.

McCartney, P. (6 December 2019). Ocean Cay receives its first cruise ship. *The Nassau Guardian*. Retrieved from, www.thenassauguardian.com.

McKenzie, N. (4 October 2019). Structural survey of Port Lucaya Market Place expected to be completed within a week or so. *Eyewitness News*. Retrieved from, www.ewnews.com.

Ministry of Tourism and Aviation. (11 November 2011). The Bahamas national aviation policy white paper. Retrieved from, www.bahamas.com.

Morgan, R. (4 December 2019a). Housing still a challenge on Abaco. *The Nassau Guardian*. Retrieved from, www.thenassauguardian.com.

Morgan, R. (16 December 2019b). Abaco airport open to int'l flights more than three months after Dorian. *The Nassau Guardian*. Retrieved from, www.thenassauguardian.com.

Myers, G. N. (30 October 2019). Map: What's open and closed in The Bahamas after hurricane Dorian. *Travel Weekly*. Retrieved from, www.travelweekly.com.

Ritchie, J. (11 December 2019). Dorian, 90+ days later. *Refresh Bahamas Incorporated*. Retrieved from, www.refreshbahamas.com.

Robards, C. (9 September 2019). Freeport airport flooded. *The Nassau Guardian*. Retrieved from, www.thenassauguardian.com.

Rolle, R. (15 August 2018). Impact of buying Grand Lucayan 'like aftermath of a hurricane.' *The Tribune*. Retrieved from, www.tribune242.com.

Rolle, R. (4 November 2019a). New report: Rising seas risk worse than feared. *The Tribune*. Retrieved from, www.tribune242.com.

Rolle, L. (29 November 2019b). More power restored in Abaco. *The Tribune*. Retrieved from, www.tribune242.com.

Sachs, A. (22 November 2019). In The Bahamas, a hard-hit island beckons again. *The Philadelphia Inquirer.* Retrieve from, www.inquirer.com.

Sealey, N. (2005). Small Hope Bay: The cycle of Casuarina-induced beach erosion. In proceedings of the Tenth Symposium on the Natural History of The Bahamas. Editors: Buckner, S. D. and McGrath, T. A. Gerace Centre, Ltd. San Salvador, The Bahamas.

Sealey, N. (2017). The climate of The Bahamas. Retrieved from, www.academia.com.

Semple, K. (6 September 2019). How one Bahamian town, nearly destroyed, is coping after Dorian. *The New York Times.* Retrieved from, www.nytimes.com.

Smith, S. (8 January 2020). Nearly 40 percent of Ragged Island solar panels installed. *Eyewitness News.* Retrieved from, www.ewnews.com.

The Tribune. (22 August 2018). Govt. purchases Grand Lucayan Resort. *The Tribune.* Retrieved from, www.tribune242.com.

The Tribune. (11 November 2019). GB water supplier set out post-Dorian strategy. *The Tribune.* Retrieved from, www.tribune242.com.

ZNS Bahamas. (11 December 2019). Solar farm underway on Ragged Island. *znsbahamas.* Retrieved from, www.znsbahamas.com.

15 Hurricane Dorian

A case for building comprehensive climate change resilience frameworks for small island developing states in the Caribbean

Teo Cooper

Background

The Bahamas became another global "poster-child" for the adverse effects of climate change on small island developing states (SIDS) following the passage of Hurricane Dorian in 2019. On September 1, the category 5 storm started moving through the northern islands of The Bahamas, first impacting Abaco then Grand Bahama, with 185 miles per hour sustained winds and wind gusts of up to 200 miles per hour (Delancy, 2019). It was dubbed "the most powerful hurricane ever recorded to hit The Bahamas" (Beaubien, 2019). In addition to extreme winds and high gusts, Hurricane Dorian brought in storm surges estimated to be between 16 and 23 feet in coastal areas and flooding a large percentage of these islands. The slow-moving superstorm pounded the islands for three days, causing damages in excess of 3.4 billion dollars to these two major islands alone (Fieser, 2020). Flooding from the ocean surges severely damaged or destroyed an estimated 1,300 homes in Abaco and Grand Bahama (Zhao, 2019). The airports, hospitals, police stations, and many of the most essential government offices were all severely compromised by flood waters. The National Emergency Management Agency (NEMA) reported that 69 persons were confirmed dead in the aftermath of the storm (UNICEF, 2019), while hundreds of others were reported missing. Hurricane Dorian became the worst natural disaster in the country's recorded history, swiftly plunging The Bahamas into a state of emergency – and unfortunately with more questions about the future of the climate resiliency of this small island state than answers.

Climate change and small island developing states

The devastating effects of climate change became most evident within the last two decades. Climate change has "developed from a rather obscure scientific topic into a key item on the global political agenda" (Bernauer & Schaffer, 2010, p. 1). Climate variation is a natural occurrence in the earth's atmosphere. However, the rapid alterations of the composition of the atmosphere observed in the last few decades have been attributed directly and indirectly to greenhouse gas emissions via human activity. Significant increases in temperature are being recorded across the globe. Sea level rise, a direct consequence of global warming, is altering the chemistry of the ocean in many regions, and predicted phenomena such as king tides and saltwater intrusion are increasingly being observed. "Over the last two decades, floods have accounted for 47% of all weather-related disasters, impacting over 2.1 billion people, causing major environmental disruption, and resulting in over one trillion USD of economic losses globally" (Dwirahmadi, Rutherford, Pung, & Chu, 2019, p. 1). Unfortunately, the effects of the changing climate are grossly disproportionate, as some countries are benefitting from the increase in temperature, for example, while many others are increasingly suffering.

SIDS are projected to shoulder the brunt of the adverse effects of climate change (Agniam, 2011; Benjamin, 2010; Nunn & Kumar, 2017). This is most unfortunate because, according to Walshe and Stancioff (2018), "islands are among the places least responsible for the emission of greenhouse gasses leading to climate change" (p. 13). In fact, SIDS are only responsible for approximately 1% of global emissions. Their extreme vulnerability to climate change can be ascribed to several attributes of SIDS, such as relatively small land masses, susceptibility to cyclones, low-lying topography, which makes them prone to flooding due to sea level rise, and a high dependence on groundwater from relatively thin and shallow freshwater lenses. Other socio-economic factors which increase their vulnerability to climate change include high population densities on some islands, short proximity of important and often poorly constructed infrastructure to the coastlines, high dependency on the importation of essential goods, economic dependence on industries which are highly susceptible to natural disasters, and limited financial resources for spending on climate resilient measures of adaptation (Benjamin, 2010; Delancy, 2019).

Sea level rise and increase in intensity of tropical cyclones (hurricanes) are the most eminent threat of climate change to SIDS. According to Layne (2017),

> Increase in sea levels can cause flooding, soil erosion, inundation and wave damage to coastlines, particularly in small island states and countries with low lying deltas. In the specific case of the Caribbean, sea levels have risen at a rate of approximately 1 mm/year during the 20th century.
>
> (p. 176)

This single consequence of climate change alone is deleterious as nearly one-third of all citizens in SIDS live less than a few meters above sea level (Hassan & Cliff, 2019). In the Caribbean, "the loss of land, tourism infrastructure, housing and other infrastructure" (Benjamin, 2010, p. 81) would be the most significant impacts of sea level rise. Temperature increases in the Caribbean support the development of more frequent and severe tropical cyclones. "Increased intensity of tropical cyclones would lead to increased storm surges and flooding events, causing infrastructural damage, loss of life, increased injuries, an increase spread of vector-borne diseases, and reduced tourist demand" (Benjamin, 2010, p. 85). The combined effects of sea level rise along with increasing intensity of tropical cyclones in the region have prompted an urgency for SIDS to swiftly accelerate the process of developing comprehensive frameworks for climate change resilience.

Building climate change resilience in the aftermath of Hurricane Dorian

Resilience refers to "the capacity or ability to anticipate, prepare for, respond to, and recover quickly from impacts of disaster" (Mayunga, 2007). The importance of building climate change resilience has been well documented in recent years. According to Dwirahmadi et al. (2019), "resilience building has been identified as one of the central concepts of all post-2015 global policy documents" (p. 2). The catastrophic impact of Hurricane Maria on Puerto Rico and the island of Dominica in 2017, and now Hurricane Dorian on The Bahamas unequivocally calls for the governments of SIDS to prioritize climate change resilience as national development goals. However, the research on this topic to inform the development of policies and practice is very limited currently. Hurricane Dorian's impact on The Bahamas and activities in the aftermath of the storm provide a unique opportunity to imagine the way forward in building strong climate resilience frameworks for SIDS in the Caribbean.

Human and social factors should be the primary focus of climate change resilience plans for SIDS. Overwhelming evidences have shown that even with their greatest of efforts to implement climate change mitigation strategies, they will yield negligible results. The limited research on this topic related to SIDS in the Caribbean has focused on advancing geographic and scientific understanding of climate change. Post-mortem reports on the aftermath of all three storms mentioned above reveal that geographic and scientific information alone have had only marginal benefits for helping governments of SIDS empower citizens to plan for and recover from these inevitable events. A critical assessment of activities in the aftermath of Hurricane Dorian suggests that comprehensive climate change resilience frameworks for SIDS must address key issues of development, governance, and sustainability as well.

Development in building climate change resilience

According to Sem (2009), "Small Island Developing States (SIDS) comprise small islands and low-lying coastal countries that face the development constraints of a small population, limited resources, remoteness, vulnerability to natural disasters, and susceptibility to external shocks" (p. 8). Therefore, addressing these issues inherent in the development of SIDS is central to building a strong framework for climate change resilience.

Developments along the coastlines are perhaps of greatest concern. Given the small size of many of these island nations, critical infrastructure such as hospitals and airports are in relatively proximity to the shores. For example, the airports, hospitals, and many of the schools and government buildings destroyed by Hurricane Dorian were all within approximately 10–15 miles of the coastline. The University of The Bahamas' campus on Grand Bahama island was among those critical infrastructures destroyed during the storm and was also constructed within the same coastal radius.

Limited guidelines and lack of stringent regulations in SIDS often lead to poor development practices, such as over dredging, removal of mangroves, and destruction of coral reef ecosystems. This not only leads to a myriad of environmental issues, including increased chances for flooding and habitat loss, but also to significant economic loss from tourism, fisheries, and other industries that benefit from the resources in coastal zones. To address these issues, "Environmental Impact Assessments (EIAs) should be made compulsory before, during, and after industrial production activities" (Igbokwe-Ibeto, 2019). In The Bahamas, EIAs are required by the government before major coastal developments are approved to begin. However, "Environmental Impact Assessment (EIA) processes are not well understood or developed and have not been applied consistently throughout The Bahamas" (Organization of American States, n.d.). It is also uncertain if monitoring mechanisms are effectively implemented over the duration of construction projects, and to what extent they continue once the development is complete.

SIDS also spend considerable amounts of their relatively small annual budgets on adaptations to protect coastal developments. Building codes are implemented throughout The Bahamas to regulate structural developments, and hardened shorelines (seawalls, bulkheads) are the most common adaptation to protect them from ocean intrusion. However, according to Silver et al. (2019), "Hardened shorelines can be expensive to build and maintain, and can lead to unintended shoreline erosion, degradation or loss of habitat, and impacts on communities that depend on healthy coastal ecosystems for protection, subsistence, and livelihoods". Seawalls can be observed along shorelines of many coastal developments in The Bahamas; however, these traditional mechanisms are now proving to be inadequate protection against the intensity of recent tropical cyclones (Silver et al., 2019), as demonstrated by Hurricane Dorian. Additionally, there have been issues with the construction quality and maintenance of some seawalls throughout the island. For instance, the seawall in High Rock, an area hardest hit by Dorian and where many lives were lost, was improperly built in 2004, and no maintenance plan was put in place for upwards to 14 years post-construction (Adderley, 2018).

There are variations in building code requirements throughout various municipalities in The Bahamas. For example, in the city of Freeport, the building codes are considerably more stringent than in other settlements on the same island (Delancy, 2019). Building codes for the City of Freeport are developed and regulated by the Grand Bahama Port Authority, a privately held corporation responsible "for the development, administration and management, and provision of services within an area called the 'Port Area' (230 sq. miles)" (Grand Bahama Port Authority, n.d.). Delancy (2009) suggests that this may explain why so many of the buildings on the eastern end of Grand Bahama were severely damaged by the storm. The archipelagic nature of The Bahama islands also makes it challenging to effectively enforce building codes, due to the limited availability of experts and resource capacity in this area (Delancy, 2009). Structural integrity can be severely compromised when building codes are not strictly adhered to.

Governance in building climate change resilience

Climate change governance is another critical component of building robust climate change resilience frameworks for SIDS. Foremost, the political system of a country has significant implications for how climate change and climate resilience are governed (Bernauer & Schaffer, 2010). For instance, Hovi, Sprinz, and Underdal (2009) propose that term limited governments may be a hindrance to nation states effectively dealing with the problem of climate change. Climate change issues and resilience strategies require long-term commitments and continuity, and often, when new governments are elected, priorities and strategies change simultaneously. Additionally, Bernauer and Schaffer (2010) suggest that these governments may have more pressure to meet public demands because of their interest in re-election, which at times may not be in the best interest of national development. The Bahamas is a democracy with term limited governments which in recent decades have changed every five years. It is possible that this factor may have affected the continuity of some efforts on climate change resilience.

The literature suggests that another limitation of democratic government structure is that the responsibility for climate change resilience is often placed within the portfolio of government officials who have other significant duties and responsibilities as well (Agniam, 2011). As a result, they may not be able to commit the necessary attention that building and managing a comprehensive climate change resilience framework requires. This has also been found to be true for The Bahamas, where the official appointed as Minister of the Environment has responsibilities for Housing as well. Subsequent to the passage of Hurricane Dorian, a new government ministry was created as part of the Office of The Prime Minister responsible for Disaster Preparedness, Management, and Reconstruction. It remains to be seen how the bureaucratic linkage of the new ministry to the Office of The Prime

Minister and co-existence of the old Ministry of Environment will influence the advancement of a climate change resilience framework for the country.

Collaborative governance approach

Climate change activities in SIDS involve the participation of many important stakeholders. Therefore, a collaborative governance approach has been found to be effective for managing climate change (Kalesnikaite, 2019). In this context, "collaboration is a process that aims to ameliorate complex public problems, which single organizations may not solve successfully alone" (Kalesnikaite, 2019, p. 866). Some of the stakeholders involved in the complex process of coordinating climate change activities in SIDS are the government, government agencies, community-based organizations, private institutions, research institutions/university, non-governmental organizations, international civic organizations, foreign governments, and international governing bodies. Benefits of collaborative governance include sharing knowledge, skills, material resources, information, and human resources.

This governance structure will provide policy guidelines and compliance regulations for all stakeholders involved (Dwirahmadi et al., 2019) and will ensure that participation is centred on a set of common priorities outlined in the national climate change resilience plan. Certainly, managing collaboration between all these entities is a mammoth undertaking and can sometimes be counterproductive. Kalesnikaite (2019) found, however, that the type of partnerships matters when seeking to achieve the best outcomes. That is, an effectively designed collaborative governance framework can coordinate the right types of partnerships within its structure that can promote very productive climate change resilience activities. Presently, a shared governance entity for climate change resilience does not exist in The Bahamas. The National Emergency Management Agency (NEMA) most closely resembles this concept, by having a committee of representatives from various public and private agencies to advise on hurricane preparedness and distribution of resources in the aftermath.

Perhaps the most common instance where a collaborative governance framework can be most effective is when it comes to management of disaster relief aid. A breakdown in the coordination of this significant component of recovery in the aftermath of a climate change disaster can be counterproductive to the resiliency goals. For example, Dwirahmadi et al. (2019) found that the most influential barrier to building community resilience in the aftermath of a storm is the high dependency of citizens on external aid. People may choose not to plan adequately or enact their own contingency plans in anticipation of the availability of external aid. In the aftermath of Hurricane Dorian, there were mass distributions of aid across the affected areas. Thousands of people stood in lines daily to receive disaster relief aid packages and meals. However, reports soon began to surface about a myriad of challenges, including inappropriateness of some items such as appliances donated to areas where there is no electricity and insurmountable issues with shipping logistics (Global Village Space, 2019). Systemic coordination through a collaborative governance framework can ensure efficient, equitable, and appropriate management of the disaster relief aid process. It can also provide mechanism to ensure that relief aid is accessible to the most vulnerable in communities and a plan to help citizens develop and execute their own disaster contingency plans.

Legislation and policies for climate change governance

Legislation and policies are the primary instruments of governance. Unfortunately, many SIDS do not have adequate and specific legislation with respect to climate change (Nachmany, Abeysinghe, & Barakat, 2017). One reason may be the paucity of local research in this area to inform national climate change legislation and policy development. According to Oulu (2015), climate change governance itself is a new area "in which policy and practice tend to precede theory or advance simultaneously" (p. 227). Unfortunately, the establishment of new climate change legislation and policy frameworks in SIDS often result from experiential learning in the aftermath of a natural disaster, like Hurricane Dorian. This is truly a high price to pay for delayed action in this regard.

Legislation and policy development work is a resource and time-intensive process, which may be another reason for procrastination. Some countries may opt to simply amend existing legislation to include climate change in the essence of expedience. This is not the best practice because "despite being time- and resource consuming, enactment of stand-alone framework climate change legislation is preferred over piecemeal amendments to relevant laws" (Oulu, 2015, p. 227). Policy development work, though not as protracted as passing legislation, can still be a laborious endeavour. Nevertheless, the current state of climate change demands that SIDS embrace this responsibility head-on.

Though The Bahamas has adopted many international climate change policies, such as the Paris Agreement in 2016, and passed legislation to reduce emissions (Ministry of Environment and Housing, n.d.), no comprehensive stand-alone legislation for climate change exists. The most relevant piece of legislation, The Disaster Reconstruction Authority Bill, was passed in 2019 in the aftermath of Hurricane Dorian. It was to establish a governing body that "will be responsible for the management of reconstruction and restoration in areas designated disaster zones" (Office of The Prime Minister, 2019). In 2005, The Bahamas government developed the National Policy for the Adaptation to Climate Change. This policy sought to identify areas of vulnerability, while recommending appropriate adaptation measures and strategies for addressing the eminent threats. However, once these policies are developed, their outcomes need to be monitored to control for the "'word-deed' gap, which appears to be larger in democracies than in autocracies" (Bernauer & Schaffer, 2010, p. 18). The 40-page document only provided a cursory overview, and a critical review of the same suggests that greater than half of the recommended actions have not yet been implemented to date (Bahamas National Climate Change Committee, 2005).

Governance of climate migration

Climate change events have the potential to displace millions of people. Yet, migration policies, legislation, and programs are not included in the climate change governance frameworks (Ferris, 2019). "The very first report of the Intergovernmental Panel on Climate Change in 1990 predicted that one of the major consequences of climate change will be the large-scale movement of people" (Ferris, 2019, p. 426). Climate change events can result in internal as well as external migration. Internal migrants represent the largest group of displaced persons and their movements are confined within the borders of their home country, whereas external migrants are those displaced persons who choose to migrate internationally.

Tens of thousands of Bahamians were displaced in the aftermath of Hurricane Dorian. According to UNICEF (2019), "4,861 evacuees had been registered by the Department of Social Services as of 18 October" (p. 2). Cruise ships and airplanes were commissioned to provide relief transportation for displaced migrants from the two islands most affected by the storm. While most citizens migrated within the borders of the country, many opted to migrate internationally. One cruise ship was permitted to carry 1,550 evacuees into the United States (Cranley, 2019). However, this intervention was soon halted by U.S. authorities, and subsequent ships and planes were only allowed to bring in visitors holding U.S. Visas (Mansoor, 2019). Most migrants reportedly lived with relatives; however, thousands had to be housed in temporary shelters for many months after the storm.

Ferris is one of a few scholars who have written extensively on the governance aspect of climate change migration. She urged that "Migration should be incorporated into national development plans, climate change adaptation plans, and disaster risk management policies" (Ferris, 2019, p. 456). Beyond the policy level, she further recommended that

> The development of national laws which could apply to those displaced by disaster and climate change could include measures such as ensuring that displaced children will have access to education even if they do not have this school records or that the government will take action to ensure the protection of property and other assets left behind after the people are displaced because of the effects of climate change.
>
> (Ferris, 2019, p. 440)

The urgency of including migration plans as part of a comprehensive climate change resilience framework for SIDS cannot be understated. Its urgency is further emphasized by the anti-immigrant climate presently developing globally, which will inadvertently inhibit any hopes for international frameworks embracing climate migration in the foreseeable future.

Governance of human rights and climate change

Climate change poses a direct threat to human rights of people, particularly those of vulnerable populations (Mukherjee & Mustafa, 2019). The poor, disabled, elderly, and children are deemed to be most disadvantaged. Therefore, it is incumbent upon governments of SIDS to also consider the well-being of these vulnerable groups, especially in relation to climate change. Hurricane shelters were reserved for the elderly and disabled before the arrival of Hurricane Dorian. However, flood waters from the storm severely compromised these shelters and persons had to be evacuated during the storm. The Grand Bahama Children's Home received flooding during the storm, and the children and workers had to be evacuated from there as well (K. Moore, 2019). These incidents demonstrated not only the need to consider the structural integrity of shelters housing these vulnerable populations in the climate change resilience plans, but also their locations. Emergency evacuation plans for all shelters should also be included, if they, too, become compromised in the middle of a storm.

The human rights of illegal immigrants within states must also be considered a critical aspect of the legislative and policy frameworks for climate change governance in SIDS. The governments must ensure that their basic human rights to life and protection are preserved in the event of a threat of and recovery from a natural disaster. The island of Abaco, for example, has been home to thousands of illegal immigrants in The Bahamas. Most of them lived in a popular "shanty town" communities known as The Mudd and Pigeon Peas (T. Moore, 2019). Synonymous with its name, The Mudd is a swamp land area that is especially prone to flooding from heavy rains alone, as is Pigeon Peas. It was reported that many of these residents refused to leave their poorly constructed homes as Hurricane Dorian approached, despite numerous warnings by the officials. Videos immediately began to flood the internet of these immigrants attempting to flee from their communities during the storm from the first day it began (Dwilson, 2019; Ward & Fiola, 2019). Many lives from these communities were lost in the storm, and hundreds of others are still reported missing. The survivors were evacuated to the nation's capital, New Providence, where the government provided temporary food and shelter. However, debates began soon after about whether these immigrants would be deported or given some form of protected status (Knowles, 2019). There is also an ongoing dispute regarding the future of these "shanty town" communities and whether they should be allowed to rebuild considering historic development and safety concerns in the area (T. Moore, 2019).

Sustainability in building climate change resilience

Sustainability is commonly defined as the ability to meet the resource demands of the present without compromising their availability for the future. In the context of climate change, attention is given primarily to the availability of those essential resources which are most vulnerable to the adverse effects of changing weather patterns. Lately, the increasing intensity and frequency of catastrophic cyclones (hurricanes) in the Caribbean demand that greater attention be focused in this area. "Climate change undermines the environmental determinants of health: clean air and water, sufficient food and adequate shelter" (WHO, 2008). However, the two resources most vulnerable to the effects of climate change in SIDS are enough food and clean water, as they also have potential to become national security concerns. Therefore, it is imperative to consider the sustainability of these precious assets as a central component of building a comprehensive climate change resilience framework.

Sustainability of food resources

Food security is an important aspect of sustainability and one of the most significant threats of climate change in SIDS. Many developing states in the Caribbean are not self-sufficient in food production and depend heavily on imports from other countries. According to the Food and Agriculture Organization of the United Nations (n.d.), "Almost all Caribbean and Pacific SIDS import over 60% of food; 50% of islands import over 80%". Therefore, access to food supplies can be significantly impeded by the inability of vessels to traverse in severe weather or when the local entry ports are inaccessible. Also, "a population that does not eat well is susceptible to diseases and poverty" (Igbokwe-Ibeto, 2019).

The likelihood of this occurrence became a harsh reality for residents of Abaco and Grand Bahama during the events of Hurricane Dorian. Food supplies at local grocery stores on the islands became very scarce in the days leading up to the disastrous superstorm. In the aftermath, all the major food stores located in Marsh Harbour (capital of Abaco) were destroyed (Beaubien, 2019), along with two of the four major food stores on Grand Bahama island (Maycock, 2019). For several weeks following, the demand for some basic grocery items was greater than the supplies could support. When relief food items began to come in, some food safety concerns with respect to expiry dates began to emerge, as well as the overall impact of relief quality foods for health (Global Village Space, 2019). Therefore, emergency long-term food security, self-sufficiency, and food production must also be sufficiently addressed in climate change resilience frameworks for SIDS.

Sustainability of water resources

Climate change poses a significant threat to the sustainability of water resources and quality in SIDS. "Many SIDS already experience water stress.

Owing to factors such as limited size, geology and topography, water resources in small islands are extremely vulnerable to changes and variations in climate, especially rainfall levels" (Sem, 2009, p. 27). Most water resources in Caribbean states come from groundwater enclosed in shallow freshwater lenses. This factor makes them highly susceptible to contamination as well as to saltwater intrusion from ocean surges due to sea level rise.

The lack of quality water for cooking, drinking, and sanitary purposes can lead to the outbreak of many diseases and ultimately even death. Ocean flood waters from Hurricane Dorian covered much of Abaco and Grand Bahama islands for days. This, in addition to upsurges of brackish water, led to high levels of saltwater intrusion in most of the islands' water tables ("Gb water supplier", 2019). Official advisories were released for weeks indicating that the waters were unsafe for drinking or sanitary purposes, prohibiting many institutions, including schools and restaurants, from being able to reopen. This major occurrence has prompted the urgency to explore alternative methods of water harvesting, revised water use policies, desalination technology, and improved methods of water resource management as vital parts of building a comprehensive climate change resilience plan for SIDS.

Conclusion

The mandate to build a robust, comprehensive climate change resilience framework for SIDS is certainly no easy feat. Yet, the impact of Hurricane Dorian on the Northern Bahama islands suggests that this has become a matter of urgency for the region. Climate change is not going away. States must strengthen their ability to prepare for, manage, and recover from the adverse effects of changing weather patterns globally. Moreover, the demand for developing and implementing a comprehensive climate change framework can only be achieved when SIDS in the Caribbean are willing to invest strategically in capacity building.

Local experts with the relevant knowledge, skills, and resources are needed in order to manage all aspects of climate change resilience. "In the Caribbean there is a limited local awareness and capacity regarding climate and climate science and as such, decision makers are often not in a position to make robust decisions applicable for the local context" (Layne, 2017, p. 179). The quote also suggests that the amount of climate change research specific to SIDS in the Caribbean is scarce. Greater strides are also needed in the area of building digital capacity in the region (Halais, 2019). Local experts are needed to innovate and implement new technological solutions for adaptation, mitigation, and construction of stronger climate change resilience plans.

Finally, the most important yet most overlooked aspect of capacity building for climate change in SIDS is empowering civilians by fostering strong social capital within communities. Involving citizens in climate change planning activities could be a very effective means of building social capital. The people aspect should be prioritized over the technical, financial, natural, social, and institutional aspects of any climate change action plan. Dwirahmadi et al. (2019) suggest that a people-centred approach that considers the needs, concerns, and demographics of target communities is most effective for building climate change resilience. For example, the socio-economic status of the people may directly influence their willingness to concern themselves with climate change issues (Mukherjee & Mustafa, 2019), and thereby negatively impact their preparation and recovery. However, another key lesson from Hurricane Dorian is that capacity building by way of fostering strong social capital can be an indispensable factor in climate change resilience, even when financial resources are limited.

References

Adderley, R. (2018, April 16). Issues with high rock seawall seed to be fixed. Bahamas Information Services. The Government of The Bahamas. Nassau, Bahamas. Retrieved from https://www.bahamas.gov.bs/wps/portal/public/gov/government/news.

Agniam, O. (2011, December 8). Climate change diplomacy and Small Island Developing States. *Our World*. United Nations University. Retrieved from https://ourworld.unu.edu/en/climate-change-diplomacy-and-small-island-developing-states.

Bahamas National Climate Change Committee. (2005). Bahamas national policy for the adaptation to climate change. Bahamas Environment, Science and Technology Commission. Retrieved from https://www.greengrowthknowledge.org/national-documents/bahamas-national-policy-adaptation-climate-change

Beaubien, J. (2019, October 15). Little miracles, huge problems: The Bahamas a month after Dorian. *NPR*. Retrieved from https://www.npr.org/sections/goatsandsoda/2019/10/15/770107636/after-dorians-wrath-little-miracles-amid-a-painful-recovery.

Bernauer, T., & Schaffer, L. (2010, July). Climate change governance. CIS Working Paper No. 60. *SSRN Electronic Journal*. doi: 10.2139/ssrn.1661190. Retrieved from https://papers.ssrn.com/sol3/papers.cfm?abstract_id=1661190.

Benjamin, L. (2010). Climate change and Caribbean small island states: The state of play. *The International Journal of Bahamian Studies*, (16), 78–91. doi: 10.15362/ijbs.v16i0.129.

Cranley, E. (2019, September 7). A cruise ship sailed 1,500 Hurricane Dorian evacuees from the Bahamas to Florida. *Insider*. Retrieved from https://www.insider.com/bahamas-evacuess-cruise-ship-to-florida-2019-9.

Delancy, C. (2019, November). Reconnaissance report on the built environment in the aftermath of Hurricane Dorian. The Government of the Commonwealth of The Bahamas. Nassau, Bahamas. Retrieved from https://www.bahamas.gov.bs/wps/wcm/connect/d7ebcbad-f9b6-42e3-aff2-79f83bd91810/Bahamas%2BBuilding%2BCode%2B3rd%2BEd.pdf?MOD=AJPERES

Dwilson, S. (2019, September 1). Hurricane Dorian damage in The Bahamas: Videos Show Devastation. *Heavy News*. Retrieved from https://heavy.com/news/2019/09/hurricane-dorian-damage-bahamas-videos/.

Dwirahmadi, F., Rutherford, S., Phung, D., & Chu, C. (2019). Understanding the operational concept of a flood-resilient urban community in Jakarta, Indonesia, from the perspectives of disaster risk reduction, climate change adaptation and development agencies. *International Journal of Environmental Research and Public Health, 16*(8), 1–24. doi: 10.3390/ijerph16203993

Fieser, E. (2020, January 17). Hurricane Dorian's Bahamas storm toll: $3.4 billion in damages, 3 years of rebuilding. *Insurance Journal.* Retrieved from https://www.insurancejournal.com/news/international/2020/01/17/555252.htm.

Ferris, E. (2019). Climate change, migration, law, and global governance. *North Carolina Journal of International Law & Commercial Regulation, 44*(3), 425–460. Retrieved from https://scholarship.law.unc.edu/ncilj/vol44/iss3/3.

Food and Agriculture Organization of the United Nations. (n.d.). Global action programme: Key facts and figures. Retrieved from http://www.fao.org/sids/en/.

Gb water supplier sets out post-Dorian strategy. (2019, November 11). *The Tribune.* Retrieved from http://www.tribune242.com/news/2019/nov/11/gb-water-supplier-sets-out-post-dorian-strategy/.

Global Village Space. (2019, September 14). Bahamas hit by a hurricane of donations, but alot of them aren't usable. Retrieved from https://www.globalvillagespace.com/after-dorian-bahamas-drowning-in-a-flood-of-donations/.

Grand Bahama Port Authority. (n.d.). About the grand Bahama port authority. Retrieved from https://gbpa.com/company.

Halais, F. (2019, June 4). Small island states turn to innovation to build climate Resilience. *Devex.* Retrieved from https://www.devex.com/news/small-island-states-turn-to-innovation-to-build-climate-resilience-94865.

Hassan, H. R., & Cliff, V. (2019). For Small Island Nations, climate change is not a threat. It's already here. *World Economic Forum.* Retrieved from https://www.weforum.org/agenda/2019/09/island-nations-maldives-climate-change/.

Hovi, J., Sprinz, D., & Underdal, A. (2009). Implementing long-term climate policy: Time inconsistency, domestic politics, international anarchy. *Global Environmental Politics, 9*, 20–39. doi: 10.1162/glep.2009.9.3.20.

Igbokwe-Ibeto, C. J. (2019). Climate change, food security, and sustainable human development in Nigeria: A critical reflection. *Africa's Public Service Delivery and Performance Review, 7*(1), doi: 10.4102/apsdpr.v7i1.322.

Kalesnikaite, V. (2019). Keeping cities afloat: Climate change adaptation and collaborative governance at the local level. *Public Performance & Management Review, 42*(4), 864–888. doi: 10.10880/15309576.2018.1526091.

Knowles, R. (2019, October 10). Haitian migrants, devastated by Dorian, face deportation From Bahamas. *The New York Times.* Retrieved from https://www.nytimes.com/2019/10/10/world/americas/haiti-bahamas-dorian-deport.html.

Layne, D. (2017). Impacts of climate change on tourism in the coastal and marine Environments of Caribbean Small Island Developing States (SIDS), Caribbean Marine Climate Change Report Card: *Science Review 2017*, 174–184.

Mansoor, S. (2019, September 10). After Dorian survivors are kicked off rescue ship, U.S. Border Patrol says all Bahamians welcome — Except those who aren't. *Time.* Retrieved from https://time.com/5672378/bahamas-dorian-survivors-us-visa/.

Maycock, D. (2019, September 18). Queen's highway businesses destroyed by storm surge. *The Tribune.* Retrieved from http://www.tribune242.com/news/2019/sep/18/queens-highway-businesses-destroyed-by-storm-surge.

Mayunga, J. S. (2007). Understanding and applying the concept of community disaster resilience: A capital-based approach. Summer Academy for Social Vulnerability and Resilience Building. Munich, Germany. Retrieved from https://pdfs. semanticscholar.org/03d3/985c3f6edb80aea0cc2f15a2c805d970fca9.pdf.

Ministry of Environment and Housing. (n.d.). Climate change. The Government of The Bahamas. Nassau, Bahamas. Retrieved from https://eh.gov.bs/gov_initiatives/ climate-change.

Moore, K. (2019, October 12). Grand Bahama children's home evacuated midstorm. *The Ledger.* Retrieved from https://www.theledger.com/news/20191012/ grand-bahama-childrens-home-evacuated-mid-storm.

Moore, T. (2019, September 6). Hurricane Dorian and the tragedy of marsh harbour's mud and Pigeon Pea. *Weather Concierge.* Retrieved from https://www.weather concierge.com/hurricane-dorian-and-the-tragedy-of-marsh-islands-mud-and- pigeon-pea/.

Mukherjee, V., & Mustafa, F. (2019). Climate change and right to development. *Management and Economics Research Journal, 5*(3), 1–10. doi: 10.18639/MERJ. 2019.735041

Nachmany, M., Abeysinghe, A., & Barakat, S. (2017). Climate change legislation in the least developing countries. In: Averchenkova, A., Fankhauser S., & Nachmany, M. (eds), *Trends in climate change legislation.* Edward Elgar Publishing. Cheltinham, United Kingdom.

Nunn, P., & Kumar, R. (2017). Understanding climate-human interactions in Small Island Developing States (SIDS): Implications for future livelihood sustainability. *International Journal of Climate Change Strategies and Management, 10*(2), 245–271. Retrieved from https://www.emerald.com/insight/content/doi/10.1108/ IJCCSM-01-2017-0012/full/html.

Office of the Prime Minister. (2019, November 6). PM Minnis: Disaster reconstruction authority bill advances disaster management regime. *Bahamas Weekly.* Retrieved from http://www.thebahamasweekly.com/publish/bis-news-updates/ PM_Minnis_Disaster_Reconstruction_Authority_Bill_advances_disaster_ management_regime_printer.shtml.

Organization of American States. (n.d.). The Bahamas national report integrating management of Watersheds and Coastal Areas in Small Island Developing States (SIDS) of the Caribbean. Retrieved from www.oas.org/reia/iwcam.pdf/bahamas/ bahamasreport.

Oulu, M. (2015). Climate change governance: Emerging legal and institutional frameworks for developing countries. In: Leal Filho, W. (eds), *Handbook of climate change adaptation.* Springer, Berlin, Heidelberg. doi: 10.1007/978-3-642-38670-1_9.

Sem, G. (2009). The impact of climate change on the development prospects of the least developed countries and Small Island Developing States. Office of the high representative for the least developed countries, landlocked developing countries and Small Island Developing States. Retrieved from http://unohrlls.org/about- sids/publications/the-impact-of-climate-change-on-the-development-prospects- of-the-least-developed-countries-and-small-island-developing-states-2/.

Silver, J., Arkema K., Griffin, R., Lashley, B., Lemay, M., Maldonado, S., ... Verutes, G. (2019). Advancing coastal risk reduction science and implementation by accounting for climate, ecosystems, and people. *Frontiers in Marine Science, 6*(556). doi: 10.3389/fmars.2019.00556 Retrieved from https://www.frontiersin.org/ articles/10.3389/fmars.2019.00556/full.

UNICEF. (2019). Hurricane Dorian The Bahamas situation report no. 4. Retrieved from https://www.unicef.org/appeals/files/UNICEF_Bahamas_Humanitarian_SitRep_Hurricane_Dorian_25_Nov_2019.pdf.

Walshe, R. A., & Stancioff, C. E. (2018). Small island perspectives on climate change. *Island Studies Journal, 13*(1), 13–24. Retrieved from https://www.researchgate.net/publication/324891508_Small_Island_perspectives_on_climate_change.

Ward, J., & Faiola, A. (2019, September 1). 'Pray for us': Dorian snapping trees, tearing off roofs in The Bahamas. *The Washington Post*. Retrieved from https://www.washingtonpost.com/world/the_americas/dorian-rips-apart-docks-floods-roads-in-northern-bahamas/2019/09/01/a358e27a-cc1c-11e9-9615-8f1a32962e04_story.html.

World Health Organization. (2008). Climate change and health in Small Island Developing States: WHO special initiative in collaboration with UNFCCC - Secretariat and Fijian Presidency of COP-23. Retrieved from https://www.who.int/globalchange/sids-initiative/180612_global_initiative_sids_clean_v2.pdf?ua=1

Part V
Conclusion

16 Toward an understanding of the tourism experience

Joshua Carroll

Water is a life-bearing force, and humans have been attracted to and connected with water since the dawn of time. We are born out of liquid and these early bonds seem to extend through our lifetimes, drawing us to water repeatedly as the opportunities arise. An island represents a refuge within a sea of water and provides a space for human habitation and entices visitation. With visitation comes an increased need for infrastructure and support systems to aid in the hosting of non-residents. Transportation systems, food and beverage, overnight accommodations, electrical supply, communications and others all feel the burden as a result. This often leads to the development of guidelines, rules, regulations, policies, and/or codes to aid in the proper provisioning of these experiences for both hosts and visitors.

As an island nation, The Bahamas is not just one island, but over 700 islands and cays stretching over 250,000 square miles. Travel to and between these islands requires boat or air travel and can be difficult or at times even impossible, complicated by storm situations and, at times, non-navigable waters. The Bahamas are a residentially diverse system of islands, ranging from metropolitan areas such as Nassau to remote uninhabited cays stretching across secluded seas. Because of this, there are many differing perspectives regarding both tourism and the most appropriate courses of action to handle tourism. These differing views can sometimes be challenges to tourism development on the islands. Alternatively, these views become unique opportunities for tourism and tourism development, particularly with regard to sustainability, sensible growth and how subtle changes in political atmosphere can have lasting impacts on visitors and the communities that host them. These elements work to shape the views that visitors have of a destination, and to an extent the views that the communities within these visited sites hold of themselves.

An identity of a tourism destination is developed in much the same way that a brand is created through marketing and promotion. It often begins with a vision, and then associated elements are designed and implemented to support that vision and create a full picture of the brand. A tourist destination as an entity is very similar to this, and The Bahamas has taken similar steps, whether conscious, planned, or not, that have lasting impacts on both sides of the visitation pendulum.

Over the years, the identity of The Bahamas has developed alongside the visitor, in much the same way that the expectations of the visitors have evolved to fulfil their needs. The limitless possibilities of The Bahamas have enabled it to grow from a "fun in the sun" destination to one with unsurpassed recreation opportunities in fishing, warm water snorkelling, long distance sailing and cruising, health and wellness, artistic expression, soul searching, cave diving, cuisine, cultural exchange, and much more. To say that The Bahamas has evolved is an understatement.

But this is not all always for the best. The Bahamian people have lived with an identity that portrays them as the eternal host to the visitor. Socio-economic stressors reinforce this role, as illustrated in scenarios from Guana Cay to Nassau. Whether buying conch salad on Elizabeth Island or a sport suit at the Atlantis Resort, the host roles have been established and perceptions developed often before the visitor boards a plane or boat, or the islander enters the working world. In a land of islands that have been selling themselves as "paradise" for many years, it can be a difficult reputation to live up to year after year. Further, the increasing rates of natural disasters, particularly hurricanes, as witnessed with the deadly and massive impacts of the recent 2019 Hurricane Dorian, can be foreboding.

The shift of The Bahamas tourism in late 1980s to early 1990s from one of high-end, winter escape, boutique tourism to a more mass packaging of tourism has shifted the economic impacts to the departing country. The purchasing of the experience often now takes place before the visitor leaves their home, with online purchasing and package deals where the warehouse approach leaves the host site, accommodations, and sometimes even restaurants at a loss to recoup their expenses.

Tourism relies first on an attraction or draw that creates demand and then on the resources to fulfil that demand. Tastes and interests change over time, with seasons, trends, livelihoods, family status, employment opportunities, and a variety of other factors. As such, the tourism supplier is forced to identify, forecast, and respond to these changes if it is to continue to attract the visitor. As an island nation, The Bahamas faces these challenges in an exaggerated fashion vis-à-vis its branding and marketing strategies, because of finite resources and definitive land boundaries. Though tourism can provide great promise for The Bahamas, it can also be a misleading panacea.

Throughout this text the reader is cautioned to not put all their eggs in one basket – tourism can do a lot for the country and its people, but not everything. When looking at the perceptions of residents from Abaco, Bimini, and Exuma, there are interesting results. Economic benefits do not appear to be reaching resident communities across the islands, though all respondents reported positive interactions with tourists. The level of agreement varies noticeably, with Bimini standing out as most supportive of tourist experiences and benefits, likely due to the recent focus of tourism enhancement projects on the island and direct benefits being realized. These relationships grow in complexity with concerns around the segregation of tourists from local communities, and immigrant workers replacing a Bahamian workforce.

In 2014 a study conducted in these same islands revealed that respondents not only noticed benefits of tourism on their daily lives but also recognized environmental impacts and costs associated with tourism. A study conducted on islands within the Abaco's (Carroll and Brown, 2017) revealed similar results where tourism providers (all residents) indicated not only social and environmental benefits across the tourism sector but also significant negative environmental impacts. All three of these studies point to environmental impact concerns and suggest the need for directed investigation into the Family Islands regarding local perceptions of the impacts of tourism, and the goals moving forward.

As we investigate the future, we realize that the vacation rental market is changing. Local participation in direct hosting has grown tremendously through businesses such as Airbnb, VRBO, and others. These rentals can offer visitors options that are more directly immersed in the culture, closer to a more "authentic" experience and often at greatly reduced prices compared to hotels and resorts. This has led to mixed perceptions by the hotel industries in The Bahamas. Some see these rentals as direct competition given the advantage of circumventing hotel taxes and surcharges, while others see them as an economic boost providing employment and entrepreneurial opportunities that empower local people. Local government in The Bahamas has begun working with Airbnb to help level the playing field and collect due taxes and provide additional revenue sources for the Ministry of Tourism. This is a notable finding from this text that offers strategies to deal with these changes.

Not only are the places people stay in The Bahamas changing, but the attractions themselves have also undergone an identity change, whether welcomed or not by local communities. A key example of this is the Junkanoo – Carnival transition. Junkanoo has historically been a means of cultural expression for the people of The Bahamas as a celebration of freedom from a time of racial prejudice and discrimination against blacks. The Junkanoo festival was a time when rules were relinquished, and boundaries blurred. Freedom reigned, and participants danced, sang, drummed, and marched in the streets. The tradition's history and importance run deep through the people of The Bahamas.

Carnival, on the other hand, is a Caribbean celebration, a celebration of people of the sea. But Carnival is also much more widely recognized across populations of potential visitors to The Bahamas. It connotes the types of experiences these visitors want to have. It has its own set of attractive properties and brand recognition. Recently the Government of The Bahamas began incorporating the traditional Junkanoo celebration into a Carnival celebration.

But what does this government-led alteration of a traditional and deeply rooted and meaningful celebration do for the people who align with this as part of their identity? Acceptance of this incorporation has not been widespread. An engineered festival, designed primarily for capitalistic experiences that often displace residents with preference to an affluent visiting target audience, does not make a recipe for successful tourism planning, and leaves little in reserves for resilience.

In a best-case scenario, a government provides sound decision-making, enforcement, communication, and facilitation of the necessary systems in order to promote the well-being of its people. Panarchy and resilience both have a hand in sustainability and can be key components of governments. Panarchy acknowledges the dual role of complex systems with the sometimes-conflicting characteristics of stability and change, while resilience allows the flexibility to adapt to unexpected changes or shifts in the needs of communities. Human interactions between themselves and their environment create the consequences for sustainability.

As an island nation, The Bahamas is inexorably connected to its natural world, and natural forces act upon it relentlessly. It is this same sense of connectedness and dependence upon the natural world that help to create an opportunity for residents and visitors alike to engage in experiences that are memorable and moving. As we shift from a goods and services economy to an experience economy, we realize how interdependent the site, hosts, and visitors are to one another in creating these experiences. Stages of an experience can include anticipation, engagement, and recall. Availability and types of information help shape the first stage, while the suitability of the host site and hosts as well as past experiences play an important role in the engagement phase, coming together to create the last stage of a memorable experience. It might be prudent to add the role of recent advances in technology to this equation. Social media takes a leading role in boosting memories, opportunities for recall, and sharing with friends and family.

Knowing the importance of these factors, a major advancement in tourism took place during the Bahamian Courtesy Campaign from 1955 to 1970. It was based on the notion that in order to "sell" paradise, friendliness was imperative. The target visitor came to The Bahamas to "overcome the impersonality of the urban life they leave behind." The campaign was successful in setting a stage for the friendliness of The Bahamas, but not without a price to the communities who bore the brunt of the campaign. Over the course of the campaign, modifications (e.g., Friendliness Through Understanding) were adopted to align more closely with local sentiments, but the general goals remained the same. The question posed in Chapter 1 still resonates: how does this impact the identity of a Bahamian-born citizen? And how do these impacts influence the possibilities of sustainable tourism in the Bahamas?

The UN adopted Sustainable Development Goals (SDGs) in September 2015. Chapter 10 diligently poses the questions: Are existing sustainability assessment tools applicable to Small Island Developing States (SIDS)? If not, should a SIDS-specific tool be developed? If so, what would it look like?

SIDS are unique, small, harbouring fragile systems, sharing close political links to former colonies, often containing levels of instability and comprised of comparatively small economies. After a comparative policy analysis of indictors used for sustainability assessment in the context of SIDS, a reduction of SIDS indicators to a more manageable list for SIDS, a focus aimed at ease of monitoring, and the development or amendment of additional SIDS-related indicators, a new SIDS-based tool was proposed. This new tool is recommended to be based on the 5M principles: measuring, monitoring, mapping, modelling, and managing. However, questions remain such as the cost effectiveness and the completeness of the indicators. This work represents concrete and proactive progress towards sustainability for SIDs.

Closely tied to this concept is the Blue Economy, which focusses on how ocean and marine life could sustain an economy. The UN defined a long-term strategy of supporting sustainable and equitable economic growth through oceans-related sectors and activities. It seeks improvement of human well-being, social equity, reduction of environmental risks, and ecological scarcities.

The Exclusive Economic Zone lies 200 nautical miles east of the easternmost outlying islands in The Bahamas. Renward Wells, former Minister of Agriculture and Marine Resources, points to this region as a possible avenue for unique, predominantly extraction-based tourism. Ragged Island, decimated by Hurricane Irma in 2017, is poised to take advantage of this. Although the hurricane damage was described as the "worst ever seen" and "no structures were left untouched" there is hope.

Out of destruction can come innovation. The Blue Economy provides a rebuilding plan that contains zoning improvements, advanced building codes, and mitigation strategies against climate change impacts. Ragged Island's proximity to the Great Bahamas Bank could make it ideal for commercial seafood engineers and fishermen to develop a fishing hub, acting as a Satellite Fisheries Outpost. This could ensure longer fishing days at sea, fuel storage, product storage, processing, export service, shipping, medical facilities, and a military outpost.

These opportunities are not unique to The Bahamas, but for the same reasons The Bahamas faces challenges, it can also enjoy some freedoms to innovate because of its small size, shifting economy and environmental immersion, allowing it to sometimes be more adaptable.

Adaptability has become essential in a climate changed world (Van Noy, 2019). Whether it is city officials along coastal Florida designing long-term pumping protocols to cope with rising sea levels or North Carolina mountain towns developing emergency response strategies to deal with flooding rivers, the only response is to adapt as best as possible. SIDS have constraints as mentioned earlier, and these can make them very vulnerable to climate change effects of sea level rise, increasing ocean temperatures, greater erosion, higher precipitation levels, and extreme weather events. June through the end of November constitutes hurricane season, and with it decreased attractiveness to potential visitors; not surprisingly, this is the low tourist season for The Bahamas. Adding to this is that key tourism market sectors typically have more attractive conditions in their home regions, as winter has passed and summer offers a welcome respite without the need to travel for relief.

Additional impacts of climate change on The Bahamas can further compound the issues for these distinct isles. Higher sea temperatures lead to increased likelihood of severe weather events, coral bleaching, and associated loss of divers, snorkelers, boaters, and other recreationists. These impacts place greater financial burden on SIDS because of the frequent need to divert funds for disaster relief that could be allocated for other needs such as education, sustainable planning and development, or social services. Difficult decisions need to be made about where and how to focus efforts on revenue sources, and how and where to spend the tax base across its constituents.

One recently debated revenue source is the possible legalization of marijuana in The Bahamas. Essentially, the question is, should The Bahamas legalize marijuana for the sole purpose of creating an Agro-Tourism Habitat as a sustainable development option on a remote Family Island? There are dichotomous views in the debate. On one side, there are some concerns of overuse, enhancement of the drug trade, illicit activities, and a general sense that the idea goes against basic Christian beliefs that permeate the island culture. On the other hand, when a survey was conducted on a younger population (ages 25–35 years old), results indicated over 50% of the sample supported legalization of marijuana for the sole purpose of creating an agro-tourism industry, and 60% of respondents believed this industry would increase the GDP.

The issue is more complex than merely respondent beliefs and/or support. There are environmental issues such as the water shortage across the islands and how this industry would impact that. Questions remain as to how much energy is required to run this industry and how those resources are developed and harnessed. The challenges of how to transport people to these remote Family Islands remain, as do the questions of where they stay, how do they eat, are medical services adequate, and would they want to come. There are also social and economic implications, as this would uproot the underground market and change the key players and stakeholders.

This text does, however, stress the importance of diversifying the economy to remain competitive and ahead of market changes. Additionally, millennials are the future policy makers and they showed notable support in the study. This agro-tourism idea does show creative thinking, promise a unique experience, and would be the first of its kind in the Caribbean. States in the US that have legalized marijuana have shown significant boosts in their tax base due to the selling of the product and related tourism experiences. Marijuana-based wedding events have sprung up, as have culinary parings, spiritual retreats, relaxation getaways, and many other associated tourism venues related to the legalization of marijuana.

Tourism is complex. It deals with multiple stakeholders with varying goals, demands, and resources. It hinges on human preferences and motivations. It relies on available time, money, and interest of potential travellers, and the ability to serve them through the entire trip from arrival to departure and all the needs in between, for both visitor and host. It takes a tremendous amount of planning to get it right, and sometimes the lessons learned from the mistakes are more valuable than realized at first.

Tourism planning is at its core an attempt to categorize, understand, and define the human experience. We use terms such as *visitation, attraction, motivation, resources, supply,* and *demand* in order to try and more completely understand this experience, but what matters is that the experience is fulfilling to the person who is engaging in it. What is even more important is, if the experience meets or exceeds expectations, has lasting impact, creates memories that can be told and retold in the future, and eventually draws people back. Finally, when they return, the place they remember must continue to fulfil their needs, despite how the visitor or host has changed over time. Some sites can be outgrown when the site and the visitor evolve differently through time and the relationship dissolves.

Tourism is not a commodity but an experience. An experience can be an elusive and difficult to define conglomeration of factors that come together in a unique space and time to create one event encountered by a sole individual. Therefore, two or more people can be in the same place, at the same time, doing the same activity, yet report very different experiences.

The conceptual foundation of the Water and Lands Recreation Opportunity Spectrum (WALROS) works on the premise that an activity (e.g., snorkelling, sailing) takes place in a particular setting which is made up of *physical, social,* and *managerial* attributes, and this yields an experience with several dimensions and senses and then affords greater benefits (e.g., personal, group, community, economic, environmental) (Carroll, 2009). For example, imagine the difference between snorkelling in a popular site near Nassau versus a remote offshore reef of the outlying islands and the varied experiences these would produce. The setting near Nassau might be dominated by human structures and channelized waters, with well-marked hazards, definitive rules and regulations, a high concentration of users, and limited opportunities to fully immerse oneself in the natural world. This might offer benefits of social interaction, physical exercise, and seeing a new site. The remote offshore reef setting might be dominated by an uninhabited landscape, extremely low concentration of visitors, and ample opportunities to see, hear, and immerse oneself in the natural surroundings. This might offer benefits of solitude, challenge, and skill development. The same activity, yet in different settings, can yield very different experiences, and ultimately different benefits.

Tourism should strive to offer diverse settings and opportunities for its visitors. Tourism experiences in and around Nassau or Freeport are generally very different than those experiences gained on remote islands or reefs in other parts of the country. They serve different markets and tastes, and they offer varying opportunities for economic gains to those who provide these different experiences. Tourism should not strive to be one size fits all.

One of the most unique and attractive features of The Bahamas are the shallow, crystal clear waters, extensive white sand beaches, and colourful reefs teaming with vibrant sea life. To sail, snorkel, and explore the remote islands in the less-travelled areas along the Exuma chain are experiences unsurpassed elsewhere. To witness an eight-foot eagle ray silently glide over you while snorkelling along the sea floor is an immense experience. Spending time underwater with the elegant yet massive green turtle or swimming through a colourful coral bridge can provide perspective to a human life. In 1959 The Bahamas National Trust identified Land and Sea Parks across The Bahamas in order to better protect species and habitats from human impacts. To protect the settings within which these experiences could take place is a noble and proactive endeavour for the natural environments of The Bahamas, the varying tastes of the visitors, and the economic opportunities of the communities that surround them.

The Bahamas certainly has not done everything right, and their approach to tourism is no exception. However, recognizing these opportunities and the basic human need and interest to connect with nature in an arena where those opportunities seem to be dwindling at an alarming rate is a solid first step in any tourism plan moving forward. The Bahamas is also keenly poised to take advantage of their unique geographic location and abundance of natural wonders.

The information, scenarios, study results, pragmatic discussions, ideas for future action, and personal reflections in this text provide a comprehensive base of knowledge to those interested in the discipline. Despite the unique characteristics of The Bahamas, this book is really about the challenges, opportunities, limitations, past experiences, and future promises we all face in tourism. Environmental impacts and the social implications of tourism, as well as the ability to create appropriate settings for a diversity of visitor experiences, are likely concerns at any number of tourism destinations. Because of this, this text is a guidebook of sorts. It is a tool to be used in any number of scenarios, at the hands of a wide array of people. It can serve as a practical reference to those seeking to better understand tourism and plan for its future development more sustainably.

References

Carroll, J. (2009). Conducting a Water Recreation Opportunity Spectrum Inventory on the Northern Forest Canoe Trail in New Hampshire. *Journal of Park and Recreation Administration.* 27(4), pp. 108–120.

Carroll, J., & Brown, M. (2017). An Assessment of Tourism Sustainability in Abaco, Bahamas. *Journal of Tourism Insights.* 8(1), pp. 1–22.

Van Noy, R. (2019). *Sudden Spring. Stories of Adaptation in a Climate-Changed South.* Athens: University of Georgia Press.

Index

Note: **Bold** page numbers refer to tables; *Italic* page numbers refer to figures and page numbers followed by "n" denote endnotes.

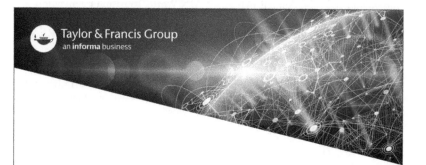